P9-CML-674

THE AZAR-HAGEN GRAMMAR SERIES

TEST BANK FOR UNDERSTANDING AND USING

English Grammar

FIFTH EDITION

Kelly Roberts Weibel

**Understanding and Using English Grammar, Fifth Edition
Test Bank**

Copyright © 2017, 2009, 2001 by Pearson Education, Inc.
All rights reserved.

No part of this publication may be reproduced,
stored in a retrieval system, or transmitted in any
form or by any means, electronic, mechanical,
photocopying, recording, or otherwise, without the
prior permission of the publisher.

Pearson Education, 221 River Street, Hoboken, NJ 07030

Azar Associates: Sue Van Etten, Manager

Staff credits: The people who made up the *Understanding and Using
English Grammar, Fifth Edition, Test Bank* team, representing
content creation, design, manufacturing, project management, and
publishing, are Pietro Alongi, Rhea Banker, Stephanie Bullard, Warren
Fischbach, Nancy Flaggman, Gosia Jaros-White, Amy McCormick,
Brian Panker, Lindsay Richman, Robert Ruvo, and Paula Van Ells.

Contributing Editor: Jennifer McAliney
Text composition: Aptara

ISBN 10: 0-13-427546-2
ISBN 13: 978-0-13-427546-8

Printed in the United States of America
3   18

CONTENTS

INTRODUCTION

This test bank accompanies *Understanding and Using English Grammar, Fifth Edition.* Instructors can choose from over two hundred and sixty quizzes and tests to use for assessment. Teachers familiar with the fourth edition of the test bank will find updated content as well as some new material created for this fifth edition.

QUIZZES

Each chapter contains a series of quizzes keyed to individual charts in the student book, followed by two chapter tests. The quizzes are intended as quick checks of student understanding for both teacher and student. Mastery of a quiz is a strong indicator that students are ready to progress to the next section.

CHAPTER TESTS

The tests at the end of each chapter are comprehensive, covering as many points from the chapter as possible. The formats of the questions in the chapter tests follow those used in previous quizzes. The two chapter tests are identical in format so that one may be used as a practice test if desired.

EXAMS

Two midterm exams covering chapters one through ten and two comprehensive final exams are included in this test bank. They can be used in conjunction with the other quizzes and tests, or used separately.

FORMAT

Because students bring a variety of learning styles to the classroom, there is a wide selection of test formats, including sentence completion, sentence connection, multiple choice, and error analysis, as well as more open completion. To maximize the use of the answer key, open-ended writing practice has been kept to a minimum. Teachers wishing to incorporate more writing into the tests are encouraged to add their own material at the end of the chapter tests.

ANSWER KEY

An answer key for all quizzes, tests, and exams can be found in the back of the text.

DUPLICATION

The material has been formatted so teachers can easily make copies for their students. Permission is granted to duplicate as many copies as needed for classroom use only.

Acknowledgments

To Pat, always my consultant on "native-speaker English"—thanks for your love and patience. To Stacy Hagen, Ruth Voetmann, and Gosia Jaros-White—thanks for your support on this new edition. To my students—thanks for keeping me on my toes with your questions about English grammar! I couldn't have done this without you.

CHAPTER 1 Present and Past; Simple and Progressive

QUIZ 1 Simple Present and Present Progressive   (Chart 1-1)

Directions: Choose the correct completions.

SITUATION: *The Morning Train*

Example: Every morning many people ((get)/ *are getting*) up early to take the train to work.

1. Every morning passengers (*stand / are standing*) in line to board the trains at
   Chiswick Station.

2. The train to London (*departs / is departing*) promptly at 7:13 A.M. daily.

3. This morning, the train (*is not running / does not run*).

4. Right now engineers (*try / are trying*) to figure out the problem.

5. It is now 7:30 A.M., but the passengers (*still wait / are still waiting*) for the train.

6. Mike Berkley (*takes / is taking*) the train to London every morning.

7. Mike (*works / is working*) 9:00 to 5:00 every day.

8. Mike (*sits / is sitting*) on a bench now.

9. Now he (*taps / is tapping*) his foot impatiently.

10. He (*calls / is calling*) his boss now.

QUIZ 2 Simple Present and Present Progressive   (Chart 1-1)

Directions: Complete the sentences. Use the simple present or present progressive form
of the verbs in parentheses.

A. It is a warm, sunny day. Many people are at Greenlake Park. Cathy and Joyce
   (*walk*) _____are walking_____ near the lake. Some children (*play*) _____
                    1   2
   at the playground, and a dog (*swim*) _____ in the water. Everyone
                                              3
   (*enjoy*) _____ the beautiful day.
                  4

B. Josh (*be*) _____ a typical American teenager. He (*do*) _____
                    1   2
   his homework every day after school. He (*clean*) _____ his bedroom
                                                              3
   before dinner every day. He (*ride*) _____ his bike every weekend.
                                              4
   Sometimes he (*play*) _____ games on his computer. Right now
                              5
   Josh (*talk*) _____ with his friends on the Internet. They
                     6
   (*use*) _____ a chat program to have a conversation.
                7

Directions: Complete the sentences. Use the simple present or present progressive form of the verbs in parentheses.

SITUATION: *In Math Class*

Example: Our math class (*start*) _____ starts _____ at 9:45 every morning.

1. Our math teacher (*give*) _____ us homework every day.

2. I (*study*) _____ every weekend.

3. Right now I (*take*) _____ a test. I (*relax, not*) _____.

4. I (*worry*) _____ a lot when I take tests.

5. Math tests (*be*) _____ stressful and (*make*) _____ me nervous.

Directions: Complete the sentences with *Do*, *Does*, *Is*, or *Are*.

Example: _____ Are _____ all of the students in class today?

1. _____ you like math?

2. _____ your math teacher helpful?

3. _____ your math teacher explain math problems clearly?

4. _____ you have any homework tonight?

5. _____ you taking your math book home with you?

Directions: Choose the correct completions.

Example: My brother (*is looking /*(*looks*)) like my father.

1. My uncle (*is appearing* / *appears*) on a TV program today. We have to watch it!

2. That fish (*is smelling* / *smells*) terrible. Are you certain it is fresh?

3. Greg (*is thinking* / *thinks*) over his career plans. He doesn't like his current job.

4. Right now the chef (*is tasting* / *tastes*) the meat dish.

5. You are lucky to have a good sense of humor. People (*are loving* / *love*) your jokes!

Directions: Complete the sentences. Use the simple present or present progressive form of the verbs in parentheses.

Example: (*you, understand*) __*Do you understand*__ the instructions?

1. Right now I (*care, not*) _____ about the election results.

2. Julia and Tim (*see*) _____ a financial advisor now, so they can't come to the phone.

3. What (*you, think*) _____ of our new boss? Do you think she's doing a good job?

4. Mr. Goddard (*feel, not*) _____ well right now. He has a severe headache.

5. My brother-in-law (*dislike*) _____ his job at the post office.

QUIZ 7 **Simple Past Tense** (Chart 1-4)

Directions: Write the simple past tense for each verb.

Example: buy _____*bought*_____

1. stop _____	11. cost _____
2. make _____	12. study _____
3. catch _____	13. find _____
4. meet _____	14. ring _____
5. stand _____	15. speak _____
6. drive _____	16. hear _____
7. read _____	17. wear _____
8. drink _____	18. quit _____
9. write _____	19. play _____
10. sleep _____	20. choose _____

Directions: Complete the sentences with the correct simple past form of the verbs.

SITUATION: *An Unusual Accident*

Example: Last Monday, a very strange accident (*happen*) _____happened_____ on the
freeway near Seattle.

1. A large truck (*have*) _____ 450 boxes with 5 million honeybees in them.

2. The bees (*be*) _____ on their way to a farm.

3. The truck driver (*drive, not*) _____ slowly enough, and the truck

    (*crash*) _____.

4. The bee boxes (*spill*) _____ onto the road, and many bees

    (*get*) _____ out.

5. Special workers (*come*) _____ to catch the bees, but they

    (*catch, not*) _____ all of them.

6. The bees (*fly*) _____ everywhere.

7. Finally, firefighters (*kill*) _____ many of the bees with spray.

Directions: Choose the correct completions.

Example: (*Did* / (*Were*)) the Smiths at the wedding last weekend?

1. (*Did* / *Were*) Mark and Jan go to Asia last year?

2. (*Was* / *Were*) I late for the meeting?

3. (*Was* / *Did*) you eat breakfast this morning?

4. (*Was* / *Were*) you and your husband at the movies last night?

5. (*Did* / *Were*) I get a good grade on the test?

6. (*Was* / *Did*) the kids have fun at the park?

7. (*Was* / *Were*) your brother a good student in high school?

8. (*Was* / *Were*) Frank and Joe at the grocery store yesterday?

9. (*Were* / *Did*) we eat all the cake?

10. (*Did* / *Were*) Miriam pass her driving test on Friday?

Directions: Choose the correct completions.

Example: The reporter ((asked) / *was asking*) many questions at the press conference yesterday.

1. While Miki (*listened* / *was listening*) to the lecture in class, her phone rang.

2. Billy was very sad when he (*lost* / *was losing*) his favorite toy.

3. While Emily (*drove* / *was driving*) on the freeway, her car ran out of gas.

4. When Helena (*heard* / *was hearing*) the joke, she laughed.

5. Mark (*ate* / *was eating*) dinner when his parents came by. He was surprised to see them.

6. The earthquake happened while I (*watched* / *was watching*) TV last night.

7. The policeman (*cleaned* / *was cleaning*) his shoes when he got a call about a robbery.

8. Joe (*ran* / *was running*) the 10K race in 45 minutes. He was happy with his time.

9. Michael (*played* / *was playing*) in the soccer game yesterday.

10. Lisa (*traveled* / *was traveling*) on business when she heard the news about her boss' illness.

Directions: Complete the sentences. Use the simple past or past progressive form of the verbs in parentheses.

A. Last year while Giorgio (*work*) _____was working_____ on his house, he
    (*fall*) _____ off a ladder. He (*break*) _____ his
    ankle. Giorgio's neighbor (*take*) _____ him to the hospital.
    Giorgio (*be, not*) _____ able to walk for six weeks.

B. Last August, my family and I (*take*) _____ a Caribbean vacation.
    We (*stay*) _____ in a beautiful hotel near the beach. Every day
    we (*spend*) _____ hours on the white sand beaches, and we
    (*eat*) _____ delicious food in colorful restaurants. One evening
    while we (*have*) _____ dinner, a band (*play*) _____
    lively music. Many people (*dance*) _____ to the Caribbean rhythms.
    After dinner we (*walk*) _____ on the beach.

Directions: Correct the errors.

Example: While Ted ~~is~~ writing the email, his computer crashed.

(above "is" is written) was

1. Michiko was chopping some vegetables when she was cutting her finger with the knife.

2. While Travis is working on his homework, he was listening to the radio.

3. When Fatima woke up, she was making a cup of tea for herself.

4. When Janice was breaking her leg, she was skiing.

5. Geoff is working on his report while he was riding the train.

6. While Faruz is shopping for a new computer, he ran into an old friend.

7. When Ana was being in Orlando, she went to Disney World every day.

8. When Carrie was dropping her tablet computer, she started to cry.

9. James was washing the dishes when he finished reading the newspaper.

10. It was starting to rain when my mother was coming by for a visit.

QUIZ 13 Unfulfilled Intentions: *Was / Were Going To*   (Chart 1-6)

Directions: Choose *yes* if the speaker is expressing an intention or plan. Choose *no* if not.

Example: I was going to call you, but I lost your number.	(Yes)	No
1. We were going to the grocery store when our car broke down.	Yes	No
2. I was going to give the book to my sister, but she didn't want it.	Yes	No
3. Mario was planning to retire this year but decided not to.	Yes	No
4. Julia was thinking about her upcoming vacation.	Yes	No
5. We were going to cancel the newspaper, but we forgot.	Yes	No
6. I was texting you when you called me.	Yes	No
7. Charlotte was thinking about watching a movie last night.	Yes	No
8. Mr. Marshall was intending to visit his brother in the hospital.	Yes	No

CHAPTER 1 – TEST 1

Part A *Directions:* Choose the correct completions.

1. A: _____ you usually work on Saturday?

   a. Are   b. Do   c. Does

   B: No, I don't. I _____ from Monday to Friday.

   a. worked   b. am working   c. work

2. A: Abdullah _____ me yesterday. Right now he is visiting his relatives in Chicago.

   a. emails   b. email   c. emailed

   B: That's nice. He _____ them last year, too.

   a. visited   b. did visit   c. visits

3. A: Mr. Smith _____ our office this week.

   a. visit   b. visits   c. is visiting

   B: Really? I _____ that.

   a. don't know   b. didn't know   c. am not knowing

4. A: What _____ at this exact time last year?

   a. did you do   b. did you doing   c. were you doing

   B: I _____ the ruins in Athens. They were fantastic.

   a. toured   b. was touring   c. tour

Part B *Directions:* Complete the sentences. Use the simple present, simple past, present progressive, or past progressive form of the verbs in parentheses.

1. My brother (*have*) _____ a car accident last year, so now he is a more careful driver.

2. The clock in the living room (*stop*) _____ six hours ago. It shows 3:00, but it's 9:00 now.

3. Mrs. Mitchell (*call*) _____ the police right now. Someone stole her jewelry.

4. Andrew (*go, usually*) _____ skiing in Austria in January.

5. Some friends from South America visited Carl last summer. While they (*visit*) _____, they went to a museum, the zoo, and the beach.

Part C *Directions:* Complete the sentences in the paragraph. Use the simple present, simple past, present progressive, or past progressive form of the verbs in parentheses. More than one answer may be possible.

Hani often (*find*) _____ a lot of interesting information on
                          1
the Internet. One unusual Web site (*be*) _____ "Weird News."
                                              2
It (*report*) _____ on strange events from around the world. Yesterday,
              3
Hani (*read*) _____ about a Japanese "air-conditioned jacket."
              4
The jacket (*have*) _____ two tiny fans to keep you cool. Hani
                    5
(*buy*) _____ because she wants to stay cool in hot weather.
         6

Part D *Directions:* Correct the errors.

1. Every summer Sarah's cousin from England visit her.

2. Ibrahim was very upset when he was hearing the news.

3. You can't talk to Mr. James right now because he talks to another student.

4. While I writing my essay, I was also surfing the Internet.

5. Karen is very kind and always helping the teachers with their work.

Part E *Directions:* Answer the questions with complete sentences. Use simple or progressive verbs.

1. Did Charles help you fix your car yesterday?

   No, he _____.

2. Was your computer working OK last night?

   Yes, it _____.

3. Does Alice spend a lot of time on her phone?

   Yes, she _____.

4. Did the workers finish putting in the new window?

   Yes, they _____.

5. Are Ken and Lisa planning to go on a vacation this summer?

   No, they _____.

Part A *Directions:* Choose the correct completions.

1. A: Marissa _____ in her journal every day.

   a. writes　　　b. is writing　　　c. was writing

   B: I know. She _____ right now.

   a. exercises　　b. is exercising　　c. was exercising

2. A: Yesterday, Phil _____ three cups of coffee before 8:00 A.M.

   a. drinks　　　b. was drinking　　c. drank

   B: He usually _____ too much coffee.

   a. is drinking　　b. was drinking　　c. drinks

3. A: Monica _____ an award for outstanding service to the company.

   a. receives　　b. received　　c. did receive

   B: Wonderful! She _____ it.

   a. earned　　b. earns　　c. was earning

4. A: Mr. Lin _____ in from China at 11:00 last night.

   a. flew　　　b. is flying　　c. was flying

   B: I'm sure he _____ really tired today.

   a. felt　　　b. fell　　c. is feeling

Part B *Directions:* Complete the sentences. Use the simple present, simple past, present progressive, or past progressive form of the verbs in parentheses. More than one answer may be possible.

1. Chris (*wake*) _____ up at 6:55 every morning.

2. When I was a child, my parents (*work*) _____ hard to take care of our family.

3. While I (*wait*) _____ in line for coffee, I got several text messages.

4. This semester I (*take*) _____ a German class. It's hard, but fun.

5. My best friend was upset about her low grade. She (*discuss*) _____ her test with the instructor when I left class.

Part C *Directions:* Complete the sentences in the paragraph. Use the simple present or the present progressive form of the verbs in parentheses. More than one answer may be possible.

      In the Pacific Ocean, various species of whales (*swim*) _____ thousands
                                   1

of miles twice a year. In the winter, they (*live*) _____ in warm tropical
                                      2

seas near Mexico. In the summer, they (*move*) _____ to cooler
                                     3

oceans near Alaska. My dad (*be*) _____ a scientist and now he
                             4

(*study*) _____ marine mammals. Because of his work, my family
             5

(*go*) _____ whale watching every spring and fall when the whales
        6

(*migrate*) _____.
        7

Part D *Directions:* Correct the errors.

1. The workers were very tired and forget to lock the door when they left for the day.

2. I didn't knew about the party for my birthday. It was a surprise.

3. David was very busy yesterday, so today he takes the day off.

4. Steven is in the library. He reading a book.

5. The little boy buys another toy because he broke the first one.

Part E *Directions:* Answer the questions with complete sentences. Use simple or progressive verbs.

1. Did Kathy leave her keys on the hall table?

   No, she _____.

2. Were you sleeping at ten o'clock last night? I tried to call you.

   Yes, I _____.

3. That movie was really funny. Did the kids like it?

   Yes, the kids _____.

4. It's almost dinnertime. Is Jun cooking dinner?

   No, Jun _____.

5. Does Rob usually watch the evening news on TV?

   Yes, he _____.

CHAPTER 2

Perfect and Perfect Progressive Tenses

QUIZ 1 **The Past Participle**   (Charts 2-1 and 2-2)

Directions: Write the simple past and the past participle for each verb.

1. go ___went___ ___gone___
2. see _____ _____
3. take _____ _____
4. buy _____ _____
5. teach _____ _____
6. fly _____ _____
7. make _____ _____
8. eat _____ _____
9. win _____ _____
10. steal _____ _____
11. fall _____ _____
12. build _____ _____
13. feed _____ _____
14. ride _____ _____
15. lose _____ _____
16. give _____ _____
17. forget _____ _____
18. hold _____ _____
19. sing _____ _____
20. tell _____ _____
21. shake _____ _____
22. study _____ _____
23. write _____ _____
24. drink _____ _____

QUIZ 2 **Present Perfect:** *Since and For*   (Chart 2-3)

Directions: Complete the sentences with *since* or *for*.

Example: The Internet connection hasn't worked _____*since*_____ Saturday.

1. The Robinsons have lived in Northridge _____ a long time.
2. Charlie has been in Sri Lanka _____ about three months.
3. The floodwaters have gone down a lot _____ the rain stopped.
4. Selma and Paulo have been married _____ 2004.
5. Travel to Europe has gotten more expensive _____ last summer.
6. I have been waiting here _____ a half hour. Why are you late?
7. The clock tower in the train station hasn't been rebuilt _____ the earthquake.
8. There hasn't been a drought in this country _____ fifteen years.
9. Patricia has worked for a Fortune 500 company _____ January.
10. I have thought about you many times _____ you left. I really miss you.

Directions: Choose the correct completions.

Example: George (*never /(still)*) hasn't read any interesting books.

1. My brother has (*ever / never*) traveled outside the United States.

2. I have lost a lot of weight (*for / since*) I started working out regularly.

3. My sister hasn't graduated from the university (*still / yet*). She hopes to graduate next spring.

4. We have (*already / for*) eaten all of the chocolate. Sorry.

5. Has Mrs. Josenhans (*ever / never*) learned another language?

6. She (*already / still*) hasn't met all of her husband's relatives. He has a large family.

7. I haven't been to the library (*for / since*) months. Have you?

8. My parents have traveled to Germany, Korea, and Canada (*for / so far*) this year. They also plan to travel to Greece.

9. They have lived in Alexandria (*for / since*) January, 2015. They like Egypt very much.

10. We have just (*recently / still*) moved to this city. So far, we like it a lot.

QUIZ 4 **Present Perfect** (Charts 2-3 and 2-4)

Directions: Use the given words to complete the sentences. Use the present perfect form of the verbs in parentheses.

Example: The traffic (*be*) _____has been_____ terrible for hours.

1. The team (*win*) _____ all of its games so far this season.

2. My baby (*get, already*) _____ her first tooth.

3. How many times (*you, call*) _____ Trisha?

4. Layla (*promise*) _____ to text us when she arrives in New York.

5. I (*eat, never*) _____ snake meat. Is it good?

6. You (*learn, not*) _____ how to write an essay yet.

7. Harry (*try*) _____ to contact his great uncle several times.

8. Mr. Polley (*drive*) _____ a city bus since 2009.

9. Writing a book (*be, not*) _____ easy.

10. His education (*give*) _____ him many good opportunities.

Directions: Choose the correct completions.

Example: Joe _____ to check his email last night.

    (a) forgot   b. has forgotten

1. I _____ a cup of coffee since this morning.

    a. didn't have   b. haven't had

2. Norita _____ French in Paris last year.

    a. studied   b. has studied

3. Ms. Field _____ English in Thailand in 2014.

    a. taught   b. has taught

4. We _____ to the art museum several times since last year.

    a. went   b. have gone

5. My son _____ his driving test three times so far.

    a. failed   b. has failed

6. Luka _____ home right after school yesterday.

    a. walked   b. has walked

7. Sam _____ Swiss cheese.

    a. never ate   b. has never eaten

8. Rachael _____ her video project two hours ago.

    a. finished   b. has finished

9. My uncle _____ since last Thursday for his package to arrive.

    a. waited   b. has waited

10. Stephanie _____ a journalist for ten years, from 2002 to 2012.

    a. was   b. has been

Directions: Complete the sentences. Use the present perfect or the simple past form of the verbs in parentheses.

Example: Janice (*talk, not*) _____has not talked_____ to her college roommate for
many years.

1. Patrick (*catch*) _____ several big fish so far this weekend.

2. I (*text*) _____ my mother this morning.

    I (*text, not*) _____ my dad yet.

3. Miss Ames (*give*) _____ the students a lot of quizzes so far
this term.

4. I just (*meet*) _____ Suzanne three months ago. I really

    (*know, not*) _____ her long.

5. Beth (*work*) _____ as a business manager for many years.
She loves her job.

6. You (*change*) _____ a lot since we

    (*see*) _____ you last year. Your hair

    (*grow*) _____ at least six inches since then.

Directions: Choose the correct completions. In some cases, both answers are correct.

Example: I ((have studied)/(have been studying)) English since I was in middle school.

1. Rob (*has worked / has been working*) on his report for two hours. He isn't finished yet.

2. Sarah (*has gone / has been going*) to that museum four times.

3. Niko (*has taken / has been taking*) several computer classes this semester.
   He is enjoying them.

4. You (*have worked / have been working*) in your garden all afternoon.

5. Ruth (*has seemed / has been seeming*) sick since Monday.

6. Martha (*has read / has been reading*) that book several times.

7. The Marshalls (*have lived / have been living*) in Boston for five years.

8. I (*have known / have been knowing*) my best friend since elementary school.

9. Faisal (*has not visited / has not been visiting*) his grandmother yet.

10. Teresa (*has chatted / has been chatting*) online with friends since she got home from school.

Directions: Complete the sentences. Use the present progressive or the present perfect progressive form of the verbs in parentheses.

Example: The boys (*swim*) _____*are swimming*_____ at the beach right now. They

(*swim*) _____*have been swimming*_____ since this morning.

1. It's almost 3:00 now and the train is late. I (*wait*) _____ at the

   station for about 20 minutes.

2. Right now Rick (*take*) _____ some pictures of his friends. He

   (*take*) _____ photos of them for 30 minutes.

3. Please be quiet. The movie (*start*) _____ now.

4. I'm really tired this morning. I (*sleep, not*) _____ well since

   last week.

5. Mr. and Mrs. McEnroe (*plan*) _____ their daughter's wedding

   since last year.

6. The weather is terrible today. It (*rain*) _____ now. The wind

   (*blow*) _____ really hard now, too.

Directions: Complete the sentences with the words in parentheses. Use the past perfect.

Example: When I called my parents, they (*hear, already*) _____*had already heard*_____ about my

   car accident.

1. Mr. Holton said that he (*finish, not*) _____ his coffee yet.

2. The chef (*put*) _____ too much pepper in the soup. It was too spicy.

3. By the time Harriet took the quiz, she (*forget*) _____ most of the

   vocabulary words.

4. The kids (*break*) _____ the window with a rock, so their mother

   was angry.

5. I didn't recognize my aunt when she got off the plane yesterday. She

   (*lose*) _____ about 30 pounds!

6. Ivan couldn't ride his bike. It (*have*) _____ a flat tire for weeks.

7. The bread (*become*) _____ stale, so it didn't taste good.

8. The woman was wearing a beautiful silk dress. She (*buy*) _____ the

   dress in Hong Kong.

9. The sunset was orange, pink, and gold. I (*see, never*) _____ anything

   so colorful.

Directions: Choose the correct completions.

Example: My brother (*looked* / (*had looked*)) for his glasses for an hour by the time I arrived.

1. Sarah (*already finished* / *had already finished*) reading her email when her computer shut down.

2. The students (*didn't finish* / *hadn't finished*) their tests when the teacher told them to stop working.

3. The old man (*died* / *had died*) by the time the ambulance (*came* / *had come*).

4. John woke up at 8:30. Charles woke up at 10:30. In other words, John (*was* / *had been*) up for two hours by the time Charles woke up.

5. When Mimi (*arrived* / *had arrived*) at the theater, the show had already started.

6. Mr. Johnson was worried about his wife. It was 10:00 P.M. and she (*didn't call* / *hadn't called*) yet.

7. My teacher (*already left* / *had already left*) by the time I got to her office.

8. Yesterday, I (*played* / *had played*) tennis with my sister.

9. Before yesterday, Mark and Rita (*never visited* / *had never visited*) such a big city. They had a lot of fun.

10. I found the perfect gift for my father. When I (*wanted* / *had wanted*) to pay for it, I realized that I (*forgot* / *had forgotten*) my money at home. I (*was* / *had been*) so embarrassed!

Directions: Read about Linda's day. Then complete the sentences with the past perfect or the past perfect progressive form of the verbs in parentheses.

Linda had a horrible day yesterday.
> She woke up late.
> She didn't have coffee.
> She missed her bus.
> Her computer at work crashed.
> She lost some important work.
> Her boss was unhappy.
> Linda got a terrible headache.

Example: Linda (*dream*) _____*had been dreaming*_____ about a vacation at the beach before she woke up.

1. When Linda's alarm clock rang, she (*sleep*) _____ very deeply.

2. She discovered that she (*forget*) _____ to buy coffee.

3. When Linda got to the bus stop, the bus (*leave, already*) _____.

4. By the time the next bus arrived, Linda (*wait*) _____ for 30 minutes.

5. Before Linda's computer crashed, she (*save, not*) _____ some important documents.

6. When her boss came in, Linda (*try*) _____ to recover the documents for an hour.

7. When Linda's boss realized that Linda (*lose*) _____ some important documents, he was unhappy.

8. Linda (*get*) _____ a headache.

9. Her headache (*stop, not*) _____ by the time she got home from work.

10. Linda (*have, never*) _____ such a terrible day.

Directions: Choose the correct completions.

Example: When I ((had finished)/ have finished) my lunch, I went back to the library.

1. Ray (*has been seeing / has seen*) a doctor several times about his allergies. I think he is feeling better.

2. The concert (*had just begun / just began*) when the power went off.

3. I (*have never been / had never been*) to Asia, but I would like to visit.

4. The apartment manager (*had told / has told*) us about the meeting, but we weren't able to attend.

5. Megan and Scott (*have been seeing / have seen*) each other for two months. They are falling in love.

6. José (*has been sitting / had been sitting*) at the computer for two hours. His eyes are tired.

7. The basketball team (*has won / had won*) all their games until last night. They lost by 3 points.

8. By the time we left the café, we (*have been talking / had been talking*) for nearly two hours.

Part A *Directions:* Choose the correct completions.

1. Apple Computers _____ many different iPads since 2010.

   a. produced   b. has produced

2. Charlie _____ too much chocolate cake at the party last night.

   a. ate   b. has eaten

3. Jason _____ on the soccer team, the Switchbacks, for eight years.

   a. plays   b. has been playing

4. Mr. and Mrs. Lohman _____ in Heidelberg for five years, but now they live in Berlin.

   a. lived   b. have lived

5. The Odens _____ in Korea for 15 years. They live in Seoul, the capital.

   a. lived   b. have been living

6. Tim _____ any good movies lately.

   a. didn't see   b. hasn't seen

7. Last week I _____ my dog to the veterinarian.

   a. took   b. have taken

8. _____ the new book by Stephanie Bond yet? It's really exciting!

   a. Did you read   b. Have you read

9. My parents _____ members of the swim club since 2009.

   a. were   b. have been

10. Nathan _____ me a text message two hours ago.

    a. sent   b. has sent

Part B *Directions:* Complete the sentences. Use the present perfect, past perfect, or perfect progressive form of the verbs in parentheses.

      The Museum of Modern Art in New York City is an extraordinary place. It houses more than 150,000 works. My cousin, Tina, (*visit*) _____ the museum
1
several times. The painting she (*enjoy*) _____ the most is *The Starry*
2
Night by Vincent van Gogh. She (*learn*) _____ a lot about art from
3
her museum visits. Every time she goes to the museum, there is something new. The
last time she was there, she saw a painting that she (*see, never*) _____
4
before. After Tina (*look*) _____ at paintings for several hours, the
5
museum closed, so she had to leave.

Part C *Directions:* Complete the sentences. Use *since*, *for*, *already*, *yet* or *just*. Use each word once.

1. Philip has been waiting for the results of the medical tests _____ three weeks.

2. We haven't seen Ben and Judy _____ we got home from our vacation last month.

3. I don't know which dress I like better. I haven't decided _____ .

4. Maja had _____ forgotten the address and had to look it up again.

5. Have you met Anne's new boyfriend? I _____ met him yesterday. He's really nice.

Part D *Directions:* Look at the time line of events in violinist Max Dubosy's life. Complete the sentences. Use the present perfect, past perfect, or a perfect progressive form of the verbs in parentheses. More than one answer may be possible.

1993	Max Dubosy is born in Salt Lake City, Utah.
1996	Dubosy has his first violin lesson, and loves it.
2003	At age ten, Dubosy performs a solo with the Utah Symphony Orchestra.
2004	Dubosy performs at Carnegie Hall in New York.
2005	Dubosy travels weekly to Los Angeles to study violin.
2008	Dubosy moves to Los Angeles to attend high school and study violin at the Colburn School.
2008	Dubosy starts to perform in cities around the world, including London, Hong Kong, and Berlin.
2012	Dubosy wins a $50,000 scholarship to continue his music studies.
2012–2014	Dubosy spends part of the summer teaching young violinists at Aspen Music Camp.
2013	Dubosy comes back to his hometown to perform with the Utah Symphony.
2014	Dubosy signs with an agency to continue his professional career.

Max Dubosy was born in Utah and (*play*) _____ the violin nearly

his whole life. By the time he was ten years old, he (*play*) _____
                                                                    2
the violin for seven years. After Dubosy (*study*) _____ violin in
                                                        3
Utah for several years, he started studying with a teacher in Los Angeles. He finally

moved to Los Angeles after he (*travel*) _____ there to study violin
                                              4
for three years. Since then, Dubosy (*perform*) _____ in concerts all
                                                    5
over the world and (*cause*) _____ great excitement among classical
                                  6
music fans. He (*encourage*) _____ other children to learn the violin.
                                  7
His fans (*watch*) _____ him develop into a world-class violinist.
                        8
Since he first started playing the violin, Dubosy (*become*) _____
                                                                    9
one of America's most popular young classical musicians. In fact, he

(*win*) _____ the hearts of classical music fans around the world.
            10

Part A *Directions:* Choose the correct completions.

1. My wife and I _____ dessert after dinner on Saturday.

   a. have shared   b. shared

2. Eric _____ his homework until 11:30 P.M. last night.

   a. hasn't finished   b. didn't finish

3. My brother repairs cars. He _____ on three different cars so far today.

   a. has worked   b. worked

4. Mai can't find her notebook. _____ it?

   a. Has anyone seen   b. Did anyone see

5. Clara _____ from Stockholm University in 2012.

   a. has graduated   b. graduated

6. The weather _____ especially warm and sunny lately.

   a. has been   b. was

7. Chang _____ for his vocabulary test for two hours yesterday.

   a. has studied   b. studied

8. My mother _____ a cake in years. She always buys one at the bakery.

   a. hasn't baked   b. didn't bake

9. David likes to listen to music. Over the last two years, he _____ many songs on his phone.

   a. has downloaded   b. downloaded

10. Nicola's daughter _____ the piano since 2:00.

    a. has been practicing   b. practiced

Part B *Directions:* Complete the sentences in the paragraphs. Use the present perfect, past perfect, or perfect progressive form of the verbs in parentheses. More than one answer may be possible.

    A. Kyoto was Japan's capital from 794 to 1868. Since that time, Kyoto

        (*become*) _____ a tourist and cultural center. UNESCO, part of the
        ₁

        United Nations, (*make*) _____ Kyoto a "World Heritage Site" because
                      ₂

        of the city's historic buildings such as palaces and temples. Many of the traditional

        buildings (*be*) _____ restored, and thousands of tourists visit them
              ₃

        every year.

    B. Christopher and his wife (*be*) _____ interested in China for
                              ₁

        a long time. They went to China last year. Up to that time, Christopher

        (*read*) _____ many books about Chinese history and culture,
           ₂

        and he (*study*) _____ the Chinese language for several years.
                  ₃

Part C *Directions:* Complete the sentences. Use *since, for, already, yet,* or *just*. Use each word once.

    1. My parents have _____ been so generous. I can't accept more money

      from them.

    2. The taxi driver hasn't had an accident _____ 15 years. He's a

      great driver.

    3. I _____ heard about Paula's accident a few minutes ago. I hope

      she's okay.

    4. Mike went to Washington, D.C., last summer. He hadn't been there

      _____ he was ten years old, and the city had changed a lot.

    5. Dana is still waiting for Russ. He hasn't arrived _____ .

Part D *Directions:* Look at the time line of events in robotics expert Jennifer Lundquist's life. Complete the sentences. Use present perfect, past perfect, or a perfect progressive form of the verbs in parentheses. More than one answer may be possible.

1971	Jennifer Lundquist is born in Portland, Oregon, U.S.
1977	Lundquist gets her first Lego toys and begins building things.
1990	Lundquist studies at the University of Notre Dame and takes her first class in robotics.
1991	Lundquist and her classmate, Charlie Miles, win a robotics competition.
2000 & 2002	Lundquist wins awards for her work.
2004	Lundquist becomes the Director of Robotics at Milton Technology.
2011	Milton Technology invents a robot that can help children with homework.
2013	Lundquist leaves Milton Technology and devotes her time to designing robotic toys.
2014	Lundquist and her business partner Loren Graham form the Robotkids organization.

Jennifer Lundquist is an unusual woman with an amazing career. She (*build*) _____ things since she was a little girl playing with blocks.
1

Lundquist (*work*) _____ in robotics since 1990, and she
2

(*be*) _____ a central figure in the development of industrial and
3

household robotics since that time. When Lundquist and a classmate, Charlie Miles, won

a robotics competition in college, Lundquist (*learn, already*) _____
4

a lot about robots and how to design them. She continued her work, and by 2002,

she (*win*) _____ two awards in design. Because of her
5

hard work and great ideas, Lundquist was very successful, and by 2004, she

(*become*) _____ the Director of Robotics at Milton Technology. By
6

2011, Lundquist (*lead*) _____ the company in the development
7

of an amazing HomeworkBot. By 2013, Lundquist (*work*) _____
8

at the company for many years, so she quit her job at Milton Technologies. Since

then, she (*design*) _____ robots for kids. In 2014, Lundquist
9

and her partner started an organization to teach kids about robots. So far they

(*give*) _____ science scholarships to hundreds of young people.
10

Future Time

QUIZ 1 Simple Future: Forms of *Will* and *Be Going To*   (Chart 3-1)

Directions: Complete the predictions. Use **will** and **be going to** with the verbs in parentheses.

Example: a. In 3 months, speaking English (*be*) _____*will be*_____ easier for me than it is now.

   b. In 3 months, speaking English (*be*) _____*is going to be*_____ easier for me than it is now.

1. a. In 5 years, I (*graduate*) _____ from the university.

   b. In 5 years, I (*graduate*) _____ from the university.

2. a. In 10 years, my mother (*have*) _____ grandchildren.

   b. In 10 years, my mother (*have*) _____ grandchildren.

3. a. In 15 years, children (*take*) _____ a solar-powered bus to school.

   b. In 15 years, children (*take*) _____ a solar-powered bus to school.

4. a. In 20 years, cars (*fly*) _____ .

   b. In 20 years, cars (*fly*) _____ .

5. a. In 25 years, humans (*live*) _____ on the moon.

   b. In 25 years, humans (*live*) _____ on the moon.

QUIZ 2 *Will* vs. *Be Going To*   (Chart 3-2)

Directions: Decide if each verb in *italics* expresses a *prediction*, a prior *plan*, or *willingness*.

Example: My mom *is probably going to call* today.   (prediction) plan willingness

1. Hilary said she *is going to go* to Texas after the conference.   prediction plan willingness

2. I think it*'s going to be* an exciting soccer season.   prediction plan willingness

3. The windows are really dirty. I *will wash* them today.   prediction plan willingness

4. Barry *will probably be* here soon.   prediction plan willingness

5. Shirley has a beautiful voice. She *is going to be* a big success.   prediction plan willingness

6. I'm so tired. I *am not going to go* out tonight.   prediction plan willingness

7. A: Calum, your room is a mess.
   B: I*'ll clean* my room later, Mom. I promise.   prediction plan willingness

8. Marcel *is going to start* his new job next week. He's excited.   prediction plan willingness

9. Pam *will be* late. She's always late.   prediction plan willingness

10. Mr. Mars needs this report by 5:00, so I *am going to finish* it.   prediction plan willingness

Directions: Complete the sentences. Use ***be going to*** if the speaker is expressing a prior plan. If you think he/she has no prior plan, use ***will***.

Examples: Ann: What time does the library open?

Barry: It opens at 8:00 A.M. I (*leave*) _____am going to leave_____ at 7:30.

Meg: What time does the library open?

Bryan: I don't know. I (*check*) _____will check_____ the schedule on their website.

1. Nolan: It's starting to get a little chilly.

   Mary: I (*get*) _____ your sweater for you.

2. Erica: With your car in the shop, how are you going to get to work?

   Dan: I (*take*) _____ the bus.

3. Chester: Have you made plans for New Year's Eve?

   Emma: Yes. We (*go*) _____ to a party at my sister's house.

4. Mr. Smith: I need to stop at the bookstore before we go to lunch.

   Mr. White: Oh, so do I! I (*meet*) _____ you in front of the building at noon.

5. Frank: What are Fareed's plans after graduation?

   Abdul: He (*work*) _____ for a year before he goes to graduate school.

6. Chris: What are Gary's plans after graduation?

   Julie: He isn't sure. Perhaps he (*work*) _____ for a year and then begin graduate school.

7. Amy: What are you going to do this weekend?

   Sue: I (*clean, probably*) _____ out the garage. On Saturday night, I (*go*) _____ to the theater.

8. Carrie: Oh, no! We're too late. The copy shop is closed!

   Oliver: Don't worry. I (*get*) _____ up early tomorrow and copy the documents before our appointment.

9. Ruth: How many people do you expect at the party?

   David: About 20 people (*come*) _____ .

   Ruth: That's nice.

Directions: Make **negative** sentences about the future using the given words. Use *will* or *be going to* to express the meaning given in parentheses. More than one answer may be possible.

Example: Katarina \ leave \ until Saturday \ not (*prior plan*)

Katarina isn't going to leave until Saturday.

1. my parents \ let \ me \ drive \ on the freeway \ not (*refusal*)

   _____

2. Teri and George \ come \ to the wedding \ not (*prior plan*)

   _____

3. that dog \ stop \ barking \ not (*refusal*)

   _____

4. Luigi \ pass \ his math class \ this semester \ not (*prediction*)

   _____

5. Nathan and Lucy \ live \ in Bellingham \ after this year \ not (*prior plan*)

   _____

6. you \ get \ to the airport \ in this traffic jam \ never (*prediction*)

   _____

7. my neighbor \ turn down \ his music \ at night \ not (*refusal*)

   _____

8. I \ win \ a prize \ at the carnival \ not (*prediction*)

   _____

9. my sister \ let \ me \ borrow \ her clothes \ not (*refusal*)

   _____

10. we \ see \ a movie \ tonight \ not (*prior plan*)

    _____

Directions: Choose the correct completions.

Example: When I ((go)/ will go) to New York next month, I (visit /(am going to visit)) my friend Don.

1. As soon as the game (*ends / will end*), the winning team (*receive / will receive*) a prize.

2. When she (*finishes / is going to finish*) sewing the button on, she (*irons / is going to iron*) the shirt.

3. I (*wait / will wait*) here until you (*park / are going to park*) the car.

4. Mark is going to Sweden. After he (*arrives / will arrive*) in Stockholm, he (*rents / is going to rent*) a car.

5. The water is heating now. When it (*boils / is going to boil*), Sally (*makes / will make*) tea.

6. Next year, after I (*get / will get*) my degree, I (*travel / am going to travel*) around the world.

7. Bill hates his job. When he (*finds / is going to find*) a new job, he (*is / will be*) happier.

8. The scientists (*go / will go*) home as soon as they (*finish / will finish*) their experiment.

9. My dad (*stops / will stop*) smoking after the doctor (*tells / is going to tell*) him to.

10. People (*love / are going to love*) this song as soon as they (*hear / will hear*) it.

Directions: Use the given words to complete the sentences. Use **will**, **be going to**, or the simple present tense.

Example: Francis will leave for Vermont on Friday. After he

(*spend*) _____ *spends* _____ a week there, he

(*go*) _____ *will go* _____ to New Hampshire.

1. My birthday is next Tuesday. After I (*celebrate*) _____ with my family, I (*have*) _____ a party with friends.

2. Rami's train is going to arrive at 7:32. I (*wait*) _____ in the station until it (*come*) _____ .

3. Gary is going to order a book online. Before the book (*arrive*) _____ in the mail, Gary (*pay*) _____ for it with his credit card.

4. The movie will begin at 7:15. The audience (*be*) _____ quiet as soon as the movie (*start*) _____ .

5. Kevin doesn't have a car yet, but when he (*buy*) _____ his first car, he (*give*) _____ his friends a ride.

6. Belinda is going to stay up late tonight. She (*watch*) _____ movies until she (*go*) _____ to bed.

Using the Present Progressive and the Simple Present to Express Future Time (Chart 3-4)

Directions: Decide if each sentence expresses *now, habitually,* or *in the future.*

Example: Nancy goes dancing every weekend.   now   (habitually)   in the future

1.	My brother is getting a new computer next week.	now	habitually	in the future
2.	Diane usually arrives on time.	now	habitually	in the future
3.	I'm waiting for the elevator.	now	habitually	in the future
4.	We're going to Morocco in December.	now	habitually	in the future
5.	My biology class starts at 8:00 A.M.	now	habitually	in the future
6.	We are spending a week at the beach this summer.	now	habitually	in the future
7.	The coffee shop closes in ten minutes.	now	habitually	in the future
8.	That store charges too much for clothes.	now	habitually	in the future
9.	My friends and I are going shopping this weekend.	now	habitually	in the future
10.	Look! It's snowing!	now	habitually	in the future

Using the Present Progressive and the Simple Present to Express Future Time (Chart 3-4)

Directions: Complete the sentences. Use the simple present or present progressive form of the verbs in parentheses to express future time. More than one answer may be possible.

Example: Next Thursday, the orchestra (*play*) _____*is playing*_____ a concert.

The concert (*start*) _____*starts*_____ at 7:00 P.M.

1. The vegetable market (*open*) _____ at 10:00 A.M. tomorrow.
   Let's go early.

2. My uncle (*come*) _____ for a visit soon.

3. Flight 726 (*leave*) _____ Portland at 7:23 A.M.

4. Next summer, we (*visit*) _____ relatives in Calcutta. I'm excited!

5. My boss (*leave*) _____ in a few minutes, so I need to talk to her now.

6. Hurry up! My favorite program (*begin*) _____ at 8:00 P.M., and I
   don't want to miss it.

7. Ruth and David (*go*) _____ on vacation for ten days. I'm jealous!

8. We (*buy*) _____ a new stove next week. Our old one isn't working.

9. The library (*close*) _____ at 5:00 P.M. tomorrow because it's Friday.

10. I (*meet*) _____ my parents for dinner after work today.

Directions: Complete the sentences. Use *will* and the future progressive form of the verbs in parentheses.

Example: Next Thursday, Pranab (*drive*) _____*will be driving*_____ from London
to Newcastle.

1. Steve: Tomorrow from 10 A.M. to 12 P.M. Tracey (*take*) _____
   her driving test.

   Dave: And you (*worry*) _____!

2. Mary: The twins (*graduate*) _____ from different universities
   on the same day in June.

   Reggie: Soon they (*look*) _____ for jobs.

   Mary: Yes, and at this time next year, they (*work*) _____.

3. Next weekend, my wife (*travel*) _____ to a conference in Milan.
   I (*take*) _____ care of our children at home.

4. Our family will be busy this Saturday. My husband (*clean*) _____
   the garage, my son (*wash*) _____ the car, and I
   (*relax*) _____.

QUIZ 10 **Future Perfect and Future Perfect Progressive** (Chart 3-6)

Directions: Complete the sentences. Use the future perfect form of the verbs in parentheses.

Example: By the time Martin comes home from work, his children
(*finish*) _____*will have finished*_____ their homework.

1. I love pizza. When I finish this piece of pizza, I (*eat*) _____
   three pieces.

2. John is going to Canada for a week. By the time he comes back home, the workers
   (*finish*) _____ painting his house.

3. The basketball team is having a great year. By the end of this season, they
   (*win*) _____ many games.

4. Dr. Munsen takes good care of his patients. When he retires next year, he
   (*be*) _____ a doctor for 25 years.

5. Yasuko is playing in a concert this Saturday. After this concert, she
   (*play*) _____ in six concerts so far this year.

Directions: Complete the sentences. Use the future perfect progressive form of the verbs in parentheses.

Example: When Mark buys his new car next year, he (*save*) ___will have been saving___ for it for a while.

1. George is playing a video game. By the time he finishes the game, he

   (*play*) _____ for several hours.

2. My brother is talking on the phone to his girlfriend. When he finally says good-bye to her,

   they (*talk*) _____ for over an hour.

3. It rained yesterday, it's raining today, and it will probably rain again tomorrow. It

   (*rain*) _____ for three days in a row.

4. I moved to Tokyo ten years ago and to Beijing three years before that. In five more years,

   I (*live*) _____ in Asia for eighteen years.

5. Alexander started learning English when he was in the first grade. By the time he

   graduates from high school, he (*learn*) _____ English for twelve years.

Directions: Correct the errors.

Example: My brother ~~came~~ *is going* to visit us next week.

1. At noon tomorrow, he will have been attending a luncheon at the Hilton Hotel.

2. As soon as the program will end, I'm going to bed.

3. By the time Mr. Wilcox reads my email, I will leave the office.

4. I will have finished my homework after school.

5. After the baby is going to stop crying, she will fall asleep.

6. Is English being an international language in 25 years?

7. The swimmers will train for several years by the time the Olympics begin next summer.

8. In six months, I am living in a new apartment.

9. Benjamin plays at a new golf club this weekend.

10. We have tickets to a play tomorrow night. We will see "The Mongol Horsemen."

Directions: Change all of the sentences to the future.

Example: By the time Joe arrived, the party had already ended.

By the time Joe arrives, the party will have already ended.

1. When my brother came home from school, he had two cookies and a glass of milk.

_____

2. The builders had been making a lot of progress since early morning.

_____

3. At 10:00, I was teaching my physics class.

_____

4. By 3:00, Junichi had finished his essay on studying in the U.S.

_____

5. After we ate dinner at the Ethiopian restaurant, we went to a movie.

_____

6. Carl was really tired. By the time the movie ended, he was falling asleep.

_____

7. As soon as I finished my homework, I called my best friend.

_____

8. After the music stopped, everyone was waiting for the next song.

_____

9. When the fireworks started, people clapped excitedly.

_____

10. Dr. Solack was seeing patients all day. She was very busy.

_____

CHAPTER 3 – TEST 1

Part A *Directions:* Read each sentence. Decide if the meaning of the verb is *now, habitually,* or *in the future.*

1. I am going to go to England during winter break.   now   habitually   in the future

2. The plane leaves at 5:30 P.M. today.   now   habitually   in the future

3. I arrive in London at noon the next day.   now   habitually   in the future

4. I am reading a travel book about England right now.   now   habitually   in the future

5. I go to England every winter.   now   habitually   in the future

Part B *Directions:* Choose all possible completions.

1. After Mary _____ her grammar lesson, she _____ on her math homework.

   a. reviews   a. work

   b. will review   b. is going to work

   c. will have reviewed   c. will have worked

2. Rob _____ 23 years old before he _____ his first full-time job.

   a. turns   a. gets

   b. will turn   b. will get

   c. will have turned   c. will be getting

3. By the time Janice _____ in November, she _____ at the bank for 37 years.

   a. retires   a. works

   b. is going to retire   b. will work

   c. will have retired   c. will have been working

4. When Margaret _____ to Asia next year, she _____ her sister in Sydney, Australia, too.

   a. travels   a. visits

   b. will travel   b. is going to visit

   c. will be traveling   c. will have visited

5. The boys _____ all afternoon by the time the hole _____ finally deep enough to plant the tree.

   a. dig   a. is

   b. will dig   b. will be

   c. will have been digging   c. will have been

Future Time   33

Part C *Directions:* Complete these short conversations with the future form of the verbs in parentheses. Use *will* or ***be going to***. More than one answer may be possible.

1. Helen: Do you want to go to the beach tomorrow?

    Yuka: Oh, I don't think so. According to the weather report, it

    (*rain*) _____ .

2. Richard: Why did your mom make so much chicken soup?

    Alex: She (*give*) _____ some to our neighbor. He is sick.

3. Marva: The kids are really hungry.

    Dan: OK. I (*make*) _____ some sandwiches for them.

4. Yung: What are your plans after work today?

    Lee: My friends and I (*go*) _____ out to dinner or see a movie.

5. Zeyad: My test grade isn't very good. I got a 69%.

    Fatima: That's too bad. Your parents (*not, be*) _____ very happy
    about that.

Part D *Directions:* Change all of the sentences to the future.

1. Barbara was working at the computer until she went out with her friends.

    _____

2. By the time Carol went to bed, she had finished correcting all her students' papers.

    _____

3. In the morning we went to the zoo, and then we ate lunch in the park.

    _____

4. When my daughter graduated from the university, I was so proud.

    _____

5. Jason had never met his girlfriends' parents.

    _____

Part E *Directions:* Correct the errors.

1. The movie starting at 7:45 P.M. and will end around 10:00 P.M.

2. As soon as I will find my key, I will open the door.

3. The book sale tomorrow will have been helping the students raise money for their trip.

4. By the time he arrives in Boston, Bert will spend three weeks cycling across the U.S.

5. I won't to lend my brother any money. He will never pay it back!

Part A *Directions:* Read each sentence. Decide if the meaning of the verb is *now, habitually,* or *in the future.*

1. I am taking three classes this term.   now   habitually   in the future

2. He's reading a really scary book.   now   habitually   in the future

3. The office opens at nine tomorrow.   now   habitually   in the future

4. Mitchell is coming as soon as he can.   now   habitually   in the future

5. Dana starts school at 7:50 A.M.   now   habitually   in the future

Part B *Directions:* Choose all possible completions.

1. Mona _____ on the accounts all day by the time she _____ home.

   a. works   a. goes

   b. will work   b. is going to go

   c. will have been working   c. will have been going

2. After Michael _____ the train to Los Angeles, he _____ writing his report on his laptop.

   a. catches   a. finishes

   b. is going to catch   b. is going to finish

   c. will have caught   c. will have finished

3. As soon as Betty _____ the ripe apples from her tree, she _____ them for an apple pie.

   a. picks   a. uses

   b. will pick   b. is going to use

   c. will have picked   c. will have been using

4. Robert _____ into his own apartment when he _____ a job.

   a. moves   a. finds

   b. is going to move   b. will find

   c. will have been moving   c. will have found

5. By the time Nikki _____ cutting the last customer's hair, she _____ on her feet for eight hours.

   a. finishes   a. is

   b. will finish   b. will

   c. will have finished   c. will have been

Part C *Directions:* Complete these short conversations with the future form of the verbs in parentheses. Use *will* or *be going to*. More than one answer may be possible.

1. Ali: Did you pass the test?

   Kristy: I'm pretty sure I did. I think I (*get*) _____ a high grade.

2. Lola: Do you have anything special planned this weekend?

   Nancy: Yes! My husband and I (*go*) _____ out to dinner for our anniversary.

3. Mark: This algebra problem is too difficult for me.

   Minsoo: Don't worry. Dennis (*help*) _____ you. He is good at math.

4. Sarah: What are Jamal's plans for his birthday?

   Adam: His girlfriend (*have*) _____ a party for him.

5. Terry: Taka had an accident and damaged his new car.

   Brad: Oh, no! The repairs (*be*) _____ expensive.

Part D *Directions:* Change all of the sentences to the future.

1. Chuck was giving a lecture in his history class.

   _____

2. She threw her old shoes away and bought some new ones.

   _____

3. By 4:00 we had been sitting on the runway for an hour. Bad weather had delayed our flight.

   _____

4. I studied until it was time to go to my appointment with my lawyer.

   _____

5. Michelle had travelled to Spain three times.

   _____

Part E *Directions:* Correct the errors.

1. Tommy will have been losing 20 pounds by December.

2. The radio station will be announced the name of the prizewinner at 4:30. We have to listen!

3. My cousins are going to send me a postcard from Bali when they will get there.

4. By the time my mom will come home, I will clean up the kitchen.

5. Mr. Ballard will have been being a very good principal for our school.

Review of Verb Tenses

CHAPTER 4 – TEST 1

Directions: Choose the correct completions.

1. Robert _____ for the International Atomic Energy Agency since 2010.

   a. is working   b. works   c. has worked

2. Mieko broke her leg while she _____ down a mountain.

   a. was skiing   b. skied   c. had been skiing

3. The children _____ into the house when it began to rain.

   a. run   b. ran   c. are running

4. Every time Nancy _____ some money, she asks her father.

   a. needs   b. needed   c. has needed

5. Kevin _____ very happy at his job until he got a new supervisor.

   a. has been   b. had been   c. is

6. Paulo _____ his family to Disneyland on vacation three times.

   a. has taken   b. takes   c. has been taking

7. Nadia will give her report to her boss as soon as she _____ a few figures.

   a. checked   b. will check   c. checks

8. By the time Fatima finishes medical school, she _____ over $60,000 to pay for her education.

   a. borrows   b. will borrow   c. will have borrowed

9. We _____ to fly to Belgrade, but it was too foggy. We had to take the train.

   a. were going   b. was going   c. have gone

10. Philip _____ most of the peanuts by the time the guests arrived.

    a. is already eating   b. has already eaten   c. had already eaten

11. When I arrived in Vienna, I _____ for 14 hours.

    a. had been traveling   b. was traveling   c. travel

(continued on the next page)

12. While David was washing the dishes, he _____ a glass.

    a. was breaking   b. broke   c. had broken

13. The movie _____ in theaters next Tuesday.

    a. will come out   b. came out   c. has come out

14. This semester, I _____ a chemistry class.

    a. take   b. takes   c. am taking

15. When Greg _____ hard, he gets good grades.

    a. studies   b. study   c. studied

16. By this time next week, I _____ painting my house.

    a. finish   b. finishes   c. will have finished

17. Wear your boots. It _____ now.

    a. is snowing   b. snows   c. will have snowed

18. By the time Mary retires, she _____ music for 35 years.

    a. is teaching   b. has taught   c. will have been teaching

19. Piet didn't hear the phone because he _____ to music with his earphones on.

    a. was listening   b. listened   c. listens

20. Dad _____ at the airport when I arrive.

    a. was waiting   b. waits   c. will be waiting

21. The Olympic swimmer _____ many races so far this year.

    a. wins   b. has won   c. won

22. As soon as Martina gets over her cold, she _____ to work.

    a. returns   b. returned   c. will return

23. At this exact time next Saturday, we _____ to Hawaii.

    a. will be flying   b. fly   c. flew

24. Last year, Tariq _____ a terrible car accident.

    a. has had   b. had been having   c. had

25. Judy _____ how to play chess for the last two days. She really likes it.

    a. is learning   b. learns   c. has been learning

Directions: Choose the correct completions.

1. This year, the Baldwins _____ skiing in Whistler, British Columbia, over New Year's.

   a. are going   b. go   c. will have gone

2. The computer _____ slowly since we installed the new operating system.

   a. was running   b. has been running   c. will run

3. When I _____ my wrecked car, I cried.

   a. was seeing   b. have seen   c. saw

4. My little sister _____ everywhere. She has a lot of energy.

   a. run   b. runs   c. running

5. I _____ call you earlier today, but I lost my phone.

   a. have gone   b. was gone   c. was going to

6. The young teacher _____ such naughty students. She had to be strict with the class.

   a. has never taught   b. had never taught   c. is never teaching

7. In the past ten years, the western United States _____ faster than other areas of the country.

   a. is growing   b. has grown   c. had been growing

8. By the time I finish the test, all of the other students _____ the class.

   a. will leave   b. are leaving   c. will have left

9. Maria _____ for the airport at 5:00 A.M. tomorrow.

   a. will be leaving   b. left   c. was leaving

10. In 2023, Collin _____ in politics for 30 years.

    a. worked   b. will work   c. will have been working

11. Right now I _____ my cell phone in my pocket.

    a. carried   b. am carrying   c. carry

12. Peter can't budget well. Last month he _____ all of his money by the 15th of the month.

    a. spends   b. was spending   c. had spent

(continued on the next page)

13. Leila _____ two great novels so far.

    a. has written   b. was writing   c. wrote

14. Maurice _____ two soccer teams next season. He loves soccer.

    a. coaches   b. has coached   c. will be coaching

15. Joann and Mark _____ a great view over the ocean from their hotel room. They enjoyed staying there.

    a. had   b. has   c. will have

16. When my father-in-law retired, my mother-in-law also _____ her job.

    a. has quit   b. quit   c. quits

17. Junko _____ in an apartment in Atlanta now.

    a. is living   b. living   c. has lived

18. While the cat _____ on Monique's lap, it fell asleep.

    a. had sat   b. was sitting   c. has sat

19. The doctor _____ to us when he has finished the surgery.

    a. talks   b. has talked   c. will talk

20. By the time the firefighters _____, the house had burned to the ground.

    a. arrive   b. arrived   c. will arrive

21. The Chinese _____ moon cakes every year during the Mid-Autumn Festival.

    a. eat   b. were eating   c. are eating

22. The teacher _____ the lesson as soon as she takes attendance.

    a. has begun   b. began   c. will begin

23. I didn't know anything about computer animation until I _____ a class.

    a. took   b. take   c. will take

24. I _____ any good movies this year. Have you?

    a. had seen   b. saw   c. haven't seen

25. When the mail carrier came to the door, I _____ on the phone.

    a. talked   b. was talking   c. have talked

CHAPTER 5

Subject-Verb Agreement

Final -s / -es: Use and Spelling   (Chart 5-1)

Directions: Use ***-s*** or ***-es*** to make the plurals of the given words. Change the ***-y*** to an ***-i*** where necessary.

Examples: bride _____*brides*_____   lash _____*lashes*_____

1. church _____
2. boy _____
3. chicken _____
4. box _____
5. kiss _____
6. land _____
7. month _____
8. tax _____
9. lady _____
10. cough _____

11. buzz _____
12. salary _____
13. list _____
14. language _____
15. friend _____
16. dish _____
17. business _____
18. minute _____
19. valley _____
20. family _____

Basic Subject-Verb Agreement   (Chart 5-2)

Directions: Choose the correct completions.

Example: Alex and his brother (*is* / *(are)*) studying French in Lyon this summer.

1.
   a. The students in their French class (*comes* / *come*) from many different countries.

   b. Every student (*needs* / *need*) a student ID card to study at the language school.

   c. Practicing French regularly (*is* / *are*) necessary if they want to speak French well.

2.
   a. These days almost everyone (*has* / *have*) a cell phone.

   b. Cell phone service in many Asian countries (*is* / *are*) cheaper than in the U.S.

   c. The phones available in the U.S. sometimes (*isn't* / *aren't*) as advanced as the phones sold in Asia.

   d. Communicating through mobile apps (*has* / *have*) become more popular in the last few years.

3.
   a. Martha, her husband, and son (*leaves* / *leave*) for vacation next Monday.

   b. Travel plans for a family vacation (*requires* / *require*) careful preparation.

   c. Each tourist site and museum (*is* / *are*) sure to be interesting for them.

Directions: Complete the sentences. Use the simple present form of the verbs in parentheses.

Example: The game (*start*) _____*starts*_____ promptly at 8:15.

1. a. Swimming, running, and cycling (*be*) _____ good examples of aerobic exercise.

   b. What (*do*) _____ your sister Jenny and her husband do for exercise?

   c. Jenny, Bob, and their son (*go*) _____ cycling every weekend.

2. a. Everyone in my family (*like*) _____ to play table tennis.

   b. My brothers playing in the table tennis competition (*have*) _____ a chance to win.

   c. Every aunt, uncle, and cousin of mine (*play*) _____ table tennis, too.

3. a. Many people in my neighborhood (*watch*) _____ football games on TV.

   b. The rules of American football (*be*) _____ unclear. I can't understand them.

   c. When a team scores, the crowd in the arena (*scream*) _____.

   d. Playing well as a team (*require*) _____ a lot of practice.

Directions: Add the word "members" where possible, or write Ø.

Example: The jury _____*Ø*_____ is going to announce its decision.

1. The audience _____ often claps at the end of good movies.

2. Every summer our choir _____ sings in the city music festival.

3. Most college faculty _____ enjoy helping students solve problems.

4. The committee _____ usually interviews several candidates for every position.

5. Crew _____ on an airplane help passengers any time there is an emergency.

6. The public _____ is happy when prices go down.

7. The soccer team _____ has practice three times a week.

8. The hospital staff _____ are not paid enough.

Directions: Choose the correct completions.

Example: One of my most serious problems with English (*is*/ *are*) my pronunciation.

1. Three-fourths of the food (*was* / *were*) cold when the waiter brought it to our table.

2. A lot of the furniture in that store (*is* / *are*) too expensive for us.

3. A number of the text messages (*was* / *were*) from my friends in Belgium.

4. One of the cartoons in the magazine (*was* / *were*) really funny.

5. (*Do* / *Does*) all of the teachers give homework every night?

6. Most of the lectures at our college (*lasts* / *last*) an hour.

7. None of the articles on this Web site (*looks* / *look*) interesting to me.

8. Some of the mail (*was* / *were*) torn during processing.

9. (*Is* / *Are*) the number of accidents on that road increasing?

10. Half of the students in the class (*doesn't* / *don't*) know the answer to the question.

Directions: Correct the errors.

Example: ~~Has~~ any of the students taken this class before?
     Have

1. Every one of the children need love and affection.

2. Seventy-five percent of the teachers in our school speaks Spanish.

3. A number of volunteers is needed to finish this cleaning project.

4. A lot of my friends recommends this apartment complex.

5. None of my friends think I should sell my car.

6. The number of restaurants in San Francisco exceed 2,000.

7. Each of these photographs are worth more than $150.

8. All of the money really belong to that man over there.

9. One of my pencils need to be sharpened.

10. Half of the airplanes leaves on time.

Directions: Choose the correct completions.

Example: How much money ((*was*)/ *were*) there in your wallet?

1. There (*is / are*) carrots, beans, and peas in my vegetable garden.

2. There (*has been / have been*) so many accidents here. They really need a stoplight.

3. Why (*isn't / aren't*) there enough seats for all of the students?

4. There (*is / are*) over 10,000 books in the university library.

5. Last night, there (*was / were*) a full moon. It was a beautiful night.

6. (*Was / Were*) there a lot of stars in the sky last night?

7. There (*isn't / aren't*) much time. We need to hurry.

8. (*Is / Are*) there anything good to eat in the refrigerator?

9. There (*has been / have been*) a lot of snow in the mountains lately.

10. How many kinds of ice cream (*is / are*) there?

QUIZ 8 Subject-Verb Agreement: Using *There + Be* (Chart 5-5)

Directions: Choose the correct completions.

Example: There (*is /*(*are*)) many excellent schools in this city.

1. There (*is / are*) so much stuff to look at on the Internet. It's amazing!

2. How many rolls of tape (*is / are*) there in the desk drawer?

3. Why (*was / were*) there so much noise outside last night?

4. There (*isn't / aren't*) enough room in the closet for all of our coats.

5. There (*is / are*) only three ways to get over a cold: drink lots of liquids, eat healthy food, and get plenty of rest.

6. How much time (*is / are*) there before we have to leave for the airport?

7. There (*has been / have been*) a lot of mistakes in news reporting recently.

8. My mother always says there (*is / are*) never too much money in the bank.

9. There (*has been / have been*) a lot of good music on the radio this week.

10. Mr. Wickham thinks there (*is / are*) an old bicycle in his garage. He will give it to me.

Directions: Choose the correct completions.

Example: The Japanese ((*live*)/ *lives*) on four major islands and many smaller ones.

1. The news about the earthquakes in Central Asia (*is / are*) very upsetting.

2. Five dollars (*is / are*) too much for a cup of coffee.

3. The United Nations (*includes / include*) more than 190 countries as members.

4. Physics and mathematics (*is / are*) really difficult for my son.

5. The police (*has / have*) come to ask questions about the accident.

6. The United Arab Emirates (*is / are*) a group of seven states called *emirates*.

7. Fish (*lives / live*) in both fresh water and salt water.

8. Rabies (*is / are*) usually spread by infected animals.

9. The disabled (*has / have*) special parking places at most American stores.

10. The London Times (*reports / report*) daily on the London Stock Exchange.

Directions: Complete the sentences. Use the simple present form of the verbs in parentheses.

Example: The news from my cousins (*be*) _____*is*_____ not good.

1. Two hundred miles (*take*) _____ at least three hours by car.

2. The people in my company (*come*) _____ from many different countries.

3. The Chinese (*be*) _____ the inventors of gunpowder and noodles.

4. The Netherlands (*be*) _____ famous for windmills and tulips.

5. The homeless (*have*) _____ little chance of finding a job.

6. Japanese (*be*) _____ a difficult language to learn because of the different alphabets.

7. The statistics about the economy (*be*) _____ very good this month.

8. Politics (*be*) _____ the major topic of conversation in the nation's capital.

9. The latest medical news (*discuss*) _____ a possible cure for cancer.

10. The police (*help*) _____ people in many different situations.

Directions: Complete the sentences. Use the simple present form of the verbs in parentheses.

Example: All of the fruit at that market (*be*) _____ is _____ very fresh.

1. Each of the cowboys (*ride*) _____ his horse with skill and grace.

2. Snowboarding (*require*) _____ strong legs, flexibility, and balance.

3. The English (*have*) _____ a long tradition of drinking tea.

4. Young people today (*remember / not*) _____ life without cell phones.

5. Diabetes (*be*) _____ a growing health concern around the world.

6. There (*be*) _____ more women with diabetes than men.

7. Only one of the children (*know*) _____ all of the words to the song.

8. Statistics (*use*) _____ a variety of methods to analyze and interpret data.

9. Three-fourths of the factory workers (*take*) _____ the train to work every day.

10. French (*have*) _____ two different words for the verb *to be*.

11. Every man, woman, and child (*need*) _____ air and water to live.

12. The office staff (*work*) _____ from Monday to Friday.

13. The number of people on earth (*be*) _____ increasing every year.

14. The United States (*have*) _____ 50 states, including Hawaii and Alaska.

15. Two hundred dollars (*be*) _____ a lot to pay for a textbook.

Part A *Directions:* Check (✓) *C* for correct or *I* for incorrect.

C   I

✓ ____ 1. Every pair of shoes in your closet needs to be cleaned.

____ ____ 2. I don't know how to correct one of the mistake on my quiz.

____ ____ 3. Studying all night before tests is not a good way to learn.

____ ____ 4. Every one of my brothers and sisters were at my wedding.

____ ____ 5. The number of Spanish speakers in the United States increase every year.

____ ____ 6. My grandmother, mother, and sister has red hair, but my hair is brown.

____ ____ 7. Each pen and pencil in the little girl's pencil box is new.

____ ____ 8. The calls she made on her cell phone was expensive.

____ ____ 9. Some of the speaker in the program look interesting.

____ ____ 10. A number of the students were unhappy with their test results.

____ ____ 11. The suggestions on that Web site about parenting is useful.

Part B *Directions:* Complete the sentences with *is* or *are*.

1. How many chairs _____ there in the conference room?

2. There _____ a lot of expensive clothing in that store.

3. There _____ excellent computer labs at my college.

4. Why _____ there bad weather every weekend?

5. There _____ an umbrella in the closet for you to use.

6. Why _____ there two tables in the kitchen?

7. There _____ a box of books on the shelf.

8. Why _____ the teacher upset with her students?

Part C *Directions:* Complete the sentences. Use the simple present form of the verbs in parentheses.

1. Japanese (*be*) _____ the most popular foreign language at my school.

2. Thirty minutes (*be*) _____ not enough time to finish this test.

3. The United States (*have*) _____ 12,383 miles of coastline.

4. Mathematics (*help*) _____ people in many different kinds of jobs.

5. The elderly often (*tell*) _____ interesting stories about their lives.

6. The news about the robbery (*be*) _____ shocking.

7. Measles (*affect*) _____ few people in the United States nowadays.

Part D *Directions:* Choose the correct completions.

My favorite place for vacation (*is* / *are*) a beautiful island called Tranquila. The weather on the island (*is* / *are*) very warm all year. There (*is* / *are*) beautiful white sand beaches all around the island. The people on Tranquila (*is* / *are*) very friendly to visitors. They (*helps* / *help*) you find the beaches or the shopping district. Many stores (*has* / *have*) handcrafted jewelry. The jewelry (*is* / *are*) beautiful and inexpensive, and $20 (*buys* / *buy*) a necklace that can cost over $100 at home. Some tourists on Tranquila (*spends* / *spend*) a lot of time shopping. Tranquila is a quiet and friendly island. Every visitor (*comes* / *come*) back from Tranquila happy and well rested.

Part A *Directions:* Check (✓) *C* for correct or *I* for incorrect.

C   I

_✓_ _____   1. My lawyer and his assistants research their cases carefully.

_____ _____   2. Each carry-on bag and purse were checked carefully at the security gate.

_____ _____   3. The number of crimes in the city are decreasing.

_____ _____   4. Growing roses are my neighbor's specialty.

_____ _____   5. The chocolates from the shop on Grant Avenue are sweet and creamy.

_____ _____   6. Some of the story was funny.

_____ _____   7. Every one of the students attend class regularly.

_____ _____   8. Half of the money is my father's.

_____ _____   9. Running marathons take discipline, endurance, and strength.

_____ _____ 10. The flowers in my garden needs a lot of water every day.

_____ _____ 11. The bookstore staff has been busy with customers this week.

Part B *Directions:* Complete the sentences with *is* or *are*.

1. _____ there any good sales at the market this weekend?

2. The weather forecast says there _____ a huge windstorm coming from the northwest.

3. I think there _____ only two ways to solve that problem.

4. Why _____ there so many cars parked in front of our house?

5. How much time _____ there until the bus comes?

6. There _____ a lot of tomatoes in the bag.

7. Why _____ there a pair of boots on the chair?

8. There _____ a lot of people at the concert.

Part C *Directions:* Complete the sentences. Use the simple present form of the verbs in parentheses.

1. Diabetes (*be*) _____ more common in women than in men.

2. The Swiss (*like*) _____ things to run on time and to run well.

3. Economics (*be*) _____ a social science.

4. Italian (*sound*) _____ similar to Spanish and Portuguese.

5. Two thousand five hundred miles (*be*) _____ the distance between Seattle and New York City.

6. Cattle (*be*) _____ expensive to breed and raise.

7. Australia (*consist*) _____ of over 8,000 islands.

Part D *Directions:* Choose the correct completions.

The Seattle to Portland Bike Ride (*happens / happen*) every year in July. Thousands of cyclists (*takes / take*) over the roads in a 200-mile ride between Seattle, Washington, and Portland, Oregon. Riders from all over the United States (*leaves / leave*) Seattle early in the morning. Men, women, and children (*rides / ride*) through the beautiful farmlands and forests of western Washington and Oregon. Along the way, there (*is / are*) several rest stops for riders. Volunteers at the rest stops (*serves / serve*) the cyclists food and drinks. Two-thirds of the cyclists (*rides / ride*) for two days. Others (*makes / make*) the trip in just one day! The number of riders (*increases / increase*) every year. The Seattle to Portland Bike Ride (*is / are*) one of the best cycling events in the U.S.

CHAPTER 6 Nouns

QUIZ 1 **Regular and Irregular Plural Nouns** (Chart 6-1)

Directions: Write the plural form of each word in the correct column.

✓ belief	deer	hero	loaf	sheep	species
bush	echo	kilo	memo	shelf	tomato
cliff	fox	life	piano	solo	wolf

-s	-es	-ves	no change
beliefs			

QUIZ 2 **Regular and Irregular Plural Nouns** (Chart 6-1)

Directions: Complete the sentences with the plural forms of the nouns in the box. Use each noun only one time.

bacterium	man	phenomenon
hypothesis	✓ medium	ticket
lady	mouse	tooth

Example: The Internet is a news source that is replacing traditional _____*media*_____ such as newspapers, TV, and radio.

1. The _____ in the old photo wore long black skirts and white blouses.

   The _____ wore suits and ties.

2. We have a lot of _____ in our mouths. We must brush our

   _____ every day to keep our mouths healthy.

3. The researchers in the lab were not sure what happened, but they had several

   _____ about why their experiment failed.

4. Mark, John, and Anthony bought their movie _____ over the Internet.
   They didn't have to wait in line at the theater.

5. Rats and _____ look similar, but rats are bigger. I don't like either of them!

6. Halley's Comet is one of many amazing _____ in space.

Directions: Complete the sentences with the nouns in *italics*. Use the singular or plural form as appropriate. Use hyphens as necessary.

Example: shoe   Simone works at a _____*shoe*_____ store. She sells ladies'
                       _____*shoes*_____ .

1. *tomato*   My grandmother makes the best _____ sauce. She
                   uses fresh _____ from her garden.

2. *storm*   We have had many summer _____ this year. The
                   _____ clouds fill the sky almost every afternoon, and
                   then it rains for a while.

3. *two + hour*   The movie was _____ long. It was a
                   _____ movie.

4. *pea*   My husband doesn't like _____ , but he likes
                   _____ soup.

5. *three + week* We were in Florida for _____ last winter. The
                   _____ vacation was long enough for us to really relax.

6. *eighteen + year + old* In the United States _____ is the legal age for voting.
                   My _____ voted for the first time last year.

7. *flower*   The _____ shop has a special on roses this week.
                   Roses are my favorite _____ .

8. *hotel*   Marcos and Jana enjoy staying in nice _____ when
                   they travel. Their last _____ room had a beautiful
                   view over a park.

Directions: Complete the sentences. Use the possessive form of the nouns in parentheses.

Example: (Nancy) _____Nancy's_____ baby was born on December 9th.

1. (*Mr. Jones*) _____ brother is a banker in downtown Chicago.

2. The baseball hit (*Marissa and George*) _____ window and broke it.

3. The (*group*) _____ decisions affected many people in our company.

4. Parents usually enjoy their (*children*) _____ musical performances.

5. My (*boss*) _____ daughter attends the University of Toronto.

6. (*Andrea*) _____ job as a reporter is always interesting.

7. The (*baby*) _____ bottle fell off the table and rolled across the kitchen floor.

8. I don't know my (*cousins*) _____ new address. They moved to Rome.

9. Last year, the (*building*) _____ owner increased the rent.

10. One (*month*) _____ rent in Manhattan is very expensive.

Directions: Choose the correct completions.

Example: An (*elephants'* / (*elephant's*)) tusk can lift up to 2,000 pounds.

1. Jim and Sam need new socks. Both (*boy's* / *boys'*) socks have holes in the toes!

2. Be careful! That (*knife's* / *knives'*) blade is very sharp.

3. (*Rhonda* / *Rhonda's*) and (*Mick* / *Mick's*) wedding was an especially happy occasion for their families.

4. I was really unhappy with the (*movie's* / *movies'*) ending. It wasn't very good.

5. The lost (*woman's* / *women's*) clothing was torn and dirty when the police found her.

6. Mark's (*parents* / *parents'*) house is on the top of a hill. They have a nice view.

7. Kirsten had problems with her (*brother's* / *brothers'*) car. She called him for help.

8. My cell (*phone's* / *phones'*) battery is dead and I don't have my charger, so I can't call anyone.

9. Someone broke into (*Tom* / *Tom's*) and (*Jerry* / *Jerry's*) cars on the same night!

10. This (*company's* / *companies'*) most popular item is the 7.5" tablet computer.

Directions: Check (✓) the correct sentences in each group. More than one correct answer may be possible.

Example: _____ The flag of Canada is red and white and has a maple leaf in the center.

_✓_ Canada's flag is red and white and has a maple leaf in the center.

1. _____ The United Nations' headquarters is located in New York City.

_____ The headquarters of the United Nations is located in New York City.

2. _____ The house's roof collapsed under the heavy snow.

_____ The roof of the house collapsed under the heavy snow.

3. _____ Today's news was mostly about forest fires in our state.

_____ The news of today was mostly about forest fires in our state.

4. _____ My country's people usually drive small cars.

_____ People in my country usually drive small cars.

5. _____ I waited for 1-1/2 hours at the doctor's.

_____ I waited for 1-1/2 hours at the doctor's office.

_____ I waited for 1-1/2 hours at the office of my doctor.

6. _____ My sister's hair is short, so it's easy to care for.

_____ The hair of my sister is short, so it's easy to care for.

7. _____ My friend's bike is red and yellow.

_____ The bike of my friend is red and yellow.

8. _____ The manager of the coffee shop wants the customers to be happy.

_____ The coffee shop's manager wants the customers to be happy.

_____ The coffee shop manager wants the customers to be happy.

QUIZ 7 Count and Noncount Nouns (Charts 6-5 → 6-7)

Directions: Add final ***-s*** / ***-es*** to the nouns in *italics* if necessary. Do not add or change any other words.

Example: There was a lot of *garbage* in the street after the parade. Many *citizens* of the town helped clean up the mess.

1. Our teacher gave us *suggestion* on how to be successful students. We appreciated her *advice.*
2. My dad bought new *luggage* for his trip. He got three large *suitcase* and a small duffle bag.
3. I just got today's *mail.* There are *bill* and a magazine.
4. Everyone admired the old man's *knowledge.*
5. Pat always puts *pepper* on his food. He likes spicy *dish.*
6. David bought *coffee, butter,* and *apple* at the grocery store yesterday.
7. The queen's necklace was made of *gold* and *diamond.*
8. Many Chinese meals include *rice, meat,* and *vegetable.*
9. Lee received twenty *dollar* for his birthday. Now he has enough *money* to buy a new game.
10. Marcos enjoys reading *poetry* in his free *time.*

QUIZ 8 Count and Noncount Nouns (Charts 6-5 → 6-7)

Directions: Complete the sentences with the given nouns. Add final ***-s*** / ***-es*** if necessary. Use each noun only one time.

beef	chicken	hair	✓ jewelry	luck	trip
chess	coffee	homework	light	orange	

Example: John gave his wife beautiful gold ___jewelry___ for their anniversary.

1. Ron has some ________________ in his yard. He gets fresh eggs almost every day.
2. My best friend gave me a four-leaf clover for good ________________.
3. Paul's grandpa plays ________________ in the park every Sunday afternoon.
4. Carrie turned off all the ________________ before she went to bed.
5. Jorge ate some juicy ________________ for a snack after school.
6. Min prepared some delicious spicy ________________ for her guests.
7. Cathy drinks ________________ for breakfast on weekends.
8. Our dog loses a lot of ________________ in the spring.
9. Steven finished all of his ________________ before he watched TV.
10. They enjoy ________________ to the mountains in the summer.

Directions: Complete the sentences with *much* or *many* and the correct form of the nouns in parentheses. Use the plural as necessary.

Example: When Eddie goes out for Chinese food, he always shares it with

(*friend*) _____many friends_____ .

1. Machiko has been teaching Japanese for (*year*) _____ .

2. I was in a hurry. I didn't have (*time*) _____ for breakfast this morning.

3. The students asked (*question*) _____ in class yesterday.

4. Hank's apartment was full of newspapers, books, and magazines. He had too

(*stuff*) _____!

5. I have too (*photo*) _____ on my phone. I need to delete some!

6. Young children don't have (*patience*) _____ and have limited attention

spans.

7. There are (*reason*) _____ for obesity in children, including diets high in fat

and sugar, and low levels of physical activity.

8. Washington state grows (*variety*) _____ of apples that are exported around

the world.

9. Australia is a country with (*sheep*) _____ . In fact, there are about ten times

more sheep than people.

10. The Internet is an amazing resource. There is (*information*) _____ on

almost any topic you're interested in.

Directions: Complete the sentences with *a few, few, a little,* or *little.*

Example: I have _____a little_____ money left. Let's go get coffee.

1. Our history teacher has _____ patience with students who talk during his

lectures.

2. The bus should be here in _____ minutes.

3. Matthew knows _____ about photography. You can ask him for help with

the photo project.

4. James has _____ relatives in the area. He usually spends holidays with his

friends.

5. This stew is not very flavorful. I think it needs _____ salt.

QUIZ 11 **Using *A Few* and *Few*; *A Little* and *Little*** (Chart 6-9)

Directions: Without changing the meaning of the sentences, replace the words in *italics* with ***a few, (very) few, a little,*** or ***(very) little.***

Example: I have lived in this apartment for five years, but I know ~~hardly any~~ *(very) few* people in the building.

1. Liam has never been to Berlin, but he has been to Munich *two or three* times.

2. Last Saturday, Julia went for a walk in the park. There were *almost no other* people. It was very peaceful.

3. The apartment was plain. There was *not much* furniture and only one window.

4. It's a good idea to ask *some* questions before you purchase any electronic equipment.

5. We have *some* time before our plane leaves. Do you want to get something to eat?

QUIZ 12 **Using *One, Each, Every,* and *Of* in Expressions of Quantity** (Charts 6-10 and 6-11)

Directions: Choose the correct completions.

Example: Cupcakes are (*one* /(*one of*)) the desserts I enjoy most.

1. (*Every* / *Every of*) cupcake is enough cake for one person.

2. (*Many of* / *Many*) cupcake stores have opened in our city in the past few years.

3. (*Each* / *Each of*) shop makes its own specialty cupcakes.

4. (*The majority of* / *The majority*) the shops sell birthday cupcakes.

5. (*One* / *One of*) the shops near my house specializes in cupcakes for kids.

6. (*Most* / *Most of*) kids' cupcakes look like clowns, princesses, or animals.

7. (*Seventy-five percent* / *Seventy-five percent of*) the cupcakes sold are chocolate.

8. (*Some* / *Some of*) cupcakes have both chocolate cake and chocolate frosting.

9. (*Many* / *Many of*) the cupcakes have sprinkles on top.

10. (*Some* / *Some of*) them have candy on top.

Directions: Choose the correct completions.

Example: We spent _____ days at the beach last summer.

        a. a great deal of   ⓑ many

1. The manager shook hands with _____ people at the meeting.

    a. each of the   b. each

2. Jennifer invited _____ friends to her birthday party.

    a. a great deal of   b. a number of

3. The boys were late, so they had _____ time to eat dinner.

    a. few   b. hardly any

4. One of the _____ fell down on stage during the concert.

    a. musicians   b. musician

5. Every _____ in the store got a free package of laundry soap.

    a. shopper   b. shoppers

6. The artist sold _____ paintings at the art fair.

    a. several of   b. several

7. Barbara has _____ laundry to do on Saturday.

    a. too much   b. too many

8. _____ the students in my computer programming class passed the final exam.

    a. Three-fourths   b. Almost all of

9. After their trip to France and Spain, Shelley and John kept _____ euros to give to their children as souvenirs.

    a. a few   b. few

10. There were _____ messages in my in-box when I got back from vacation.

    a. hundreds   b. hundreds of

Directions: Check (✓) the correct sentence in each pair.

Example: __✓__ My best friend from college is married and has three children.

_____ My best friend from college is married and has three child.

1. _____ I found several of new movies to watch online.

_____ I found several new movies to watch online.

2. _____ When Greg was a college student, he didn't have much money for going out.

_____ When Greg was a college student, he didn't have many money for going out

3. _____ My mom set the table with knives, forks, salads forks, and spoons.

_____ My mom set the table with knives, forks, salad forks, and spoons.

4. _____ The flower shop across the street has the biggest sunflowers I've ever seen.

_____ The flower-shop across the street has the biggest sunflowers I've ever seen.

5. _____ My boss gave me some good advice.

_____ My boss gave me some good advices.

6. _____ Fifty percent of my classmates is from Asia.

_____ Fifty percent of my classmates are from Asia.

7. _____ Maurice doesn't eat many vegetables, but he loves fruit.

_____ Maurice doesn't eat much vegetables, but he loves fruit.

8. _____ I have a twelve-year-old sister.

_____ I have a twelve years old sister.

9. _____ Two deers were standing near the lake in the early morning.

_____ Two deer were standing near the lake in the early morning.

10. _____ The English is an international language.

_____ English is an international language.

11. _____ Joan needs more bookshelfs in her room. She has lots of books.

_____ Joan needs more bookshelves in her room. She has lots of books.

12. _____ Steve loves basketball. He plays on a ten men team.

_____ Steve loves basketball. He plays on a ten-man team.

Part A *Directions:* Complete each sentence with the plural form of the nouns in parentheses.

1. Mr. Samuels grows (*potato*) _____ and corn on his farm.

2. Michael is only ten years old, but he is already five (*foot*) _____ tall.

3. Catherine played the same piece on several different (*piano*) _____ before she chose which piano to buy.

4. We need to put out steak (*knife*) _____ because we are having roast beef for dinner.

5. When our house caught on fire, the firefighters sprayed water on our neighbors' (*roof*) _____ to stop the fire from spreading.

Part B *Directions:* Complete each sentence with the possessive form of the nouns in parentheses.

1. The teacher collected the (*students*) _____ papers at the end of the test.

2. I am going with Linda to a party at a (*friend*) _____ house this Saturday.

3. (*Doris*) _____ dog has been missing for two weeks.

4. You can find (*men*) _____ sportswear on the third floor of the store.

5. The nurse was reviewing the (*patients*) _____ medical information when the doctor asked for her assistance.

Part C *Directions:* Add final *-s* / *-es* to the nouns in italics if necessary. Do not add or change any other words.

1. I love *snow* in the winter, especially when it falls in big *flake*.

2. The *information* on the Internet is much more current than in printed *article*.

3. Grace has had some good *job*. She really enjoys her *work* as a customer service representative.

4. *Life* is an adventure full of interesting *experience*.

5. Baxter bought a lot of *stamp*. He was unsure about how much *postage* he needed.

Part D *Directions:* Choose the correct completions.

1. Our (*office's / office*) manager is young and uses technology very effectively.

2. My nephew is going to be (*sixteen-year-old / sixteen years old*) on his next birthday.

3. Outside the train station, there is a (*bicycle / bicycles*) rack where Ron can lock up his bike.

4. I'm upset! We had a long wait at the (*office of the doctor / doctor's office*) today!

5. The manufacturer has recalled that (*baby / babies'*) food. There is something wrong with it.

Part E *Directions:* Correct the errors.

1. When Gloria went to the zoo yesterday, she took a few pictures because it was raining.

2. One of the problem facing big cities is homelessness.

3. Brian was late for work because of so many traffic on the road.

4. Every children needs to play outdoors to be healthy.

5. Most store in that mall close at 9:30 P.M.

Part A *Directions:* Complete each sentence with the plural form of the noun in parentheses.

1. My uncle's ranch has more than 200 cattle and 150 (*sheep*) _____.

2. Mr. Lee's alarm system has protected his jewelry store from (*thief*) _____.

3. You can see many (*mouse*) _____ around the tracks in the subway station.

4. The prime minister had to deal with several political (*crisis*) _____ as soon as he took office.

5. The dentist is going to clean Mary's (*tooth*) _____ when she visits him next Tuesday.

Part B *Directions:* Complete each sentence with the possessive form of the nouns in parentheses.

1. Did you read about the earthquake in (*this morning*) _____ newspaper?

2. There is a great sale going on in (*ladies*) _____ shoes this week.

3. (*Louis*) _____ car broke down on the freeway last night.

4. What is wrong with the (*city*) _____ cell phone service? They are always having problems.

5. (*Patty and Mike*) _____ apartment is only three blocks from the grocery store.

Part C *Directions:* Add final **-s** / **-es** to the nouns in italics if necessary. Do not add or change any other words.

1. Tim spent a lot of time on his *homework*. He had to finish *assignment* in chemistry and math.

2. Nina has fun trying on *dress* and *shoe*. She loves to shop for *clothing*.

3. The *garbage* didn't fit in the trash can.

4. The police found several *hair* at the crime scene while they were gathering *evidence*.

5. It was difficult to lose *weight*, but I lost thirty *pound*.

Part D *Directions:* Choose the correct completions.

1. Mr. Johnson sent his lawyer a (*six pages / six-page*) letter about his estate.

2. For breakfast I usually have eggs, toast, and (*orange / oranges*) juice.

3. The (*vegetables' / vegetable*) drawer in the refrigerator smells bad. There is something rotten in there!

4. Alex's (*eighteen-year-old / eighteen years old*) sister just got her driver's license.

5. Visitors to Dubai can get a wonderful (*city's view / view of the city*) from the top of the Burj Khalifa building.

Part E *Directions:* Correct the errors.

1. When I asked Adam for advice, he didn't have much suggestions.

2. When I got to the train station, there was plenty room in the parking lot.

3. I have a little minutes to finish writing this report before the meeting.

4. One of the actor in the play forgot his lines. It was embarrassing.

5. This store accepts both of credit cards and electronic payments.

Directions: Choose the correct completions.

Example: Mr. Seymour is reading _____ magazine.

      a. some   (b.) a   c. an

1. Joan's husband gave her _____ flowers on their anniversary.

    a. some   b. a   c. an

2. Edward bought _____ kilo of potatoes.

    a. the   b. a   c. an

3. Please put _____ mail on the kitchen table.

    a. some   b. the   c. a

4. My son didn't have _____ answer to my question.

    a. some   b. a   c. an

5. Tina and Jack haven't been to _____ concert in several months.

    a. the   b. a   c. an

6. Frederick got _____ fresh lettuce for a good price.

    a. some   b. the   c. an

7. Do you have _____ book I ordered?

    a. some   b. a   c. the

8. I need to make _____ appointment with the dentist.

    a. some   b. the   c. an

9. Teresa found _____ helpful information on a Web site.

    a. some   b. a   c. the

10. _____ wind is blowing hard today.

    a. Some   b. A   c. The

Directions: Complete the sentences with *the* or Ø. Capitalize as necessary.

Example: I hate __Ø__ homework.   __The__ homework from biology class is really difficult.

1. I can't find _____ key to my car.

2. Kevin asked his older brother for _____ advice about college.

3. Jared doesn't like _____ tomatoes. He never eats them.

4. Have you seen _____ new movie starring Mamie Elliott?

5. Sylvia lives in _____ house at the end of the street.

6. Donald works hard to earn _____ money.

7. Patrick never watches _____ sports on TV.

8. I haven't finished _____ laundry yet.

9. _____ strawberries are my favorite fruit.

10. What's wrong with _____ computer? It's making a strange sound.

Directions: Add *a / an* if necessary. Write Ø in the blank if no article is needed. Capitalize as necessary.

Example: __Ø__ ᴳgiraffes are the tallest animals on earth today.

1. _____ international airport is a busy place at any time of day.

2. _____ leather furniture is difficult to clean.

3. _____ manager is responsible for many employees.

4. _____ flag is a national symbol.

5. _____ smartphones have changed the way people communicate.

6. _____ baseball is very popular in Japan.

7. _____ piano is very heavy and difficult to move.

8. _____ oranges contain a lot of vitamin C.

9. _____ effective speaker prepares well before giving a presentation.

10. _____ children need eight to ten hours of sleep a night.

Directions: Complete the sentences with *a, the,* or *Ø* to give the noun in *italics* the appropriate meaning. Capitalize as necessary.

Example: general: My daughter has ___*a*___ new *teacher* this year.

1. general: _____ *teachers* in the U.S. usually work for 10 months.

2. general: Miss Mackey is _____ second grade *teacher* at Elmville School.

3. specific: _____ *kids* in Miss Mackey's class are active and smart.

4. general: Miss Mackey plans _____ interesting *activities* for her pupils.

5. general: Every morning the school principal rings _____ *bell* at school.

6. specific: _____ *bell* that the principal rings signals the beginning of class.

7. general: Every day there are _____ *kids* who come late to school.

8. specific: _____ *teachers* at Elmville School work hard for their classes.

QUIZ 5 General Guidelines for Article Usage   (Chart 7-4)

Directions: Complete the conversations with *a, an, the,* or *Ø*. Capitalize as necessary.

Example: A: What are you doing?

  B: I'm going to __*the*__ dentist.

1. A: You seem stressed. What happened?

   B: I had _____ early dentist appointment, but I was late.

   A: Did you call _____ office to let them know?

   B: Yes, but I hate being late!

2. A: I think I need _____ new phone.

   B: What's wrong with _____ phone you have?

   A: It keeps dropping calls, and _____ screen is cracked.

3. A: What types of movies do you like best?

   B: I really like _____ action movies and comedies.

4. A: Seattle is becoming more bicycle friendly, isn't it?

   B: Yes. The city has added _____ bike lanes to many streets.

5. A: Are you having fun?

   B: Oh, yes! I really like _____ band.

Directions: Choose the correct completions.

Frank Simms is a travel writer and TV/radio host in (*the* / Ø) United States. (*The* / Ø) Mr. Simms specializes in European travel and has hosted programs about most countries in (*the* / Ø) Europe. He encourages people to travel on their own, and to experience lesser known places as well as major tourist sites. In a recent TV program about (*the* / Ø) Czech Republic, he visited (*the* / Ø) Prague, the capital, where he showed famous sites like the Charles Bridge across (*the* / Ø) Vitava River. Then he took viewers to the delightful small town of Český Krumlov near (*the* / Ø) Šumava Mountains. Simms also writes guidebooks that have detailed travel suggestions. For example, his guidebook about (*the* / Ø) Spain includes information on going to (*the* / Ø) Canary Islands, and his book about (*the* / Ø) Italy recommends a visit to (*the* / Ø) Lake Como.

QUIZ 7 Chapter Review

Directions: Correct the errors.

Example: I don't like ~~the~~ pancakes. I never eat them.

1. Salt Lake City, Utah is named after the Great Salt Lake, which is nearby.

2. Please lock a door when you leave the house.

3. Christine often wears earrings made of the silver.

4. There was a fire in Bev's apartment last night. Smoke was terrible.

5. Josh works at movie theater where all tickets cost $4.00.

6. Seattle has many beautiful mountains nearby. My favorite is the Mount Baker.

7. Cathy often has the fresh flowers on her kitchen table.

8. Who invented the cellphones? I want to thank him or her!

9. Visitors to Yellowstone National Park often get too close to wild animals there.

10. Yesterday, Max bought black dress shoes and running shoes. Running shoes are bright red.

Part A *Directions:* Complete the conversations with *a, an, the,* or *Ø*.

1. A: Emily's parents gave her _____ laptop computer for graduation.

   B: Great! She will use _____ laptop a lot in college next year.

2. A: Do you know where _____ post office is? I need to mail _____ package.

   B: Yes, it's on First Street, next to the bank.

3. A: Mom, I need _____ new notebook, _____ scissors, and _____ eraser.

   B: OK, I'll get them for you.

4. A: I saw _____ news report on TV about _____ tornado in Oklahoma.

   B: What happened?

   A: _____ wind was blowing 100 miles an hour. It destroyed several homes.

Part B *Directions:* Choose the correct completions.

1. Last Saturday, Scott had to clean his office. His desk was covered with (*a* / *an* / *Ø*) mail, scraps of paper, coins, and (*a* / *an* / *some*) old newspapers. He took (*a* / *an* / *the*) mail and threw it away, and he recycled (*a* / *an* / *the*) newspapers.

2. Maria did her laundry last night. She sorted (*a* / *an* / *the*) clothes and put them in (*the* / *some* / *Ø*) washing machine. Then she read (*a* / *an* / *Ø*) book while she waited.

3. While I was waiting for (*the* / *some* / *Ø*) doctor, I had to write (*a* / *an* / *some*) information on (*a* / *an* / *Ø*) insurance form.

Part C *Directions:* Choose the correct completions.

1. _____ car is not necessary if you live in a city with good public transportation.

   a. Ø   b. A   c. The

2. My daughter wants to learn how to play _____ violin.

   a. Ø   b. a   c. the

3. Hawaii is the only U.S. state that grows _____ pineapples.

   a. Ø   b. a   c. the

4. Everyone should try to help _____ poor in the world.

   a. Ø   b. a   c. the

5. Do you know who invented _____ microwave oven? I couldn't cook without mine!

   a. Ø   b. a   c. the

Part D *Directions:* Check (✓) the correct sentence in each pair.

1. _____ I'd like the hamburger from Burger Hut for lunch.

   _____ I'd like a hamburger from Burger Hut for lunch.

2. _____ People who want to become accountants have to pass a certification exam.

   _____ The people who want to become the accountants have to pass a certification exam.

3. _____ The people on the bus weren't hurt in the accident.

   _____ People on the bus weren't hurt in the accident.

4. _____ Did you get text message I sent earlier today?

   _____ Did you get the text message I sent earlier today?

5. _____ There are the stamps for your letter in the desk drawer.

   _____ There are stamps for your letter in the desk drawer.

Part E *Directions:* Complete the sentences with *the* or **Ø**.

1. I read an interesting story about a Japanese man who crossed _____ Pacific Ocean in a small sailboat.

2. Many small rivers in _____ South America flow into _____ Amazon River, making it the largest river on that continent and one of the largest rivers in the world.

3. In May of 2014, 13-year-old Malavath Purna of India became the youngest girl to climb _____ Mount Everest.

4. The city of Victoria, British Columbia, Canada is on _____ Vancouver Island, but it's easy to get there on a ferry boat.

Part A *Directions:* Complete the conversations with *a, an, the,* or *Ø.*

1. A: We have _____ new manager at work. She seems nice.

   B: I hope _____ new manager will be better than your old one!

   A: Me, too.

2. A: Can you help me? I'm looking for _____ book about organic gardening.

   B: There are _____ gardening books on _____ second floor.

   A: OK. Thank you.

3. A: Do you want _____ eggs or _____ pancakes for breakfast?

   B: I'm not really hungry. I am thirsty, though.

   A: OK. Do you want _____ glass of juice? We have apple juice and orange juice.

   B: I'll have orange juice, thanks.

4. A: I just read _____ article about students who take a "gap" year.

   B: What's that?

   A: It's when students choose to take time off from _____ school between high school and

   college. Some students are tired of _____ studying by the time they graduate from

   high school, so they travel or work for _____ year before they start college.

   B: Sounds like a great idea!

Part B *Directions:* Choose the correct completions.

1. People collect (*an* / *the* / *Ø*) things for different reasons. I have (*a* / *an* / *Ø*) friend who collects
   (*a* / *an* / *Ø*) rocks. He has (*a* / *an* / *Ø*) different story to tell about each rock.

2. My aunt has (*a* / *an* / *Ø*) unusual painting that she bought for ten dollars.
   (*A* / *The* / *Some*) painting is now worth over two hundred dollars. My aunt is
   (*a* / *an* / *Ø*) lucky woman!

3. I am not feeling well today. I have (*a* / *an* / *the*) awful headache and
   (*a* / *an* / *the*) fever. I think I need (*a* / *an* / *some*) medicine.

Part C *Directions:* Choose the correct completions.

1. I usually don't eat _____ eggs in the morning.

   a. Ø   b. a   c. the

2. An American named Chester Carlson invented _____ photocopier in the 1930s.

   a. Ø   b. a   c. the

3. Young people should respect _____ elderly for their experience and wisdom.

   a. Ø   b. a   c. the

4. My parents just bought _____ piano, so now I can play whenever I want.

   a. Ø   b. a   c. the

5. _____ bottlenose dolphin is one of the most intelligent animals on earth.

   a. Ø   b. A   c. The

Part D *Directions:* Check (✓) the correct sentence in each pair.

1. _____ There is a black sock under the bed.

   _____ There is the black sock under the bed.

2. _____ Jorge wants to borrow new headphones that I bought.

   _____ Jorge wants to borrow the new headphones that I bought.

3. _____ It's starting to rain. Do you have an umbrella that I can borrow?

   _____ It's starting to rain. Do you have the umbrella that I can borrow?

4. _____ The movie that I saw last night was really scary!

   _____ A movie that I saw last night was really scary!

5. _____ Most cars have electronic keys that are expensive to replace.

   _____ Most cars have the electronic keys that are expensive to replace.

Part E *Directions:* Complete the sentences with *the* or *Ø*.

1. _____ Lake Balaton, in Hungary, is a popular tourist destination from June to August.

2. My brother-in-law has an appointment with _____ Dr. Hernandez, a diabetes specialist.

3. "The Blue Danube Waltz," by Viennese composer Johann Strauss II, was named for _____ Danube River, which runs through Vienna on its way to _____ Black Sea.

4. _____ Rocky Mountains extend 3000 miles from north to south through North America.

CHAPTER 8　Pronouns

QUIZ 1 **Pronouns and Possessive Adjectives**　　(Chart 8-1)

Directions: Identify the antecedent for each personal pronoun in *italics*. Write the antecedent on the line.

Example: Rosa gave her boyfriend a wallet for his birthday. He liked *it* very much.

　　　it = _____*wallet*_____

1. Angelo is a good employee. *He* works very hard and always helps others.

    He = _____

2. My sister lives in Michigan. I visit *her* every summer.

    her = _____

3. Most cats are quite independent. *They* have very distinct personalities.

    They = _____

4. Our soccer team won the championship game. *It* was very exciting!

    It = _____

5. My parents and I visited my grandma last Sunday. She baked *us* a delicious cake.

    us = _____

6. Coffee, tea, and cola all have caffeine. Too much of *it* can keep you awake.

    it = _____

7. Coffee, tea, and cola all have caffeine, but I drink *them* anyway.

    them = _____

8. What was the point of the lecture? I didn't understand *it* at all.

    it = _____

9. Rita is the tallest girl in our class. *She* is 6'0" tall.

    She = _____

10. Sean and Adam's mom wants *them* to do well in school.

    them = _____

QUIZ 2 Pronouns and Possessive Adjectives   (Chart 8-1)

Directions: Complete the sentences with subject or object pronouns: *she, her, he, him, it, we, us, they,* or *them.*

Example: Ted and his wife are expecting a baby in August. _____*They*_____ are very excited.

1. Sarah is very clever. _____ works as a scientist in a university research lab. Last year, the university gave _____ an award for excellence.

2. Julia met her parents at the theater, and _____ watched a play together. Afterwards, Julia took _____ out for dessert and coffee.

3. Something was wrong with the door to our apartment. When I tried to open _____, I broke my key. We asked our landlord, Joe, for help. _____ fixed the lock and gave _____ new keys.

4. James was in a car accident last week. Fortunately, _____ wasn't hurt. However, the police gave _____ a ticket.

5. Cell phones have changed the way my sons and I communicate. Now _____ can send text messages to each other anytime.

QUIZ 3 Pronouns and Possessive Adjectives   (Chart 8-1)

Directions: Choose the correct completions.

Example: (Me /(My)) brother is the mayor of Newton, Illinois.

1. This book is (*my* / *mine*) and that one on the table is (*your* / *yours*).

2. (*Their* / *Theirs*) basketball team plays more games every year than (*our* / *ours*) does.

3. Maggie is wearing a pink sweater. Pink is (*she's* / *her*) favorite color.

4. Tyler needs a haircut. (*His* / *He's*) hair is too long.

5. (*Your* / *Yours*) desktop computer is much more powerful than (*my* / *mine*) laptop.

6. (*Their* / *They*) house is at 5488 Greenough Place. (*Its* / *It's*) about a mile from here.

7. Tammy is a tax accountant. (*Her* / *Hers*) busiest time is in February and March when people have to pay (*their* / *they're*) income taxes.

8. (*Our* / *Ours*) best friends just got a new puppy. It is full of energy and likes to chase (*its* / *it's*) tail.

Directions: Complete the sentences with the correct possessive form.

Example: Laura teaches science in a middle school. _____*Her*_____ students are
all between twelve and fourteen years old.

1. Last night, a cat was stuck in our tree. _____ loud meowing woke us up.

2. _____ new smartphone has a cool application for tracking exercise.
   Now I can track how many steps I take each day.

3. Marie is on the Internet several hours a day. This upsets _____ parents.

4. I can't find an eraser. Can I borrow _____, Mickey?

5. Caitlin and Terry moved to Florida last summer. _____ house is
   on the beach.

6. _____ family is huge! We have eight aunts, eight uncles, and eighteen cousins.

7. Ms. Paulos cooks wonderful Greek food. She is very proud of _____ moussaka.

8. My shoes are size 8, but my brother's are size 13. _____ feet are very large!

Directions: Complete the sentences with pronouns or possessive adjectives. More than
one answer may be possible. Choose the correct singular or plural form of the verbs in
parentheses as necessary.

Example: A parent is responsible for taking care of _____*his or her*_____ children.

1. A doctor has to communicate well with _____ patients.

2. I have a lot of respect for the faculty at Edmonds Community College.
   _____ (*is / are*) very caring instructors.

3. Somebody forgot _____ calculator in math class today.

4. A firefighter risks _____ life to help other people.

5. Anyone can learn to speak a foreign language if _____ (*practices / practice*).

6. Everybody in the class had _____ own opinion on the subject of dating and
   marriage.

7. Frank is on the city planning committee. _____ (*has / have*) seven
   members.

8. Nobody (*forgets / forget*) _____ computer password as often as I do!

Directions: Choose the correct completions.

Example: Maria made this hat (*myself* / *himself* /(*herself*)).

1. Don't copy your work from Junichi. Do it (*myself* / *yourself* / *himself*).

2. The girls took pictures of (*herself* / *yourselves* / *themselves*) and posted them on Facebook.

3. My uncle told me that he had built the small greenhouse by (*myself* / *himself* / *herself*).

4. My parents always told me to take good care of (*myself* / *himself* / *themselves*).

5. The cruise ship staff were extremely helpful. They prided (*itself* / *himself* / *themselves*) on good service.

6. No one helped us with this project. We did it (*myself* / *ourselves* / *yourselves*).

7. Kara got a new bag. Her mom offered to buy it, but she wanted to pay for it (*yourself* / *himself* / *herself*).

8. The Miller's dog is a smart animal. The dog uses its paws to open doors by (*itself* / *themselves* / *yourself*).

Directions: Complete the sentences with reflexive pronouns.

Example: Mark is a funny guy. He sings to _____*himself*_____ when he is happy.

1. My friends have a new picnic table. They built it _____.

2. Roberta sews all her own clothes. She taught _____ to sew.

3. Rick is really proud of _____ because he has learned so much about photography.

4. I _____ do not believe in ghosts.

5. I'm sorry. I can't help you with your test. You have to do it _____.

6. We are planning our summer vacation, but we're not using a travel agent. We are making all of the reservations _____.

7. My grandpa lives by _____ on a small farm in Alabama.

8. The children entertained _____ with a game while they were waiting for their parents.

Directions: Choose the correct completions.

Example: I have two <u>brothers</u>. One of my brothers has brown hair and
(*another* / (*the other*)) has blonde hair.

1. These shoes don't fit me. Are there (*other* / *others*) in a larger size?

2. Tyler dropped his phone and now it doesn't work. He has to buy (*another* / *the other*) one.

3. There are two pieces of chocolate cake left. You can eat one, and I will eat (*another* /
   the other).

4. I'm taking two art classes this semester. Books for art classes are usually expensive. Some
   aren't too bad, but (*the others* / *others*) can cost as much as $150.

5. I already ate one sandwich, but I'm still hungry. May I please have (*other* / *another*)?

6. George has seven cousins. One lives in Chicago, (*another* / *the other*) lives in Dallas, and
   (*another* / *the others*) live in San Francisco.

7. I like this jacket. It's quite different from (*another* / *the others*) I tried on.

8. I have a new boss, but I don't really like him. I've liked my (*other* / *others*) bosses better.

QUIZ 9 **Common Expressions with *Other*** (Charts 8-6 and 8-7)

Directions: Complete each sentence with a word or expression from the box.

another	every other	one after the other	other than
✓ each other	in other words	one another	the other

1. Miguel and Selma are getting married next month. They love ____each other____
   very much.

2. The children took turns playing the game. They threw the ball _____.

3. My friends from Italy come to the U.S. about _____ year. I wish they
   could come more often.

4. The scientists wanted to spend _____ three years doing research, but they
   didn't have enough money to continue the work.

5. Julie and Kathy are best friends. They tell _____ all their secrets.

6. A: Have you talked to Kevin lately?

   B: Yes. He called me just _____ day, and we had a long conversation.

7. I am not fond of anchovies. _____, I don't like them.

8. No one _____ members is allowed into the private club.

Directions: Choose the correct completions.

Example: Javier is sixteen. (*He's* /⟨*His*⟩) brothers are thirteen and eleven.

1. Good employees do (*his or her* / *their*) job well.

2. Anna and (*me* / *I*) will fly to Toronto on Sunday.

3. Everybody on the bus was on (*hers* / *her*) cell phone.

4. I was happy when I saw (*myself* / *me*) in the picture. I looked good!

5. Ted worked there for two years. The first year was in accounting and (*another* / *the other*) was in marketing.

6. In my grammar class, some students are from Korea, (*others* / *the others*) are from China, and (*other* / *the others*) are from Vietnam.

7. Maria wanted to use my phone, so I lent it to (*she* / *her*).

8. Mr. Carlson forgot (*his* / *him*) jacket on the bus yesterday.

9. My family travels to Japan every (*other* / *another*) year.

10. Susan's family (*are* / *is*) large. She has five brothers and three sisters.

11. The businessmen introduced (*himself* / *themselves*) at the meeting.

12. The support staff in our company (*consists* / *consist*) of 50 people.

13. (*We* / *Us*) and our parents have dinner together every week.

14. Where did you park (*yours* / *your*) car?

15. Willy repaired the computer by (*himself* / *him*) and saved a lot of money.

Part A *Directions:* Choose the correct completions.

1. Last night after dinner, (*I / me / my*) gave Sergei (*I / my / mine*) dessert because (*he / him / his*) asked (*me / my / mine*).

2. Yesterday, Susan forgot (*she / her / hers*) magazine on the bus when (*she / her / hers*) went downtown.

3. Amelie got a bad grade on (*she / her / hers*) test in Mr. Thomas' class. (*She / Her / Hers*) is going to talk to (*he / him / his*) in (*he / him / his*) office tomorrow.

4. Grace and Karl took (*they / their / theirs*) baby to the doctor for a checkup. (*They / Them / Their*) need to take (*he / him / his*) in every four months.

5. John doesn't want anybody to touch (*he / him / his*) things, and Julie doesn't want anyone to touch (*she / her / hers*).

Part B *Directions:* Identify the antecedent for each personal pronoun in *italics*. Write the antecedent on the line.

1. The class is too big. The school needs to move *it* into a larger room.

    it = _____

2. The people in my family are quite tall. All of *them*, including the women, are over 5'10".

    them = _____

3. A bus driver has a very stressful job. *He or she* often needs to deal with heavy traffic and angry customers.

    He or she = _____

4. The young couple won a trip to Hawaii. *They* also received a color TV.

    They = _____

5. The committee consists of representatives from different parts of the city. *It* even includes members from the financial district and the industrial area.

    It = _____

6. Somebody parked *his or her* car in my driveway. I can't drive into my garage.

    his or her = _____

Part C *Directions:* Complete the sentences with reflexive pronouns.

1. When Nathan fell down the stairs, he hurt _____ very badly.

2. I didn't think that I would, but I really enjoyed _____ at Jane's party last night.

3. Sayako promised _____ that she would do better next time.

4. The members of the team are very proud of _____ after winning the city championship.

5. If you don't take care of _____, no one will.

6. We forgot to leave a tip for the waiter. We were so ashamed of _____ .

7. We had a fire at our house last year. The house _____ didn't burn down, but our garage was totally destroyed.

Part D *Directions:* Complete the conversations with **another, the other, other, the others,** or **others**.

1. Customer: Do you have anything for people on special diets?

   Waitress: Yes, we do. Some dishes are low-fat, and _____ are vegetarian.

   Waitress: And what would the children like to drink?

   Customer: She'll have a root beer, and _____ will have milk.

   Waitress: For dessert, we have a wonderful apple pie.

   Customer: I really don't like pie. What _____ desserts do you have?

2. Waitress 1:   What a horrible day!

   Waitress 2:   What happened?

   Waitress 1:   Well, at one table, a child kicked me when I was walking by, and I dropped a tray of drinks. Later, _____ child wouldn't stop screaming, and all _____ customers were very annoyed.

Part E *Directions:* Complete each sentence with a word or expression from the box.

another	in other words	one another	the other
every other	one after the other	other than	

1. I swim on Sundays, Tuesdays, and Thursdays. I go to the swimming pool
   _____ day.

2. My mother told me that, in a good relationship, the two people communicate with each
   other, help _____, and forgive each other.

3. My brother has two close friends. One is Kent, and _____ is Bill.

4. _____ fish, no pets are allowed in this apartment building.

5. Jenny cheered as her team members ran across the finish line, _____.

6. I am thinking about buying _____ pair of shoes.

7. I can help you with the budget report, but I'm very busy today. I have to finish this
   project summary and meet with my boss. _____, I can't help you until
   tomorrow.

Part F *Directions:* Complete the sentences with personal pronouns that refer to the antecedents
in *italics*.

1. *Robert* is taking classes at Clearwater College this semester. Last year,
   _____ was working at a car factory in Milpitas. _____
   didn't enjoy _____ job.

2. Many *people* find a great job after _____ go back to school and finish
   _____ degree.

3. *My family* used to live in Kansas, where the land is very flat and rich.
   _____ had a wonderful vegetable garden behind _____
   house.

4. *Someone* left _____ dictionary in the classroom last Friday.
   _____ can go to the department office to claim it.

5. *Personal computers* have changed education. When _____ were invented in
   the early 1980s, _____ cost more than $2,000 each. Today, people can buy
   _____ much cheaper in discount stores and on the Internet.

Part A *Directions:* Choose the correct completions.

1. (*We / Us / Our*) are worried that we won't find a renter for (*we / us / our*) apartment because no one has called (*we / us / our*) about it yet.

2. Barbara went to (*she / her / hers*) nephew's birthday party yesterday. (*She / Her / Hers*) gave (*he / him / his*) a book that a friend of (*she / her / hers*) had recommended.

3. Teresa bought a sweater as a gift. She is going to give it to (*he's / his / her*) brother. She also bought some towels. She is going to give (*it / they / them*) to a friend as a wedding present.

4. If (*you / your / yours*) don't finish (*you / your / yours*) homework on time, the teacher will ask (*you / your / yours*) to correct it by yourself.

5. My brother and (*I / my / mine*) are planning an anniversary celebration for (*we / our / ours*) parents. (*They / Their / Them*) will celebrate their 25th year together.

Part B *Directions:* Identify the antecedent for each personal pronoun in *italics*. Write the antecedent on the line.

1. Katie's parents were worried. She didn't tell *them* where she was going or when she was coming home.

   them = _____

2. A dentist not only cleans patients' teeth, but *he or she* also checks for diseases and infections that can cause tooth decay.

   he or she = _____

3. The people in the audience clapped loudly for the actors. *They* appreciated the wonderful performance.

   They = _____

4. Everyone who paints knows how to take care of *his or her* paintbrushes.

   his or her = _____

5. The team won a gold medal in volleyball. *It* was honored to represent its country.

   It = _____

6. Most faculty are going to come to the president's meeting. *They* want to find out about the new Internet use policy.

   They = _____

Part C *Directions:* Complete the sentences with reflexive pronouns.

1. I always talk to _____ about important things that I am thinking about.

2. Because we were in a hurry, we carried our bags up to our hotel room

   _____ .

3. While Alex was working on his car, he cut _____ on a sharp edge.

4. After rehearsing for two hours, the musicians allowed _____ a ten-minute

   break.

5. Rita was very angry at _____ for missing the important meeting.

6. The dog scratched _____ happily as it lay in the sun.

7. If you want a job done right, you have to do it _____ .

Part D *Directions:* Complete the sentences with *another, the other, other, the others,* or *others*.

1. Waitress: There are two specials on the menu tonight. The first is a delicious broiled sea

   bass. _____ is an oven-roasted chicken with rosemary.

   Customer: I'll have the bass, please.

2. Waitress: Are you ready to order?

   Customer: There will be five of us, but only three of us are here. We'll wait until

   _____ arrive before we order.

3. Mary: Where should we go for dinner?

   John: How about Ray's Boathouse on the waterfront?

   Mary: Have you ever eaten there? Is it any good?

   John: I've never eaten there, but many _____ have and recommend it

   highly.

   Mary: Well, I don't have any _____ suggestions. If we don't like it, we

   can find _____ place.

Part E *Directions:* Complete each sentence with a word or expression from the box.

another	every other	one after the other	the other
each other	in other words	other than	

1. John can't go with us to the museum on Thursday, so he will have to see the Picasso exhibition on _____ day.

2. During the war, my mother and father wrote to _____ every day. In fact, they still have all their letters.

3. My job working in the factory is very boring. All day long I put together electronic parts. They come down the assembly line, _____, and I put them together.

4. I have two scarves, but I can't decide which one to wear. One is black, and _____ one is gray.

5. Firenz doesn't have any plans this weekend _____ studying. He is a serious student.

6. Online education uses the Internet to connect teachers and students. _____, you need a computer to take an online class.

7. My bridge club meets on the first and third Saturdays of the month. I usually play bridge _____ Saturday.

Part F *Directions:* Complete the sentences with personal pronouns that refer to the antecedents in *italics*.

1. If *people* drive above the speed limit, _____ should expect to get a speeding ticket. When the police officer gives _____ a ticket, _____ should just accept it quietly.

2. Have you seen my *purse*? I left _____ on this desk. _____ is brown with a gold clasp.

3. I want *everyone* at my party to have a good time. _____ should relax and have fun. If _____ want to take off _____ shoes, that's OK with me.

4. The *government* announced last night that _____ was going to help the earthquake victims in the south. _____ voted to approve $100 million in assistance and supplies.

5. A *professor* has many responsibilities. First and foremost, _____ has an obligation to help students learn. Second, _____ should do research that will improve the prestige of _____ college.

CHAPTER 9   Modals, Part 1

QUIZ 1 Necessity and Prohibition: *Must / Have To* and *Must Not / Not Have To*   (Charts 9-2 and 9-3)

Directions: Choose the correct completions.

Example: At the Schmidt's house, the children _____ do their homework immediately after dinner.

          (a.) must / have to   b. must not   c. doesn't have to

1. If Americans want to travel abroad, they _____ have a passport.

    a. must / have to   b. must not   c. don't have to

2. Students _____ cheat on tests or exams.

    a. must / have to   b. must not   c. don't have to

3. You _____ have any special equipment to go jogging, but a good pair of shoes helps.

    a. must / have to   b. must not   c. don't have to

4. The store opens at 10:00 A.M., so I _____ be there to work by 9:30.

    a. must / have to   b. must not   c. don't have to

5. Children _____ be impolite to adults. They should be respectful.

    a. must / have to   b. must not   c. doesn't have to

6. To make a contract valid, both people agreeing to the contract _____ sign it.

    a. must / have to   b. must not   c. don't have to

7. Tomorrow is Saturday. It's my day off, so I _____ go to work.

    a. must / have to   b. must not   c. don't have to

8. Good photographers _____ take pictures carefully to make sure there is nothing strange in the background.

    a. must / have to   b. must not   c. don't have to

9. On most freeways in Washington state, drivers _____ drive over 60 miles per hour, or they will get a speeding ticket.

    a. must / have to   b. must not   c. don't have to

10. Our plane leaves at 8:30 A.M. The airport shuttle is picking us up at 6:00 so we _____ take our car.

    a. must / have to   b. must not   c. don't have to

Directions: Complete the sentences with **must** (**not**) or (**do not**) **have to** and the verbs in parentheses. More than one answer may be possible.

Example: Kumi's visa is good until July. After that she (*return*) __must / has to return__ to Japan.

1. Jason's mom says he (*go*) _____ to bed at 10:00 P.M.

2. If you want to get a good grade, you (*study*) _____ hard.

3. We (*go, not*) _____ shopping today if you don't want to. You decide.

4. Leslie failed her Spanish class. She (*take*) _____ it again next year.

5. Visitors (*smoke, not*) _____ in the hospital. It is not allowed.

6. Mr. Lehmann just had a major heart attack. The doctors (*do*) _____ emergency surgery right away.

7. Marcia (*worry, not*) _____ about her grade in my class. Her work is very good.

8. Carlos borrowed $500 from his brother. He (*pay*) _____ it back in a month.

Directions: Read each sentence. Decide if it expresses advice, a duty, a suggestion, or a warning.

1. Children shouldn't watch more than an hour of television daily.

   (a.) advice   b. duty   c. suggestion   d. warning

2. Police officers ought to protect the public in dangerous situations.

   a. advice   b. duty   c. suggestion   d. warning

3. You'd better not park in the loading zone. You'll get a ticket.

   a. advice   b. duty   c. suggestion   d. warning

4. Sharon could take some time off next month.

   a. advice   b. duty   c. suggestion   d. warning

5. Liz shouldn't talk so much. She is extremely talkative.

   a. advice   b. duty   c. suggestion   d. warning

6. Visitors to any country ought to follow that country's rules.

   a. advice   b. duty   c. suggestion   d. warning

Directions: Complete the conversations with **must, have to, should,** or **had better**. More than one answer may be possible.

Example: Karen: What time does the concert start?

        Mark: Seven-thirty. We _____*had better*_____ hurry if we want to get good seats.

1. Anita: Dad, can I borrow your camera tomorrow for school?

   Dad: Yes, but you _____ not lose it. It was expensive.

   Anita: OK. I'll be very careful.

2. Mr. Moore: If you want this apartment, you _____ sign the rental agreement by Friday or we'll rent it to someone else.

   Willy: Thank you for letting me know.

3. Amy: I _____ work next weekend, so I'm going to miss Gretchen's party.

   Wendy: That's too bad.

4. Sam: Hello. This is Sam. Is Erica home?

   Jessie: No, she's not here right now, but you _____ try her cell phone. Do you have the number?

   Sam: Yes, I'll try that. Bye.

5. Linda: Michael stayed up late last night and fell asleep on the train to work.

   Vick: Oh, no! He _____ go to bed earlier tonight. He has got to work tomorrow, too.

6. Barry: I am going to San Francisco during spring break. Do you want to come?

   Paul: Oh, I'd love to, but I can't. I _____ stay here and study for my medical school exams.

7. Philip: Look at that little boy who fell off the swing!

   Susan: Oh, here comes his mom. She _____ watch him more carefully or he's going to get hurt.

8. Chris: We _____ leave on time or we'll miss our connecting flight in Houston.

   Harry: Yes, I hope we leave at 9:45 like we're supposed to.

Directions: Choose the correct completions.

Example: Martha: You ((should)/ *could*) not eat such sugary foods. It's unhealthy.

Adam: You're right. I really (*should* / *could*) be eating healthier foods.

1. Anya: Theo isn't sure about his plans for the weekend. He (*should* / *could*) go to the beach, but he's not sure if he wants to.

   Claire: Maybe he's too tired. He (*should* / *could*) also stay home and relax.

2. Derik: I have a problem and I don't know what to do. My roommate is driving me crazy.

   Sam: Well, you (*should* / *could*) find a new roommate, but that takes time. I think you (*should* / *could*) talk with your roommate about whatever is bothering you.

3. Carlos: My English teacher says students (*should* / *could*) speak English every day if they really want to improve their communication skills.

   Martin: That's great advice. I (*should* / *could*) try to speak English every day, too. I need the practice.

4. Alexis: How are we going to get from the airport to our hotel?

   Nick: We (*should* / *could*) take a taxi, but that's a little expensive. There's also an airport bus.

5. Cate: I need a new phone, but I can't decide what to buy.

   Sarah: You (*should* / *could*) do more research before you go shopping. Then you'll have more information to make your decision.

6. Gary: Alice has a terrible headache.

   Tomas: That's too bad. She (*should* / *could*) take two aspirin and lie down.

7. Nora: I'm excited about going to New York next month. There are so many things to do there. For example, we (*should* / *could*) see a Broadway show or go to the Museum of Modern Art.

   Chris: We (*should* / *could*) also visit the Statue of Liberty. Whatever we do, we (*should* / *could*) try to purchase tickets online before we go.

Directions: Answer the questions in complete sentences. Choose an answer from the box.
Use *be supposed to*.

bring a passport or ID	exercise regularly	✓ pay your friend back
call the police	help patients	turn off your phone

1. What are you supposed to do if you borrow money from a friend?

    You are supposed to pay your friend back.

2. What are travelers supposed to bring when visiting a foreign country?

    _____

3. What are you supposed to do if your cell phone rings during a meeting?

    _____

4. What are people supposed to do to stay healthy?

    _____

5. What is a driver supposed to do if there's a traffic accident?

    _____

QUIZ 7 Expectation: *Be Supposed To / Should* (Chart 9-5)

Directions: Rewrite the sentences with *should*.

Example: I expect you to clean your room. It's really messy.

    You should clean your room.

1. I expect John to call soon. It's almost 10:00.

    _____

2. I expect your parents to be here soon. They are going to pick you up.

    _____

3. You have studied hard for the test. I expect you to pass.

    _____

4. I'm waiting for the bus. I expect it to come in a few minutes.

    _____

5. Everyone expects the weekend to be warm and sunny.

    _____

Directions: Rewrite the sentences using *be able to*.

Example: Jim can work on Saturday.

Jim is able to work on Saturday.

1. Josh can eat a whole pizza at one meal.

_____

2. Can you carry my bag, please? It's too heavy for me.

_____

3. I can see really well in the dark.

_____

QUIZ 9 Ability: *Can, Know How To, Be Able To*   (Chart 9-6)

Directions: Rewrite the sentences using *know how to*.

Example: Mr. Ponce can make beautiful silver jewelry.

Mr. Ponce knows how to make beautiful silver jewelry.

1. Misty can make her own yogurt.

_____

2. My brother can ride a motorcycle.

_____

3. Can you speak Spanish as well as English?

_____

QUIZ 10 Ability: *Can, Know How To, Be Able To*   (Chart 9-6)

Directions: Make the sentences negative.

Example: I know how to cook a Spanish omelet.

I don't know how to cook a Spanish omelet.

1. Ms. Wilson is able to play tennis for hours at a time.

_____

2. Jessie knows how to iron shirts perfectly.

_____

3. I can send you a text message later today.

_____

Directions: Choose the correct completions to express *possibility*. More than one answer may be possible.

Examples: Poor sleep (*can* / *may* / *might*) ruin one's health.

I (*can* / *may* / *might*) go to bed early tonight.

1. Driving too fast (*can* / *may* / *might*) cause an accident.

2. It's easy to get from the airport to the city center. You (*can* / *may* / *might*) take the subway.

3. We (*can* / *may* / *might*) need to buy gasoline before we leave.

4. These days you (*can* / *may* / *might*) learn a new language online.

5. Taking a test (*can* / *may* / *might*) be stressful.

6. The weather (*can* / *may* / *might*) be rainy and cool tomorrow.

7. Mr. Roberts (*can* / *may* / *might*) want your email address to contact you.

8. Dogs are smart. You (*can* / *may* / *might*) teach them how to follow simple commands.

9. Mami (*can* / *may* / *might*) come to visit us next weekend.

10. You (*can* / *may* / *might*) get a fishing license at a hardware store.

QUIZ 12 **Polite Requests** (Charts 9-8 and 9-9)

Directions: Read each sentence. Decide if it expresses a request or permission.

Example: Will you please help me open this door?	request	permission
1. Could you bring me a glass of water, please?	request	permission
2. May I have another cookie?	request	permission
3. Would you mind if we sat here?	request	permission
4. Will you come to my party on Friday?	request	permission
5. May we come in?	request	permission
6. Would you mind stepping to the left a little?	request	permission
7. Would you please put away your clothes?	request	permission
8. Would you mind calling me back in ten minutes?	request	permission
9. Could I go to Europe next summer?	request	permission
10. Would you mind if I didn't eat dinner tonight? I'm not hungry.	request	permission

Directions: Complete the polite requests with *I* or *you*.

Example: Could __I__ borrow five dollars?

1. Could _____ send me a text when you get to the office, please?

2. May _____ use your phone, Dad?

3. Could _____ go to the movies with Jason, please? He invited me.

4. Would _____ make me a sandwich?

5. Will _____ call me tomorrow?

6. Can _____ have another piece of pizza?

7. Could _____ please give me a ride to school?

8. Would _____ mind closing the window?

9. Can _____ help me wash the dishes?

10. Could _____ please borrow your car?

QUIZ 14 Polite Requests with *Would You Mind*   (Chart 9-9)

Directions: Change each sentence into a polite request.

Examples: I want to cook dinner tonight. Would you mind __if I cooked dinner tonight?__

I want you to cook dinner tonight. Would you mind __cooking dinner tonight?__

1. I want you to help me with my homework.

   Would you mind _____?

2. I want to go to a café.

   Would you mind _____?

3. I'm tired. I want to take a nap.

   Would you mind _____?

4. This box is too heavy. I want you to carry it.

   Would you mind _____?

5. I want you to wait for me.

   Would you mind _____?

Directions: Complete the conversations with appropriate pronouns. If no pronoun is needed, write *Ø*.

Example: Waiter: Good afternoon, Madame. Shall _____*I*_____ take your coat for you?

         Lady: Yes, thank you.

1. Bob: What do you want to do tonight, Georgia?

   Georgia: I'm tired. Let's _____ just stay home.

   Bob: OK. Why don't _____ watch a movie?

   Georgia: That would be nice, thanks.

2. Ms. Babcock: Miss Jones? Do you have the number for the accountant's office?

   Miss Jones: Yes, Ms. Babcock. Shall _____ get him on the phone

               for you?

   Ms. Babcock: Yes, please. I need to ask him a question.

3. Sam: Mom, I'm bored.

   Mom: Why don't _____ invite a friend to come over?

   Sam: Can I? That's a good idea.

4. Maggie: Let's _____ go to the zoo this weekend, Daddy.

   Daddy: I'm sorry, but I think it's going to rain. Why don't _____ go

               bowling instead?

5. Bill: Jim, did you get a new car?

   Jim: Yes. Why don't _____ get in, and I'll take you for a ride.

6. Students: Mrs. Dann, what are we going to practice?

   Mrs. Dann: Students, we'll be playing "Für Elise" today. Shall _____

               begin?

7. Junko: I've been studying for three hours. My brain is numb.

   Mariko: Why don't _____ take a break?

8. David: Our meeting starts at 8:30 A.M. What time shall _____ pick

               you up?

   Charlie: How about 7:45?

   David: See you then.

Directions: Choose the correct completions.

Example: (*Let's*/ *Shall*) go to the market on Saturday.

1. (*May* / *Would*) I borrow your grammar book, please?

2. (*Should* / *Could*) you please turn the air-conditioning off? I'm cold.

3. Mr. Sutherland is rich. He (*doesn't have to* / *had better not*) work for a living.

4. If you lose your credit card, you (*supposed to* / *should*) cancel the card immediately.

5. (*Let's* / *Why don't*) you call me tomorrow?

6. High school (*can* / *may*) often be very stressful for American teenagers. They have a lot of homework and exams.

7. Billy (*must* / *have to*) go to bed at 8:30 tonight.

8. When people are sick, they (*should* / *ought*) to stay home.

9. It's getting dark outside. I think it (*might* / *can*) rain.

10. I'm hungry. (*Let's* / *Why don't*) get something to eat.

Part A *Directions:* Complete the sentences. Use *must, must not, have to,* or *don't have to.*
More than one answer may be possible.

1. Max: What do I need to do to get my U.S. passport?

   Nan: Three things: You _____ prove that you are an American citizen,
   bring a photo, and pay a fee.

2. Lisa: When _____ we _____ turn in our quarterly reports?

   Mark: I think they're due on the 15th.

3. Here is the last point in my safety lecture. You _____ operate these machines
   if your hands are wet. You could get a serious shock.

4. Joe: I'm surprised to see you on the bus. Is your car still having problems?

   Pat: Yeah. I _____ take it to the garage, but I never seem to find time.

5. Lucy: I'm so relieved

   Bill: Why?

   Lucy: Originally, our essays were due on Friday, but the teacher has changed the due
   date. Now we _____ hand them in until next Wednesday.

Part B *Directions:* Read the paragraph. Then complete the sentences with *should, ought to, had
better,* or *could.* Use the information in parentheses to help you.

You and your friend Jimmy are walking to class. You have a test today, but Jimmy doesn't feel
well. He was up all night coughing, and he slept very little. Now he has a slight fever and a
headache. Jimmy is clearly not well enough to take a test.

1. Jimmy _____ not be at school today. (*advice*)

2. Jimmy _____ talk to the teacher about the test and maybe take it later. (*possibility*)

3. The teacher _____ send Jimmy home. (*responsibility*)

4. You _____ not get too close to Jimmy. You may get sick. (*advice*)

5. Jimmy _____ go home so other students don't get sick, too. (*warning*)

Part C *Directions:* Choose the correct completions.

1. Tom: Everyone's using the Internet for business these days. I (*ought / know how*) to learn more about it if I want to get a better job. What can I do?

   Phil: Maybe you (*can / have got to*) take classes at a business school or try an online lesson. However, I think the best idea is to take a class at the community college first. You (*ought / should*) make sure you like computers before you spend a lot of money.

   Tom: Thanks for the suggestion. I (*may / know how to*) look into that sometime soon. I want to (*can / be able to*) get a job that pays well.

2. Jane: I'm so tired. I'm really happy that tomorrow is a holiday and I (*must not / don't have to*) go to work. I can sleep late. (*Let's / Why don't*) we do something fun?

   Dan: Not me. We took last Friday off, so I still (*have to / might*) go to work tomorrow.

   Jane: I'm planning to go downtown and do a little shopping. I also have some errands to run.

   Dan: Speaking of errands, (*would / should*) you pick up some stamps for me at the post office?

   Jane: No problem. I (*had better / have to*) mail a package, so I can do both things at the same time.

Part D *Directions:* Complete the polite questions. Add the subject where necessary and use the verbs in parentheses.

1. I want to open the window. Would you mind (*open*)

   _____

2. I want you to help me wash the dishes. Could (*help*)

   _____

3. I want you to take me to the airport. Would you mind (*take*)

   _____

4. I want to go to a movie tonight. May (*go*)

   _____

5. I want you to vacuum the carpet. Would (*vacuum*)

   _____

Part E *Directions:* Correct the errors.

1. Would you mind if I using your pen?

2. In the United States, children are suppose to go to school until age sixteen.

3. May you please help me move this table?

4. Silvia must to send out her thank-you notes soon.

5. Would you mind to call me tomorrow?

Part A *Directions:* Complete the conversations. Use *must, must not, have to,* or *don't have to.* More than one answer may be possible.

1. Jenny: You aren't leaving the party already, are you?

   Lucas: I'm really sorry, but I _____ go. I've had a wonderful time.

2. Mr. Bix: This presentation is very important if we want to attract new business. There _____ be any problems.

   Jose: Don't worry, sir. I'm sure everything is ready.

3. Pat: I'm going to leave work early today. I _____ see my doctor.

   Ann: Are you sick?

   Pat: Yes, I _____ blow my nose every five minutes, and I have a cough.

4. Sara: I think we can finish this by ourselves now. You _____ stay. You can go home.

   Allen: I can stay longer. I _____ do anything else tonight.

   Sara: Thanks, but you've worked long enough. Go home and relax.

Part B *Directions:* Read the paragraph. Then complete the sentences with *should, ought to, had better,* or *could.* Use the information in parentheses to help you.

You are going out for the evening with your spouse. A babysitter is going to look after your kids. Before you leave, you give the kids some rules of behavior. They may not watch TV or play video games, and they have to go to bed at 9:00. They are allowed to have a snack before bed.

1. You _____ give the babysitter your cell phone number in case of an emergency. (*responsibility*)

2. The kids _____ obey the rules while you're gone. (*warning*)

3. You _____ let the children watch a movie with the babysitter. (*possibility*)

4. The babysitter _____ play cards or read with the kids. (*advice*)

5. You _____ be home by midnight. (*possibility*)

Part C *Directions:* Choose the correct completions.

1. Paul: Hi! What are you doing tomorrow evening?

   Yuka: I don't have any plans. Why?

   Paul: I was thinking that we (*could / have to*) do something together.

   Yuka: (*Must / Should*) we go out to dinner and then to a movie?

   Paul: That would be really fun. What do you want to see?

   Yuka: (*Let's / Why don't*) see Secrets of the Dark Woods. I hear that it's good and scary.

   Paul: Sounds great. If I meet you at the theater, (*should / would*) you drive me home? I'll probably go directly to the theater from work.

   Yuka: No problem. Well, I (*had better / could*) go and finish my work. See you tomorrow.

2. Carl: Wow! This box is heavy. What's in it?

   Pete: My old college textbooks. I (*could / have to*) make room for my new sound system, so I'm putting these in the garage.

   Carl: You (*should / must not*) sell them. There's a used bookstore on 24th Street. (*Why don't / Let's*) we take your records there and see if they'll buy them?

   Pete: They're awfully heavy. (*May / Would*) you drive me down there in your car?

   Carl: No problem, but I need to be at my parents' house for dinner in an hour, so if you want to go, we (*have to / ought to*) go now.

Part D *Directions:* Complete the polite questions. Add the subject where necessary and use the verbs in parentheses.

1. I want you to put the laundry away. Could (*put*)

   _____

2. I want to get a drink of water. Would you mind (*get*)

   _____

3. I want you to tell me what time it is. Would (*tell*)

   _____

4. I want to go shopping. May (*go*)

   _____

5. I want you to empty the garbage. Would you mind (*empty*)

   _____

Part E *Directions:* Correct the errors.

1. Matthew should not falls asleep at work.

2. I must to help my parents in their store after school, so I can't play basketball.

3. Lindsay has better calling me tonight.

4. Would you mind if I leaving work early today?

5. When does Ben had to be at the train station?

QUIZ 1 Using *Would* to Express a Repeated Action in the Past   (Chart 10-1)

Directions: Check (✓) the correct sentence/sentences in each pair. In some cases, both sentences are correct.

Example: __✓__ When I was a child, we used visit my grandma in Helena every summer.

__✓__ When I was a child, we would visit my grandma in Helena every summer.

1. _____ Before Tom got his own cell phone, he always used to use his brother's old phone.

    _____ Before Tom got his own cell phone, he would always use his brother's old phone.

2. _____ Alex used to work for Microsoft, but now he is working for Apple Computer.

    _____ Alex would work for Microsoft, but now he is working for Apple Computer.

3. _____ I used to study at Kirk College before I transferred to the University of Georgia.

    _____ I would study at Kirk College before I transferred to the University of Georgia.

4. _____ Every night when my dad got home from work, he used to sit down in his armchair, read the newspaper for five minutes, and fall asleep.

    _____ Every night when my dad got home from work, he would sit down in his armchair, read the newspaper for five minutes, and fall asleep.

5. _____ In 2012, Mary used to live in a chic apartment in midtown Manhattan.

    _____ In 2012, Mary would live in a chic apartment in midtown Manhattan.

QUIZ 2 Using *Would* to Express a Repeated Action in the Past   (Chart 10-1)

Directions: Complete the sentences with the given words. For a repeated action in the past, use *would*. For a past state, use *used to*.

Examples: I (*ride*) _____would ride_____ my bike to work when I lived in Taylorville.

Alan (*be*) _____used to be_____ a veterinarian, but now he is retired.

1. Last semester, Jake (*be*) _____ late for class every morning because he had a job on the night shift.

2. Lisa (*be*) _____ able to speak Chinese when she was younger, but she can't anymore.

3. When my Uncle Stanley was alive, he (*take*) _____ us children for rides in his sports car.

4. My grandmother (*work*) _____ in her garden every day until she developed arthritis in her knees.

5. Dennis (*be*) _____ a poor speller. Spell-check has really helped him!

Directions: Change the sentences to the past.

Example: We have to buy fresh vegetables at the market on Saturday.

We _____*had to buy*_____ fresh vegetables at the market on Saturday.

1. Nelson has got to talk to the tech specialist about his computer virus.

   Nelson _____ to the tech specialist about his computer virus.

2. The police officer ought to give that driver a ticket for speeding.

   The police officer _____ that driver a ticket for speeding.

3. Maureen must buy her plane tickets and make hotel reservations a year before her trip.

   Maureen _____ her plane tickets and make hotel reservations a year

   before her trip.

4. My aunt and uncle don't have to pay any extra taxes this year.

   My aunt and uncle _____ any extra taxes last year.

5. Roy shouldn't leave the kitchen dirty after cooking. It's a mess.

   Roy _____ the kitchen dirty after cooking. It was a mess.

6. My teenaged children are supposed to be home by 10:00 P.M.

   My teenaged children _____ home by 10:00 P.M.

7. I've got to finish sending this text before my phone battery dies.

   I _____ sending that text before my phone battery died.

8. I don't remember my homework assignment. I should listen carefully during class.

   I don't remember my homework assignment. I _____ carefully

   during class.

9. John's train isn't supposed to arrive until midnight.

   John's train _____ until midnight.

10. After the soccer match ends, we have to take the express bus home.

    After the soccer match ended, we _____ the express bus home.

Directions: Read each story. Then complete the statements about it with **should have** or **shouldn't have**.

Example: You are in a restaurant in the non-smoking section. A man at the next table lights a cigarette. You speak to the waiter, who then asks the man to move to a different table.

The man ___*shouldn't have*___ sat in the non-smoking section.

A. Kate recently started surfing the Internet, and she discovered all the different stores that offer online shopping. Many of them offered really good bargains. Kate bought books, CDs, clothes, toys for her nephews, and even an expensive big-screen TV. Yesterday Kate got her credit card bill. She found she had spent more than $2,500 last month. She was shocked.

1. Kate _____ been more careful with her online shopping.

2. Kate _____ bought an expensive TV.

3. Kate _____ spent so much money

4. Kate's credit card company _____ limited her credit.

B. Mr. and Mrs. Taylor read about a new play at the City Theater. Mr. Taylor promised to buy tickets. Unfortunately, he always had to do something else first. When he finally went to the box office two weeks later, the show was sold out. His wife was very disappointed.

5. Mr. Taylor _____ disappointed his wife.

6. Mr. Taylor _____ gone to the box office sooner.

7. Mr. Taylor _____ waited to buy the tickets.

8. Mrs. Taylor _____ bought the tickets herself.

C. Marcia went shopping for a new suitcase with her mother. Marcia's mother recommended that she buy the TravelPro suitcase for $250. Marcia's mother had one, and she said it was very good quality. A similar suitcase was on sale for $100, so Marcia bought the cheaper suitcase. Within a year, the suitcase lost a wheel and a zipper broke. Marcia's mother's TravelPro suitcase is still in good condition and works well.

9. Marcia _____ ignored her mother's advice.

10. Marcia _____ spent more money on her suitcase.

11. Marcia's mother _____ given Marcia money for a TravelPro suitcase.

12. The suitcase _____ started falling apart so soon.

Directions: If possible, rewrite the sentence with **could** to express a past ability. If it isn't possible, write **no change**.

Example: As a sound technician, Galen was able to operate all kinds of electronic recording equipment.

As a sound technician, Galen could operate all kinds of electronic recording equipment .

1. My mother was able to tap dance when she was 12 years old.

_____

2. Sam was able to attend Rutgers University because he got a scholarship.

_____

3. The baby horse was able to stand up immediately after being born.

_____

4. Eddie was able to walk when he was only ten months old.

_____

5. We were able to buy delicious fresh bread at the Great Harvest Bakery.

_____

QUIZ 6 **Expressing Past Ability** (Chart 10-3)

Directions: Choose the correct verb. In some cases, both verbs are correct.

1. My roommate _____ meet me at the airport, so I didn't have to take a taxi.

   a. could   (b.) was able to

2. Ruth broke her foot and _____ drive for six weeks.

   a. couldn't   b. wasn't able to

3. Susan and Lucas _____ visit their son in Port Angeles last month.

   a. could   b. were able to

4. When I lived in San Diego, I learned to surf. I _____ ride on big waves.

   a. could   b. was able to

5. The dog was old but _____ see and hear well.

   a. could   b. was able to

6. We _____ spend a couple of hours at the Field Museum when we were in Chicago.

   a. could   b. were able to

Directions: Choose the correct completions.

Example: My sister ((might)/ must) come to visit next weekend. I'm not sure yet.

1. The boys have been playing computer games all afternoon. They (may / must) love those games.

2. I wonder how many people will come to our party this weekend. We (may / must) have twenty or thirty guests.

3. My dog is standing by its food dish, but it (couldn't / mustn't) be hungry. I just fed it 30 minutes ago.

4. I don't know what my husband is getting me for my birthday. It (may / must) be jewelry or perfume.

5. The weather (might not / must not) be very good for a picnic this weekend. The forecast is predicting rain.

6. Movies about the American West (might / must) be popular in other countries. I'm not sure.

7. Natasha is in really good shape and has muscular arms. She (might / must) exercise regularly.

8. Mick (might not / must not) like potato salad. He never eats it.

9. I'm not sure where Julia went. She (could / must) be doing her laundry, or she (might / must) be studying at the library.

10. I have an important meeting this morning. I (mustn't / couldn't) be late.

Directions: Complete the sentences. Use ***must, may, might,*** or ***could***. More than one answer may be possible.

Examples: Tanya's boyfriend wrecked her new car. She _____*must*_____ be angry.

I don't know what the weather forecast is. It _*may / might / could*_ rain today.

1. Helen's son just got a big promotion at work. She _____ be very proud of him.

2. I'm not sure what our homework assignment for tomorrow is. It _____ be pages 250 to 255, but I can't remember for sure.

3. Debra eats dinner out in a restaurant almost every night. She _____ not like to cook!

4. We're trying to make plans for a trip this summer. We'd like to go to Scotland, but we _____ visit the Virgin Islands instead.

5. Mr. and Mrs. Jackson just became grandparents. They _____ be excited about their new granddaughter.

6. I found a Web site for an online dating agency called "Marry an Ugly Millionaire." This _____ not be a real dating agency! It's too strange!

7. The problem with online shopping is that you _____ spend more money than you realize because you usually have to pay taxes and shipping charges.

8. Jessica just tried to call Anita's cell phone, but she didn't answer. Her phone _____ be off, or she _____ not have it with her.

9. Andy is carrying five books, his laptop, and a bottle of water in his backpack. That _____ be heavy!

Directions: Complete the sentences. Use the past forms of ***must,*** or ***may, might,*** or ***could*** and the correct form of the verbs in parentheses. More than one answer may be possible.

Example: We (*get*) _____could have gotten_____ tickets to the hit show, but they were too expensive, so we decided not to go.

1. I'm not sure what Chuck did last weekend. He (*go*) _____ camping.

2. A: What did you get on the quiz?

   B: I got 100%!

   A: That's impossible! You (*get, not*) _____ 100%! You didn't even study!

3. I wonder where Sharon is. She's not usually late. She (*have*) _____ a late appointment today.

4. Last week someone stole Mitch's wallet with $200 in it. He (*be*) _____ angry.

5. Jasmine looked really tired this morning. She said there was a lot of noise outside her apartment last night. She (*sleep, not*) _____ well.

6. I'm not sure what happened, but Uncle Seth's car has a big scratch on the hood and one headlight is broken. He (*hit*) _____ a tree or something.

7. I'm not sure when Max got back from Germany. He (*come*) _____ back last week or the week before.

8. Mia told me that she and her boyfriend had broken up. She (*be, not*) _____ very upset about it though because she was smiling and wanted to go out dancing.

9. The airline pilots went on strike last week. It (*be*) _____ because of vacation pay or salaries. I don't really know.

10. When the earth was formed, there (*be*) _____ incredible forces that shaped it.

Directions: Read each situation. Use past modals to restate the sentences in parentheses. More than one modal may be possible.

Example: (Maybe Brian went to the grocery store.) Brian ___may / might have gone___ to the grocery store.

SITUATION 1: I am supposed to meet my friend Mona at a local coffee shop. I've been waiting for 30 minutes and she hasn't come yet. I tried to call her, but she didn't answer her cell phone.

1. (Maybe Mona forgot her cell phone at home.)

_____

2. (It's not possible that Mona forgot our meeting. I talked with her this morning.)

_____

3. (I'm 95% sure that Mona left her office late. She told me she had a lot to do today.)

_____

SITUATION 2: Jim can't find his car. He parked it on the street across from the post office, but now it isn't there. He is really worried.

4. (It's possible that Jim parked his car on a different street.)

_____

5. (A post office worker is 95% sure the police towed the car away. He saw a tow truck in front of the post office.)

_____

6. (Jim is guessing that he probably didn't park the car legally.)

_____

7. (Maybe Jim had many unpaid parking tickets before this.)

_____

Directions: Using the information about each situation, complete the sentences.

Example: SITUATION: The students are taking a two-page quiz. There are five minutes left for the quiz. Who will finish the quiz?

INFORMATION: The last two questions on **Ron's** paper are still blank.
Sheila is working on the last question.
Wendy is still working on the first page of the quiz.

a. _____Wendy_____ won't finish the quiz.

b. _____Ron_____ might finish the quiz.

c. _____Sheila_____ should finish the quiz.

SITUATION 1: People are running in a 26-mile marathon. Who will finish the marathon?

INFORMATION: **Mark** is in very good shape and ran a marathon last year.
Jane has never run a marathon before, and she trained for only two weeks.
Martha has never run a marathon before, but she has been training for three months.

a. _____ might not finish the marathon.

b. _____ could finish the marathon.

c. _____ ought to finish the marathon.

SITUATION 2: We are at the airport in Chicago. Whose flight will arrive on time?

INFORMATION: **Alice's** plane left on time and has had no problems in the air.
Kay's plane had a mechanical problem and left an hour late.
Jack's plane left fifteen minutes late, but a strong tail wind helped the plane go faster.

a. _____ should arrive on time.

b. _____ might arrive on time.

c. _____ won't arrive on time.

SITUATION 3: Several people were interviewed for a job. Who will get the job?

INFORMATION: **Mr. Anton** answered all the questions well, and he is well qualified for the position.
Mrs. Chu answered the questions well, but she lacks some job qualifications.
Ms. Callahan was extremely nervous and did not make a good impression.

a. _____ won't get the job.

b. _____ should get the job.

c. _____ may get the job.

Directions: Complete the sentences. Use the appropriate progressive forms of **must,** **should**, or **may** / **might** / **could** and the verbs in parentheses.

Example: Laura had a lot of homework and came home late from the library.

　　　She (*study*) _____*must have been studying*_____ .

1. Nora has been on the phone for an hour! I wonder who she is talking to. She

　(*talk*) _____ to her sister.

2. A: Do we turn right or left at the corner?

　B: I'm not sure. I (*listen*) _____ more carefully when

　　　Lawrence gave us directions to his house.

3. Johann looked really sleepy when he came to the door. I'm not sure, but he

　(*take*) _____ a nap when I arrived.

4. A: Where's Cassie?

　B: She (*eat*) _____ lunch in the cafeteria. A few minutes

　　　ago, she told me she was really hungry and wanted a hamburger.

5. My house is a mess and I have guests coming tomorrow.

　I (*clean*) _____ now, but I don't feel like it. I'll clean later.

6. Alex's car was badly damaged in the accident. He (*drive*) _____

　too fast.

7. I (*sleep*) _____ at 3:00 A.M, but a police siren woke me up.

　Then I couldn't go back to sleep.

8. A: Where is Khaled?

　B: I don't know. He (*wash*) _____ his car or maybe he's gone

　shopping.

9. Margaret looks upset and her eyes are red. She (*cry*) _____ .

10. A: What are you doing?

　B: I'm reading a novel, but I (*pay*) _____ bills instead.

Directions: Complete the sentences. Use ***would rather*** and the appropriate form of the verbs in parentheses.

Example: I (*stay*) _____would rather have stayed_____ home last night.

1. Paul (*take*) _____ his driving test next week.

2. Ruth (*have*) _____ fish than chicken for dinner. She's going to stop by the fish market.

3. I (*watch, not*) _____ TV. Let's play a card game instead.

4. I'm so tired! I (*sleep*) _____ right now, but I have to study.

5. My kids really wanted to go to Disneyland, so we did.

   I (*go*) _____ on a vacation to the beach. Maybe next year!

6. Ann (*visit*) _____ Seattle than Los Angeles anytime. She likes Seattle's green environment.

7. My grandfather likes the fruit trees in their garden, but my grandmother

   (*plant*) _____ roses.

8. Yumi got 88% on her grammar test. She (*get*) _____ a higher grade on it.

9. It's 8:00 A.M. on Saturday, and Tomás is taking a college entrance exam.

   He (*take, not*) _____ the exam. He

   (*play*) _____ basketball with his friends this morning.

10. My sister wanted to see a scary movie, so we did. I (*see*) _____ a comedy. Maybe next time.

Directions: Choose the correct completions.

Example: Joe (*should have* /(*must*)) finish his homework tonight.

1. Alice (*must have forgotten* / *must forget*) her phone at home. She doesn't have it with her.

2. Children (*have got to* / *supposed to*) go to bed early on school nights.

3. The meeting with our attorney (*should* / *would rather*) start at 9:30 A.M.

4. Dan (*had better not* / *isn't able*) use bad language around his parents.

5. When I arrived yesterday, Susan (*could meet* / *met*) me at the airport.

6. Jason (*shouldn't have spent* / *should have spent*) so much money on my birthday present. It was too expensive.

7. Emily, (*shall* / *will*) you lend me twenty dollars until Saturday?

8. May I (*borrow* / *could borrow*) your dictionary?

9. Students (*may have left* / *may leave*) the examination room when they finish the test. It's allowed.

10. That (*couldn't be* / *wouldn't be*) true! I don't believe it!

11. Charles (*must* / *has*) to be at work by 5:30 A.M. every morning.

12. My uncle Willy isn't going to (*be able to* / *can*) come for a visit this summer.

13. Maxine would rather (*drinking* / *drink*) coffee than tea.

14. We haven't seen John since summer. We (*maybe* / *might*) get together with him this weekend.

15. When I was growing up, I (*would* / *may*) ride my bicycle all over my hometown.

CHAPTER 10 – TEST 1

Part A *Directions:* Complete the sentences, using an appropriate modal with the verb in parentheses.

1. Those two people look so similar that they (*be*) _____ closely related. I think Julie told me they are first cousins.

2. Ben: Wow! You are an hour late. The traffic (*be*) _____ awful!

   Carla: It is. A terrible accident is blocking three lanes. The traffic is barely moving.

3. Marty: If I (*change*) _____ my reservation, I would like to leave on an earlier flight. Right now I'm booked on the 6:00 P.M. flight.

   Clerk: There (*be*) _____ plenty of room on the 4:30 flight. Saturday afternoons are usually pretty light. Let me check for you.

4. I'm sorry, but I (*need*) _____ to leave in a few minutes.

5. Julie: This speaker is so boring. Can we go now?

   Lam: No, that would be rude. He (*finish*) _____ soon.

Part B *Directions:* Using the information about each situation, complete the sentences.

SITUATION 1: The students took a difficult quiz. This is how far they had gotten five minutes before the end of the quiz. Who finished the quiz?

INFORMATION: The last two questions on **Sam's** paper were still blank.
Linda was working on the last question.
Liz had not finished one of the questions on page one, but I think she had finished the other page.

a. _____ must have finished the quiz.

b. _____ might have finished the quiz.

c. _____ might not have finished the quiz.

SITUATION 2: Mr. Anton loves to read, and his friends often give him recommendations. Which book did Mr. Anton read?

INFORMATION: **Ms. Adams** recommended *Trials by Night*. Mr. Anton has enjoyed all of the books Ms. Adams has recommended.
Mr. French recommended *The Terrible War*. Mr. Anton has enjoyed one or two of the books Mr. French has recommended.
Mrs. White recommended *The Thinking Mystery*. Mr. Anton has never enjoyed any of her recommendations, but she is a very close friend.

a. Mr. Anton may have read the book _____ recommended.

b. Mr. Anton might not have read the book _____ recommended.

c. Mr. Anton must have read the book _____ recommended.

Part C *Directions:* Complete the sentences, using the progressive forms of ***must, should,*** or ***may / might / could*** with the verbs in parentheses.

1. Mr. Black: Excuse me, Miss, are we going to take off soon?

   Attendant: Yes, Sir. There was a small problem, but it has been fixed.

   We (*leave*) _____ momentarily.

2. Audrey: Should I pack my umbrella?

   Dane: I checked the weather report, and it wasn't good. When we get there,

   it (*rain*) _____ .

3. Kellie: Oh, my! This month's water bill is over $100! Last month it was

   less than $40.

   Jack: Water (*leak*) _____ somewhere. We'd better call a plumber.

4. Mom: Johnny, why are you playing games on your phone? Your room is a mess, and

   you (*clean*) _____ your room right now.

   Johnny: All right, Mom. I'm going!

5. Vicky: Excuse me. I'm looking for the Investment Seminar. It's supposed to

   be in Room 4301.

   Ms. Lowe: If it's not in 4301, they (*meet*) _____ in Room 2301. Let me check

   for you.

Part D *Directions:* Choose the correct completions to express ability.

1. The library was already closed when we arrived. We (*can / can't / could / couldn't*)
   get any books.

2. Brenda has a new Apple watch. She (*can / can't / could / couldn't*) use it to communicate,
   track her exercise, and pay for groceries, as well as see the time of day.

3. Research has shown that children (*can / can't / could / couldn't*) learn foreign languages
   more easily before they reach age thirteen.

4. I'm really sorry, but I (*can / can't / could / couldn't*) help you this weekend. I'm going to
   be out of town.

5. When I was younger, I (*can / can't / could / couldn't*) eat a lot more than I
   (*can / can't / could / couldn't*) now.

Part E *Directions:* Complete the sentences with **would** or **would rather** and the appropriate form of the verbs in parentheses.

1. In the past, Mrs. Mitchell (*call*) _____ her sister in Illinois every week. Now she doesn't call so often.

2. I am taking a test right now, but I (*eat*) _____ lunch instead.

3. Last year, our teacher (*give*) _____ us "pop" quizzes. We never knew when we were going to have one.

4. Before 2012, the professional basketball team (*play*) _____ at least twice a week in Key Arena. Now the team plays in Fischer Pavilion.

5. Barbara lives in Miami, but she's thinking about moving to Phoenix next year. She (*live*) _____ there.

Part A *Directions:* Complete the sentences, using an appropriate modal with the verb in parentheses.

1. I have a math test tomorrow, but I (*go*) _____ to a movie with you instead of studying. I studied a little yesterday, so I (*do*) _____ OK on the test.

2. Jen said she doesn't want to go skiing this weekend, but she (*change*) _____ her mind. I'll call her on Friday to check.

3. I don't know why I told Mrs. Ramirez that I would babysit her naughty children tomorrow night. I (*be*) _____ crazy!

4. If I (*leave*) _____ work early, I (*be able to*) _____ meet you for dinner.

5. Ten years ago, it took me ten minutes to drive to work. Now the traffic is so bad that I (*get, not*) _____ to work in less than forty minutes.

Part B *Directions:* Using the information about each situation, complete the sentences.

SITUATION 1: Jean made some phone calls to her friends at 7:30 P.M., but no one answered. What were her friends doing?

INFORMATION: **Jeff** is usually at the library every evening from 7:00 P.M. to 9:00 P.M.
Eva usually eats dinner at 7:30 P.M., and sometimes she doesn't answer the telephone.
When **Ken** is at home, he always answers the telephone.

a. _____ could have been at home.

b. _____ must not have been at home.

c. _____ may not have been at home.

SITUATION 2: Mrs. Chang is in the kitchen. Her husband and three children are at home. She hears water running. Who is taking a shower?

INFORMATION: **Mr. Chang** often takes a shower after work, but he's out working in the garage.
Her son **Tom** had a basketball game that afternoon, and when he got home, he was very sweaty.
Her daughter, **Julie**, only takes a shower in the morning.
Her other son **Kevin** was working in the garden earlier, and she thinks he is still outside.

a. _____ may be taking a shower.

b. _____ must not be taking a shower.

c. _____ couldn't be taking a shower.

d. _____ must be taking a shower.

Part C *Directions:* Complete the sentences, using the progressive forms of *must, should,* or *may / might / could* with the verbs in parentheses. More than one answer may be possible.

1. Harry: That's the third time this week that I've seen you looking at employment information online. You (*look*) _____ for a new job.

   Kate: You're right. My boss and I aren't getting along, so it looks like it's time for me to go elsewhere.

2. Mom: Peter has been awfully quiet for more than an hour. What's he doing?

   Dad: I'm not sure. He (*play*) _____ a computer game, or he (*read*) _____ a comic book.

3. Karen: I haven't seen Maria all day. What's she doing?

   Rosa: She (*study*) _____ at the library. I think she has two exams tomorrow.

4. Ceci: I can't believe it's really 11:30 P.M. It's been so nice visiting with you, but we (*go*) _____ .

   Denis: And I (*get*) _____ to bed. I have to get up at 6:30 A.M.

Part D *Directions:* Choose the correct completions to express ability.

1. (*Can / Can't / Could / Couldn't*) you lift this box of books? It's too heavy for me.

2. Mr. Rodriguez (*can / can't / could / couldn't*) speak both Spanish and English when he was a little boy. Now he speaks mostly English, though.

3. My uncle Joe never learned to swim. He still (*can / can't / could / couldn't*) swim, and he's afraid to go in water.

4. Last summer, I wanted to take a long road trip, but I broke my arm and (*can / can't / could / couldn't*) drive.

5. Harriet (*can / can't / could / couldn't*) sing really well. She's in the school choir.

Part E *Directions:* Complete the sentences with *would* or *would rather* and the appropriate form of the verbs in parentheses.

1. Olivia and Guido used to work for a tour boat company. They (*take*) _____ tours to Ellis Island several times a day.

2. Nick hates flying. He (*take*) _____ a bus or a train than fly.

3. We watched a movie at home last night, but I (*see*) _____ the movie on a big screen in a theater.

4. Last semester, David failed his science class. This semester he (*pass*) _____ .

5. My nephew graduated from physical therapy school last year. It was really difficult and he (*study*) _____ for hours when he had exams.

CHAPTER 11

The Passive

Active vs. Passive   (Chart 11-1)

Directions: Decide if the sentences are Active (**A**) or Passive (**P**).

Examples: ____A____ A speeding truck hit my car.

____P____ My car was hit by a speeding truck.

1. _____ Millions of glass bottles are recycled in Australia every year.

2. _____ Almost all of our money was spent by the end of our vacation.

3. _____ The waitress is going to bring your drink very soon.

4. _____ The gift was wrapped beautifully with colorful paper and ribbon.

5. _____ Mary is taking care of Alex's son.

6. _____ Final exams are given at the end of every semester.

7. _____ Members of the audience asked many questions after the lecture.

8. _____ Several homes in Carlos' neighborhood were damaged in the windstorm.

9. _____ My brothers and sisters are helping with housework today.

10. _____ The dog is taken for a walk every morning.

11. _____ Robert visited his parents in California last week.

12. _____ They were asked to take their seats for the meeting.

13. _____ We were given two free tickets to the game.

14. _____ I'm going to ride the bus to work next week.

15. _____ I was told it might rain today.

Directions: Choose the sentence that has the same meaning as the given sentence.

Example: The hospital patients were cared for by wonderful nurses.

    a. The patients took care of wonderful nurses.

    (b.) Wonderful nurses took care of the patients.

1. John will be introduced to Tammy's parents next weekend.

   a. Someone will introduce John to Tammy's parents.

   b. John will introduce someone to Tammy's parents.

2. The teacher congratulated the students on their success.

   a. The teacher was congratulated by the students.

   b. The students were congratulated by the teacher.

3. Miriam often misunderstands her older sister, Paula.

   a. Paula is misunderstood by Miriam.

   b. Miriam is misunderstood by Paula.

4. Joel scratched his dog, Butch, behind the ears.

   a. Butch was scratched by Joel.

   b. Butch scratched Joel.

5. All of Satoshi's questions were answered by his teacher.

   a. Satoshi answered his teacher's questions.

   b. Satoshi's teacher answered his questions.

6. My grandfather's blood pressure is checked regularly.

   a. My grandfather checks his own blood pressure regularly.

   b. Someone else checks my grandfather's blood pressure regularly.

Directions: Change the verbs in **bold** to the passive. Do not change the tense.

1. Nina **answers** the phone.   The phone _____is answered_____ by Nina.

2. Nina **is answering** the phone.   The phone _____ by Nina.

3. Nina **has answered** the phone.   The phone _____ by Nina.

4. Nina **answered** the phone.   The phone _____ by Nina.

5. Nina **was answering** the phone.   The phone _____ by Nina.

6. Nina **had answered** the phone.   The phone _____ by Nina.

7. Nina **will answer** the phone.   The phone _____ by Nina.

8. Nina **is going to answer** the phone.   The phone _____ by Nina.

9. **Did** Nina **answer** the phone?   _____ the phone _____ by Nina?

10. **Has** Nina **answered** the phone?   _____ the phone _____ by Nina?

11. **Will** Nina **answer** the phone?   _____ the phone _____ by Nina?

Directions: Change the verbs in **bold** to the passive. Do not change the tense.

Example: Many people read the news online.

     The news _____is read_____ by many people online.

1. Everyone in my family **enjoys** a cup of tea after dinner.

   A cup of tea after dinner _____ by everyone in my family.

2. Scientists **are studying** the results of the experiment.

   The results of the experiment _____ by scientists.

3. Thieves **stole** two priceless paintings from the art museum.

   Two priceless paintings _____ from the art museum.

4. The board members **are going to discuss** the vacation policy at their next meeting.

   The vacation policy _____ at the next board meeting.

5. **Did** your manager **explain** the project clearly?

   _____ the project _____ clearly by your manager?

6. **Is** the college **going to give** you a scholarship?

   _____ you _____ a scholarship by the college?

Directions: Complete the sentences with the passive form of the verbs in parentheses.
Use any appropriate tense.

Example: My wallet (*steal*) _____ *was stolen* _____ out of my pocket while I was in
a busy train station.

1. Every summer on the Fourth of July, many, many hamburgers and hot dogs

   (*eat*) _____ at barbeques in the U.S.

2. The game of basketball (*invent*) _____ by Dr. James Naismith
   around 1891.

3. Josh's school project (*finish*) _____ by next Friday.

4. A new president (*elect, not*) _____ yet. The election will be in
   November.

5. An award-winning movie (*show*) _____ at the new theater
   downtown until next weekend. Let's go see it.

6. My parents (*give*) _____ some land in the mountains when
   my grandfather died.

7. The company (*feature*) _____ in many popular business
   magazines.

8. That poem (*write*) _____ by my sister. She's a wonderful poet.

9. Yesterday, three homeruns (*hit*) _____ during the baseball
   game. The balls (*catch*) _____ by fans in the stadium.

10. Algebra (*teach*) _____ formally in middle and high school, but
    the basics of algebraic thinking (*introduce*) _____ much earlier.

Directions: Complete the sentences about William Shakespeare with the passive forms of the verbs in parentheses. Use any appropriate tense.

William Shakespeare (*know*) _____*is known*_____ as one of the greatest
                                              1

writers of the English language. Shakespeare lived in the 16th and 17th centuries,

but even today, his many plays and sonnets (*read*) _____ and
                                                              2

(*study*) _____ by people everywhere. Many of Shakespeare's most
                    3

famous plays (*write*) _____ between 1594 and 1599.
                              4

During that time, *A Midsummer Night's Dream, Romeo and Juliet, Richard II*, and *The*

Merchant of Venice (*perform*) _____ for the first time. However,
                                          5

Shakespeare's plays (*publish, not*) _____ by the time he died in 1616.
                                            6

Since that time, they (*translate*) _____ into over 80 languages and
                                          7

(*print*) _____ in languages from Arabic to Zulu. Today, Shakespeare's
              8

plays (*see*) _____ on stages around the world.
                    9

Directions: Make complete sentences using the given words. Some are active and some are passive. Use the simple past.

Hurricane Betty

Example: The news about the storm \ see \ by thousands TV

_____*The news about the storm was seen by thousands on TV.*_____

1. The east coast of Florida \ hit \ by Hurricane Betty two days ago

   _____

2. Many houses \ damage \ in the storm

   _____

3. Injured people \ take care of \ by aid workers

   _____

4. The damage \ evaluate \ the morning after the storm

   _____

5. Some people \ not allow \ to go back to their homes

   _____

Directions: Complete the sentences with the words in parentheses. Use the appropriate form.

Example: a. James (*should + tell*) _____should be told_____ about the company's plans
to move their office to Texas.

b. He (*might + quit*) _____might quit_____ if he doesn't want to move.

1. a. More than 30 people (*may + injure*) _____ in the
bus accident.

    b. The bus (*should + drive*) _____ more slowly on the
dangerous road.

2. a. People (*should + not + send*) _____ text messages or emails
with spelling mistakes.

    b. Any text or email (*must + check*) _____ carefully before
it is sent.

3. a. Your homework (*have to + finish*) _____ by the time
class starts.

    b. The papers (*will + collect*) _____ at the beginning of class.

4. a. This conversation group is too large. It
(*should + divide*) _____ into two groups.

    b. A different conversation topic (*could + choose*) _____ for
each group.

5. a. According to the fire chief, the fire (*might + start*) _____
by a cigarette in the garbage can.

    b. Someone (*must + throw*) _____ a burning cigarette in
the trash.

Directions: Use passive modals to restate the recycling guidelines. Make two sentences for each rule. Use a variety of modals.

Recycling Guidelines

Example: Recycle clean paper, plastic, cans, and glass.

Clean paper, plastic, cans, and glass should be recycled.

Clean paper, plastic, cans, and glass can be recycled.

1. Rinse all food from plastics, glass, and cans.

_____

_____

2. Press clean boxes and paper items flat.

_____

_____

3. Do not recycle any paper with food on it. Put it in the trash.

_____

_____

4. All clean recyclable items go into your recycling bin.

_____

_____

5. Put recycling bins out for pick up by 7:00 A.M. on collection day.

_____

_____

Directions: Complete the sentences with the correct prepositions. Use *about, for, from, in, of, to,* or *with.*

Example: My mother is interested _____*in*_____ art, but my dad prefers music.

1. Trish was really disappointed _____ her grade in biology last semester. Her average was 85 percent.

2. Parents are always concerned _____ their children, no matter how old the children are.

3. Bill has been married _____ his wife for 40 years.

4. The new computer lab is equipped _____ the latest technology.

5. The applicants were all well qualified _____ the position. It was a difficult choice.

6. My tablet computer is not connected _____ the Internet at the moment.

7. I'm tired _____ seeing so many advertisements every time I open a Web page on my computer.

8. Hannah is accustomed _____ the humid Florida weather, but she doesn't like it.

Directions: Complete each sentence with the non-progressive passive form of the verb and an appropriate preposition. Use the simple present.

Example: Anton's ability to communicate in English (*limit*) _____*is limited by*_____ his lack of vocabulary.

1. I (*worry*) _____ the next test. It's going to be really difficult.

2. The state of Maine (*locate*) _____ the northeast corner of the U.S.

3. I'm going to bed now. I (*finish*) _____ my homework.

4. Michael (*scare*) _____ spiders. He always avoids spider webs.

5. My sister and her fiancé (*excite*) _____ their wedding next weekend.

6. Nikki (*satisfy*) _____ her new job, and she really likes her co-workers.

7. Jonathan (*exhaust*) _____ working so much. He worked 60 hours last week.

8. I (*annoy*) _____ the neighbor's dog. It is always barking.

Directions: Choose all possible completions for each sentence.

Example: I am getting _____, so I had better go to bed.

      a. sleep   (b.) tired   (c.) sleepy   d. late

1. When Mr. Mitchell heard that Dennis had picked all of his flowers, he got _____.

    a. annoy   b. annoyed   c. angry   d. anger

2. Jennifer got _____ during the exam and made some careless mistakes.

    a. confused   b. confuse   c. worry   d. nervous

3. Now that he has lived here for six months, Chang has gotten _____ American food.

    a. use to   b. accustomed to   c. comfortable to   d. comfortable with

4. I'm going to get _____ after I finish this chapter of the book I'm reading.

    a. readied   b. ready   c. to dress   d. dressed

5. If we don't go home soon, we are going to get _____.

    a. chilly   b. sunburned   c. sunburn   d. easy

6. You can take the children to the park if they get _____.

    a. bored   b. are bored   c. bore   d. lost

7. I don't like to go out at night. I get _____ in the dark.

    a. nervous   b. late   c. anxious   d. scared

8. Yesterday, Steve waited for 30 minutes for the bus. It was raining, and he got really _____.

    a. wet   b. worry   c. cold   d. annoyed

9. Anna has gotten very _____ in volunteering at the hospital. She volunteers three times a month.

    a. done   b. worse   c. involve   d. involved

10. The Paris subway is really _____ during rush hour.

    a. crowds   b. crowded   c. busy   d. noise

Directions: Complete the conversation with an appropriate form of *get* and the given words. Use the correct tense.

An Accident

Mary: Hi, John. It's good to see you again. How have you been lately?

John: Not too well. Unfortunately, I (*hurt*) _____got hurt_____ in a car accident
                                              1
    last month, and I missed two weeks of work.

Mary: Oh, that's too bad. What happened?

John: It was pretty bad. The other driver (*arrest*) _____ for causing
                                              2
    the accident. I'm lucky that I (*kill, not*) _____.
                                              3

Mary: Are you behind on your work?

John: I was able to take a lot of work home with me, so all my work

    (*do*) _____. Now I (*worry*) _____
                        4   5
    about my car. It (*damage*) _____.
                                      6

Mary: Can you (*fix*) _____ it _____?
                          7   7

John: I'm not sure if it's worth it. The insurance company just

    (*finish*) _____ calculating the cost of repairs.
                          8

Mary: Well, I hope your car (*take*) _____ care of soon.
                                    9

John: Thanks, Mary. In the meantime, I'm taking the bus.

    I (*accustom*) _____ to it.
                       10

Mary: That's great, John. Bus drivers rarely (*arrest*) _____ for
                                              11
    reckless driving, and you can relax on your way to work.

Directions: Choose the correct completions.

Watching Soccer

Example: I don't like watching soccer on TV. It's too (bored / (boring)).

1. Yesterday, a group of friends and I went to a (*disappointed / disappointing*) soccer game.

2. We were very (*surprised / surprising*) because not many people were there.

3. At first, the teams played well, and it was (*thrilled / thrilling*) to watch them.

4. Jim got so (*excited / exciting*) that he jumped out of his seat.

5. It was (*embarrassed / embarrassing*) because he spilled his soda on the lady in front of him.

6. She was quite (*annoyed / annoying*) and got upset with Jim.

7. We were (*shocked / shocking*) when our favorite player got hurt and had to leave the game.

8. We felt sad about the (*injured / injuring*) player.

Directions: Complete the sentences with the present (*-ing*) or past (*-ed*) participle of the verbs in parentheses.

Movies

Example: The (exhaust) _____exhausted_____ actors relaxed at the end of a long
day of work.

1. The most (*entertain*) _____ movies have lots of action and are
funny, too.

2. Jane enjoyed the romance movie. It had a (*satisfy*) _____ conclusion.

3. The (*surprise*) _____ actress had tears in her eyes. She gratefully
accepted the award for Best Performance.

4. If a movie's plot is (*confuse*) _____, the audience won't understand it.

5. The movie tickets sold out quickly, so the theater manager had to talk to several
(*frustrate*) _____ customers.

6. Some people feel (*bore*) _____ if there isn't enough action in a movie.

7. I recently saw a (*fascinate*) _____ movie about the life of Dr. Martin
Luther King, Jr.

Directions: Choose the correct completions.

Example: Ms. Haugen _____ at the Ajax Company.

    a. is employing   b. employed   c. employing   ⓓ is employed

1. I still can't believe it! My bicycle _____ last night.

    a. was stolen   b. was stealing   c. stolen   d. stole

2. The condition of neighborhoods in New York is _____ by city leaders and police.

    a. studying   b. being studying   c. being studied   d. been studied

3. The child was crying because he _____ by a bee.

    a. stung   b. had stung   c. had been stung   d. had being stung

4. Today, many serious diseases _____ successfully with modern medicines.

    a. are treating   b. can treat   c. treat   d. can be treated

5. In the past, many U.S. automobiles _____ in Detroit, Michigan.

    a. make   b. have made   c. were made   d. were making

6. The firefighters _____ for their bravery and strength in saving people from the fire.

    a. were praised   b. praised   c. were praising   d. praising

7. Today, most cars _____ technology that makes driving easier and more fun.

    a. equip with   c. equip by

    b. are equipped with   d. are equipped by

8. A lack of water is a problem in many parts of the world. In some areas, salt _____ from sea water to make it drinkable.

    a. is being removed   c. is removing

    b. has been removing   d. has removed

9. Vitamins _____ by the human body in many different ways.

    a. use easily   b. are easily using   c. are easily used   d. used easily

10. My car is at the repair shop. I think it'll _____ late this afternoon.

    a. finish   b. be finished   c. have finished   d. be finish

11. I am so happy! I _____ for the job I wanted.

    a. was hiring   b. hired   c. got hiring   d. got hired

12. Let's go ahead and start our meeting now. Nothing _____ by waiting.

    a. accomplishes   b. accomplished   c. has accomplished   d. will be accomplished

Part A *Directions:* Choose the correct completions.

1. When I woke up and looked outside, the landscape had changed. The ground had been lightly _____ with a dusting of snow during the night.

   a. covering   c. covers

   b. cover   d. covered

2. We can't even walk in this storm. Let's wait inside where we'll be _____ the strong winds until things quiet down.

   a. protected from   c. protecting from

   b. protected by   d. protecting by

3. A: _____ about the eight o'clock flight to Chicago?

   B: Not yet.

   a. Has been an announcement made   c. Has an announcement been made

   b. Has an announcement made   d. Has been made an announcement

4. Last night, a tornado swept through Rockville. It _____ everything in its path.

   a. destroyed   c. was being destroyed

   b. was destroyed   d. had been destroyed

5. Be sure to wash these vegetables thoroughly. A lot of chemical residue _____ on unwashed produce.

   a. can find   c. can be found

   b. can found   d. can be finding

6. A new bridge _____ to replace the old, damaged one. Now it's much safer to cross the river.

   a. was built   c. built

   b. gets built   d. has built

7. Before a holiday, the highways _____ people on their way out of the city.

   a. are crowding by   c. are crowded with

   b. are being crowd with   d. crowd by

8. Fortunately, the hospital's new air-conditioning system _____ by the time the first heat wave of the summer arrived.

   a. had installed   c. had been installed

   b. installed   d. had been installing

Part B *Directions:* Complete the sentences with the passive form of the verbs in parentheses. Use any appropriate tense. More than one answer is possible.

1. The robber's photo (*take*) _____ by the store's security camera, and the robber (*arrest*) _____ by the police a few hours later.

2. An announcement about the government's plans for a new economic policy (*make*) _____ at a press conference this afternoon.

3. Young people in many countries (*encourage*) _____ to get a college degree.

4. Claire (*give*) _____ a $5,000 college scholarship.

5. I think the movie is starting. The theme music (*play*) _____. Let's hurry.

Part C *Directions:* Change the following sentences from active to passive.

1. Nearly everyone uses cell phones these days.

   _____.

2. The museum lent the old book to the university.

   _____.

3. David will invite the company president to speak at the meeting.

   _____.

4. The government requires a visa for tourists to visit the country.

   _____.

5. The mechanic at Maher's Auto Repair is fixing our car.

   _____.

Part D *Directions:* Complete the sentences with the words in parentheses. Use the appropriate form, active or passive.

1. All signs and posted notices (*should + obey*) _____.

2. It's too bad you threw those steak bones away.
   They (*could + give*) _____ to the dog.

3. The birthday card I sent to my brother (*should + arrive*) _____ by tomorrow.

4. This report (*must + finish*) _____ by the end of the week.

5. The smoke from the forest fire (*can + see*) _____ from miles away.

Part E *Directions:* Complete the sentences with the correct prepositions.

1. The expensive dress is made _____ silk.

2. Marianne is interested _____ movies from the 1950s.

3. New Orleans is known _____ its great restaurants and music, especially jazz.

4. Many people are involved _____ the effort to raise money for our class trip.

5. My parents are excited _____ their upcoming trip to Thailand.

6. The director is quite pleased _____ the final cut of the movie. It will open in theaters next weekend.

7. Jacob gets really annoyed _____ noisy, crowded restaurants. He prefers quiet dining.

Part F *Directions:* Choose the correct completions.

1. My sister lives in a very (*interested* / *interesting*) part of London.

2. The mystery story was so (*excited* / *exciting*) that I stayed up until 2:00 A.M. finishing it.

3. The (*fascinated* / *fascinating*) little boy stared as the magician performed (*amazed* / *amazing*) tricks.

4. The (*frightened* / *frightening*) storm tore the roof off of the house across the street.

5. My (*embarrassed* / *embarrassing*) mother blushed when she forgot my fiancée's name.

Part A *Directions:* Choose the correct completions.

1. A: Can't we do something about the terrible noise next door?

   B: The building manager _____ right now.

   a. calls   b. is called   c. is being called   d. has been calling

2. A: Are you interested in scuba diving?

   B: Very. Undersea life is _____.

   a. fascinated   c. being fascinating
   b. fascinating   d. being fascinated

3. The university _____ by private funds as well as by tuition income and grants.

   a. is supported   b. supports   c. is supporting   d. has supported

4. My computer wasn't working well, but our technician quickly _____ the source of the problem.

   a. was discover   b. discovered   c. was discovered   d. has been discovered

5. A: Alex, please prepare those letters before noon.

   B: They've already _____. They're on your desk.

   a. prepared   b. been prepared   c. being prepared   d. been being prepared

6. A: Has the committee made its decision yet?

   B: Not yet. They are still _____ the proposal.

   a. considering   c. being considered
   b. been considered   d. considered

7. In some remote areas, health care _____ by only a small number of doctors, nurses, and other health professionals.

   a. is providing   c. provides
   b. is being provided   d. provided

8. A: How did that window _____?

   B: I don't know.

   a. get broken   b. broke   c. got broken   d. broken

Part B *Directions:* Complete the sentences with the passive form of the verbs in parentheses. Use any appropriate tense.

1. Courtney (*ask*) _____ to give a karate demonstration for the elementary school children.

2. Next year, the university entrance exams (*give*) _____ in January and February.

3. Madeline's flight (*schedule*) _____ to leave at 6:50 A.M. We'll have to leave for the airport by 4:00.

4. The contract conditions (*agree*) _____ to by both sides. The negotiations were successful.

5. The new software (*load*) _____ onto your laptop right now. The technician (*finish*) _____ in a few minutes.

Part C *Directions:* Change the following sentences from active to passive.

1. The school is giving scholarships to many students from low-income families.

   _____

2. A falling pine cone hit Michael on the head.

   _____

3. Workers check each computer five times before they pack it for shipping.

   _____

4. Someone is going to cut down the weeds on the hill.

   _____

5. An anonymous donor gave the Cancer Foundation two million dollars.

   _____

Part D *Directions:* Complete the sentences with the words in parentheses. Use the appropriate form, active or passive.

1. We have to throw this old salad out. It (*should + eat*) _____ by now.

2. I can't find my keys. I (*must + leave*) _____ them in my coat pocket.

3. My uncle Philip (*can + always + count*) _____ on for help.

4. The cake (*should + bake*) _____ at 350 degrees for about 30 minutes.

5. Tom (*may + invite*) _____ to the party. I'm not sure.

Part E *Directions:* Complete the sentences with the correct prepositions.

1. I am very worried _____ my husband's health. Although he quit smoking, he still coughs a lot.

2. Duncan's parents were satisfied _____ his grades last semester.

3. That president will be remembered _____ his generous policies.

4. Carolina is well qualified _____ a job as an editor. She has a lot of experience.

5. After exams, the students are exhausted _____ so much studying and not enough sleep.

6. I am really bored _____ this novel. I need to go to the library and get another book.

7. Matthew was really disappointed _____ his results in the marathon.

Part F *Directions:* Choose the correct completions.

1. My first date was such an (*embarrassed* / *embarrassing*) experience that I'll never forget it.

2. The chemistry experiment did not have the (*expected* / *expecting*) result. That was (*surprised* / *surprising*).

3. My teacher tries to provide (*balanced* / *balancing*) instruction; she usually has some group discussion in addition to her lecture.

4. (*Experienced* / *Experiencing*) musicians practice almost every day to keep their technique strong.

5. I love roller coasters. The roller coaster in Santa Cruz gives you a (*thrilled* / *thrilling*) ride.

CHAPTER 12

Noun Clauses

QUIZ 1 **Noun Clauses with Question Words**   (Charts 12-1 and 12-2)

Directions: Underline the noun clause in each sentence.

Example: James wants to know <u>where the meeting is going to be</u>.

1. Mr. Murphy doesn't know how much the tickets are.

2. The students will ask their teacher when the final exam is.

3. Patricia wanted to know when her dad would give her a ride to school.

4. The police are trying to find out what happened.

5. We wondered why the woman had come to the meeting.

6. Can you tell me what time it is?

QUIZ 2 **Noun Clauses with Question Words**   (Chart 12-2)

Directions: Complete the sentences with the words in parentheses. Use any appropriate verb tense. Some contain noun clauses and some contain questions.

Example: Sharon: What (*Marion, want*) __*does Marion want*__ for her birthday?

Yuki: Gosh, I don't know what (*she, want*) ____*she wants*____.
Let's ask her.

1. Alice: How much (*your tablet computer, cost*) _____?

   Fatima: I don't remember exactly how much (*I, pay*) _____ for it.
   I got it last year.

2. Jeremy: Where (*Bill, park*) _____ the car?

   Will: I'm not sure where (*the car, be*) _____. I hope it's nearby.

3. Arturo: How many tickets to the art show (*you, sell*) _____?

   Peter: I think about ten. Do you know how many (*Ted, sell*) _____?

   He said nearly everyone he knew had bought one from him.

4. Ken: Hey, look! This old bottle has a note in it!

   Simon: Really? What (*it, say*) _____?

   Ken: I can't read it. The ink is too faded.

5. Mike: Do you have a key to the supply room?

   Oliver: No, but I know where (*the key, be*) _____.

   Mike: Where (*it, be*) _____?

   Oliver: I can't tell you. Where (*it, be*) _____ is a secret.

Directions: Complete the conversations. Change the questions into noun clauses.

Example: Nan: How long has Hank lived in Memphis?

Julie: I don't know _____*how long Hank has lived in Memphis*_____.

1. Bill: Where is the nearest post office?

   John: I'm not sure, but I'll find out _____.

2. Ann: Who did Pierre visit in Paris last year?

   Sam: I don't know _____.

3. Carla: How much did Sue's car cost?

   Patty: You don't need to know _____.

4. Ali: Which pages are we supposed to study?

   Hank: Let's ask the teacher _____.

5. John: Who left the door unlocked?

   Phillip: It's not clear _____.

6. Don: How much time do we have left?

   Ivan: I don't know _____.

7. Eva: Why are they going to the police station?

   Barbara: I'm not sure _____.

8. Henry: The traffic is terrible! Why is there so much traffic today?

   Brad: I don't have any idea _____.

9. Jack: How will they solve their financial problems?

   Mary: They had better figure out _____.

10. Martha: Whose cell phone is that?

    Bella: I'm not sure _____.

Directions: Circle all the correct completions. More than one answer may be possible.

1. The Mikkelsons aren't sure _____.

   a. whether or not they will go on vacation

   b. if they will go on vacation

   c. they will go on vacation or not

   d. whether they will go on vacation

2. We would like to know _____.

   a. if or not it rains a lot in the summer

   b. does it rain a lot in the summer

   c. whether if it rains a lot in the summer

   d. whether it rains a lot in the summer or not

3. The electrician is trying to figure out _____.

   a. whether the light switch works

   b. whether or not works the light switch

   c. if the light switch works or not

   d. that if the light switch works

4. _____ is important.

   a. Whether or not I am on time

   b. Whether I am on time or not

   c. If I am on time

   d. If I am on time or not

5. Please let me know _____.

   a. if I should help you

   b. whether should I help you

   c. whether I should or not help you

   d. if I should help you or not

6. Many people wonder _____.

   a. whether there is life on other planets

   b. whether there is life on other planets or not

   c. if the life on other planets or not is

   d. if there's life on other planets or not

Directions: Complete the sentences by changing the questions into noun clauses.

Example: Is the bookstore open today?

Do you know _____*if / whether the bookstore is open today or not*_____? OR

Do you know _____*whether or not the bookstore is open today*_____?

1. Is Alice going to pass her math class?

   I don't know _____.

2. Did an express mail package arrive today?

   We can ask the mail clerk _____.

3. Does Andy like the new basketball coach?

   I don't know _____.

4. Has anyone seen the new show at the Paramount Theater?

   Let's find out _____.

5. Were Jim and Marcia at the party last night?

   I meant to ask you _____.

6. Do you prefer coffee or tea for breakfast?

   Please let me know _____.

7. Had Ken ever been to an opera before last night?

   I wonder _____.

8. Does Max usually ride his bicycle to school?

   Could you tell me _____?

9. Are the Smiths coming over for dinner on Saturday?

   I need to know _____.

10. Will Liz go to Orlando with us?

    Liz isn't sure _____.

Directions: Make sentences with the same meaning by using infinitives.

Example: Tom didn't tell me where I should meet him.

Tom didn't tell me where to meet him.
_____

1. Mick showed me how I could solve a Sudoku puzzle.

_____

2. I can't decide whether or not I should travel over the holidays.

_____

3. Julie wanted to know when she should start the barbecue.

_____

4. I wondered what I should do with my old clothes.

_____

5. Sandy and Jack discussed where they should go on vacation.

_____

Directions: Complete the sentences with your own words. Use infinitives.

Example: Sue: What are you going to fix for dinner?

Josh: I don't know. I can't decide ___*whether to have*___ fish or pasta tonight.

1. Don: Mom, can you help me with this math homework?

   Mom: Hmmm ... . Sorry. I don't know _____ that type of math problem anymore.

2. Ben: I bought a new computer, but I'm having trouble setting it up. Can you come over and help me with it?

   Jason: Sure, but you'll have to explain _____ to your house.

3. Cathy: I need a book on gardening. Can you tell me _____ one?

   Clerk: Of course. All of our gardening books are in the back of the store on the right side.

4. Yuko: I don't know _____ about my failing grade in English class.

   Mari: Try doing some homework now and then!

5. Carl: What kind of movie do you want to watch?

   Susan: I don't know _____ a comedy or an action film. What do you think?

Directions: Add the word *that* to the sentences to mark the beginning of a noun clause.

Example: I didn't know Alice had a broken leg.
                      that
                             ∧

1. Are you sure you didn't leave your cell phone in the car?

2. It's a fact there have been several robberies in our neighborhood recently.

3. Steve failed his driving test is unfortunate.

4. Did I remind you we are going shopping after work?

5. Ginger is excited she will go to Costa Rica in March.

Directions: Write each sentence in another way, but keep the same meaning. Include a noun clause.

Example: That Don isn't feeling well is obvious.

It's obvious that Don isn't feeling well.

1. It is too bad that Sarah won't be able to attend the celebration.

_____

2. That the doctor gave you the wrong prescription is unlikely.

_____

3. That the little boy survived the plane crash is a miracle.

_____

4. It surprises me that Rosa didn't finish the project on time.

_____

5. It is clear that no one will pass this class without additional help from the teacher.

_____

Directions: Match each sentence from Column A to a sentence in Column B. Then combine the sentences into one that contains a noun clause. Use *it* or ***that*** where necessary to make the noun clause. More than one answer is possible. The first one is done for you.

Column A

1. The rain isn't going to stop anytime soon.

2. Karen and Joe will arrive tomorrow.

3. Mary got an award for Teacher of the Year.

4. I have a very loving and supportive family.

5. Our soccer team is going to do well this season.

6. A meteorite hit the earth 65 million years ago.

7. A number of the tests were graded incorrectly.

8. My daughter got a job as a flight attendant with Amazon Airlines.

9. I will pay back the money I borrowed by the end of the month.

Column B

That is surprising.

I promise.

I'm lucky.

I'm pleased.

It's wonderful.

Martin is confident.

Scientists believe.

✓ That's unfortunate.

That is possible.

1. _____ *It is unfortunate that the rain isn't going to stop anytime soon.* _____

2. _____

3. _____

4. _____

5. _____

6. _____

7. _____

8. _____

9. _____

Directions: Add punctuation and capitalization.

Vacation Plans

Example: I am looking forward to summer said Anne

"I am looking forward to summer," said Anne.

1. where are you going on your vacation Ruth asked

2. we are going on a road trip to Alaska replied Anne

3. that sounds like fun said Ruth how long will you be gone

4. around three weeks answered Anne we are going to tour the southeast coast and visit a glacier we also hope to go to one of the national parks

5. I hear Alaska is beautiful said Ruth so you're sure to have a wonderful vacation

6. yes added Anne and we're sure to put lots of miles on our car

Directions. Complete the sentences by changing the quoted speech to indirect speech. Use noun clauses with past verb forms where appropriate.

Example: "Those jeans are too expensive," said Laura.

Laura said _____ *(that) those jeans were too expensive* _____.

1. "I don't want to eat my vegetables," says my little sister.

   My little sister always says _____.

2. "The earth has seven continents and five oceans," said the teacher.

   The teacher told the children _____.

3. "I've got a lot of work to do today," stated Kate.

   Kate told me _____.

4. Helena asked, "Are there any new magazines available?"

   Helena asked the clerk _____.

5. "I think that is an excellent book," said Matthew.

   Matthew commented _____.

6. "What time does the meeting start?" asked Cynthia.

   Cynthia wanted to know _____.

Directions: Complete the sentences by changing the quoted speech to indirect speech. Use noun clauses with past verb forms where appropriate.

Example: Tonya said, "I can't find my keys."

Tonya complained _____ *that she couldn't find her keys* _____.

1. Victor and Ivan said, "We may have pizza for dinner."

   Victor and Ivan said _____.

2. "How can I help you?" Mrs. Bell asked.

   Mrs. Bell wanted to know _____.

3. Ben said, "I must be at work by 9:00 A.M."

   Ben said _____.

4. My grandfather said, "Children ought to listen when adults are talking."

   My grandfather argued _____.

5. "When will the movie begin?" asked the excited children.

   The children wanted to know _____.

6. "I am going to be there in fifteen minutes," promised Kevin.

   Kevin just texted me _____.

7. Maria said, "The local radio station will have a singing contest next month. You should enter it."

   Maria said _____,

   and _____.

8. "Do I have to finish this project today?" Jonas asked. "I might not have enough time," he said.

   Jonas asked _____

   and said _____.

Directions: Write a report about each conversation. Your reports should include an accurate idea of the speaker's words, but they don't have to use the exact words. Use the formal sequence of tenses as appropriate. Answers will vary.

Example: Lynne said, "I had a wonderful vacation."

Neil said, "That's good. What did you do?"

Lynne answered, "I went skiing in Montana. The snow was perfect."

Possible answer: Lynne told Neil that she had had a great vacation. Neil wanted to know what she had done, and she told him she had gone skiing in Montana.

She added that the snow had been perfect.

1. "How was your English test?" David's mom asked.

   "It wasn't too hard," David replied.

   _____

   _____

2. Harry said, "I'm so tired today."

   Max said, "You should get more sleep."

   _____

   _____

3. Doug asked, "Where can I find the shoe department?"

   The clerk answered, "It's on the second floor."

   Doug said, "Thank you for your help."

   _____

   _____

   _____

4. "I have my first accounting class today," Susan said.

   "Who's your instructor?" Carol asked.

   "Professor Nelson," Susan replied.

   "She's great. I was in her class last year," Carol said.

   _____

   _____

   _____

   _____

Directions: Complete the sentences with the correct form of the verbs in parentheses.

A Car Accident

Example: It is important that people (*know*) _____*know*_____ what to do in case of a car accident.

1. I recommend that someone (*call*) _____ the police.

2. The police advise that everyone (*stay*) _____ calm.

3. It is vital that any seriously injured person (*go*) _____ to the hospital.

4. It is suggested that witnesses (*talk*) _____ to the police.

5. It is critical that a witness (*report*) _____ on what he or she saw.

6. It is essential that someone (*take*) _____ photos of the accident scene.

7. It is necessary that an accident investigator (*decide*) _____ what caused the accident.

8. One driver might insist that the other driver (*get*) _____ a ticket for causing the accident.

9. A driver may demand that the other driver (*pay*) _____ for damage to his or her car.

10. My parents have requested that I (*call*) _____ them if I ever have an accident.

QUIZ 16 Chapter Review

Directions: Correct the errors.

Example: My sister asked me what ~~did I want~~. *I wanted*

1. I don't know if or not we will buy a new car this year.

2. Can you tell me what time does the concert start?

3. Delia knows if that I'm going to ride to Vancouver with her.

4. The student asked her counselor which class she should to take.

5. After the flood, the president requested that everyone was helpful.

6. That Jordan was angry it was obvious.

7. Marcy wants to know how much does the bag cost?

8. I wonder is it supposed to rain tomorrow.

Part A *Directions:* Complete the sentences by changing the questions into noun clauses.

1. When does Flight 2803 arrive?

   The timetable can tell you _____.

2. Has the mail already been picked up?

   Debbie wants to know _____.

3. How did the fire start?

   Investigators are trying to find out _____.

4. What grade did I get on the last quiz?

   I wonder _____.

5. Would Jim prefer a sweater or a shirt?

   I'm not sure _____.

Part B *Directions:* Make sentences with the same meaning by using infinitives.

1. I've told you everything I know about the crime. I don't know what else I should say.

   I've told you everything I know about the crime. I _____.

2. We were completely lost. We didn't know which way we should go.

   We were completely lost. We _____.

3. The instructions for the project weren't clear. Maria wasn't sure what she should do or how she should begin.

   The instructions for the project weren't clear. Maria _____

   _____.

4. Mr. Lee can't decide whether he should go on a trip or visit his family during the holidays.

   Mr. Lee _____.

Part C *Directions:* Combine the sentences into one that contains a noun clause. Use *it* or *that* where necessary to make the noun clause.

1. James is lying. It is a shame.

    _____.

2. I am amazed. Sophie got 100% on the vocabulary quiz.

    _____.

3. Women live longer than men. That is a fact.

    _____.

4. The coffee at the Campus Café is terrible. I agree with that.

    _____.

5. It is unusual. Max's father has six names.

    _____.

Part D *Directions:* Add punctuation and capitalization.

1. I don't want to waste time said Mary so let's hurry

2. why did the mother bird fly away from the nest asked Jimmy

3. Valerie told the tour group please stay close together so no one gets lost

4. Mr. Donovan is our attorney Margaret said he is very good

5. when he saw the car coming towards them James shouted look out

Part E *Directions:* Write a report of the conversation. Use the formal sequence of tenses.

Anita: Do you sell computer accessories?

Clerk: Yes, we do. What are you looking for?

Anita: I need a wireless mouse for my laptop.

Clerk: What kind of a computer do you have?

Anita: It's a MacBook Air™.

Clerk: All of these should work with your computer.

Anita: Thanks very much.

_____

_____

_____

_____

_____

_____

Part F *Directions:* Complete the sentences with the correct form of the verbs in parentheses.

1. My daughter proposed that everyone in the family (*go*) _____ hiking.

2. I suggested that she (*choose*) _____ a place to go.

3. It is important that everyone (*dress*) _____ appropriately.

4. It is necessary that my son (*buy*) _____ some hiking boots before we go.

5. It is recommended that hikers (*take*) _____ emergency supplies with them.

Part A *Directions:* Complete the sentences by changing the questions into noun clauses.

1. How often do you go to the gym?

   I would like to know _____.

2. Did Teresa stay after school to play table tennis?

   Do you know _____.

3. What time does the movie start?

   Let's ask the ticket seller _____.

4. Where did Ana go after the lecture?

   I don't know _____.

5. Do Paul's meetings usually end on time?

   Please tell me _____.

Part B *Directions:* Make sentences with the same meaning by using infinitives.

1. Alan has two girlfriends. He can't decide which one he should invite to the school dance.

   Alan has two girlfriends.
   He _____.

2. The patient asked the doctor how often she could take the medicine.

   The patient _____.

3. The teacher gave us very clear directions for our essay. He told us how many paragraphs we should write, and when we should turn it in.

   The teacher gave us very clear directions for our essay.
   He _____.

4. The director told the actors that they should rehearse their lines more before the performance.

   The director _____.

Part C *Directions:* Combine the sentences into one that contains a noun clause. Use *it* or *that* where necessary to make the noun clause.

1. Mischa needs to study harder. That is the truth.

   _____.

2. It is too bad. Emma had to take her driving test three times before she passed.

   _____.

3. The Chinese have used traditional medicines for thousands of years. Many Chinese are proud of that.

   _____.

4. Too much sun can cause skin cancer. That is a well-known fact.

   _____.

5. The library is a quiet place to study. Jason is glad.

   _____.

Part D *Directions:* Add punctuation and capitalization.

1. are you ready to order asked the waiter

2. please help me Doug begged this box is too heavy for me to carry

3. I don't want to go home cried the angry child

4. it is an unusual problem said the scientist but I think we can find a solution

5. Ms. Bell said to the students please talk quietly in the library

Part E *Directions:* Write a report of the dialogue. Use the formal sequence of tenses.

Mr. Thomas:	You didn't do well on the quiz. What happened?
Mary:	I really didn't have enough time to study.
Mr. Thomas:	Why not?
Mary:	My mother has been sick, so I've been taking care of her.
Mr. Thomas:	You should have told me! You could have taken the quiz on a different day.

_____

_____

_____

_____

_____

_____

Part F *Directions:* Complete the sentences with the correct form of the verbs in parentheses.

1. It is necessary that our company (*have*) _____ a strong standing in the community.

2. Mr. Samuels insists that everyone in our office (*wear*) _____ professional clothing.

3. It is advised that everyone (*arrive*) _____ to work on time.

4. It is essential that the receptionist (*greet*) _____ people in a friendly manner.

5. I recommend that people (*do*) _____ business with us.

CHAPTER 13   Adjective Clauses

Directions: Choose all the possible completions for each sentence.

Example: The soccer team _____ won the city championship practiced three times a week.

     a. who   b. Ø   (c.) that   (d.) which   e. they

1. The woman _____ Jim remembered meeting several years earlier had completely changed.

     a. who   b. whom   c. that   d. which   e. she

2. The movie _____ we watched last night was so exciting that I couldn't sleep for hours afterwards.

     a. who   b. whom   c. that   d. which   e. Ø

3. I met a very interesting man _____ works as a museum curator.

     a. who   b. whom   c. that   d. which   e. he

4. My daughter had on a dress _____ was too short. I made her change her clothes before she went out.

     a. who   b. Ø   c. that   d. which   e. it

5. Mr. Scott, to _____ I sent the email yesterday, hasn't responded yet.

     a. who   b. whom   c. Ø   d. which   e. him

6. Yesterday's game, _____ was canceled due to the weather, will be rescheduled.

     a. who   b. whom   c. that   d. which   e. they

7. I don't know the man _____ Teri is engaged to.

     a. who   b. whom   c. that   d. Ø   e. he

8. The era of history _____ Gordon is most interested in is the Middle Ages.

     a. Ø   b. whom   c. that   d. which   e. it

9. The students _____ I study with are smart, hard-working, and helpful.

     a. who   b. whom   c. that   d. which   e. them

10. Larry Miller won first prize for a science project on solar power _____ he had been working on for several months.

     a. who   b. whom   c. that   d. which   e. it

Directions: Combine the two sentences. Use the second sentence as the adjective clause.

Example: Midori served tasty Japanese snacks. We enjoyed them very much.

Midori served tasty Japanese snacks which / that we enjoyed very much.

1. Robin told the children a story. The story made them laugh.

   _____

2. Jason applied for a job at the new café. I told you about it.

   _____

3. The pianist played a Mozart concerto. It was one of Mark's favorite pieces of music.

   _____

4. My roommate invited her brother to our party. I had never met him before.

   _____

5. The new computer makes my work easier. I just bought it last week.

   _____

6. Angela is the oldest child in her family. She has three younger sisters and a younger brother.

   _____

7. The elderly woman was grateful. Anne helped her with yard work.

   _____

8. Julia's husband gave her some beautiful roses. He bought them at the flower market.

   _____

Directions: Complete the sentences with **who** or **whose**.

Examples: The boy _____*whose*_____ bike was stolen was really upset.

The boy _____*who*_____ lives next door is very friendly.

1. I forgot the name of the person _____ does the bookkeeping for our office.

2. Mrs. Manzinalli is looking for the student _____ cell phone was left
   in class.

3. The neighbors _____ live upstairs are very noisy.

4. Juanita works for a company _____ employees get good salaries
   and benefits.

5. Rob knows an Iranian man _____ family immigrated here in 1997.

6. Mark and Leroy have a building manager _____ collects the rent
   every month.

7. This coat belongs to the man _____ came to the meeting with Jonathan.

8. The young woman _____ hair is blue and purple wants to be a rock star.

9. There are two students in my class _____ knowledge of American history
   is impressive.

10. Rose's uncle, _____ full name is Stanislaus, uses the nickname "Stash."

11. The children _____ live across the street are very cheerful.

12. I'm looking for the owner _____ wallet was left on the train.

13. Do you know the name of the poet _____ wrote this poem?

14. I have two friends _____ are very talented singers.

15. Meg has a cousin _____ a famous writer.

Directions: Combine the sentences with *whose*. Use the second sentence as the adjective clause.

Example: The woman lives in Los Angeles. Her daughter is an actress.
The woman whose daughter is an actress lives in Los Angeles.

1. The boy has beautiful teeth. His father is a dentist.

   _____

2. We want to do business with that company. Its products are top quality.

   _____

3. Sarah feels sorry for her neighbors. Their car was stolen last night.

   _____

4. The student came to class late every day. Her homework was never done.

   _____

5. I have never met Meg's brother. His wife is the conductor of the symphony orchestra.

   _____

6. The dog always begs for food. Its back leg is injured.

   _____

7. Ellen met a kind man. His parents died when he was very young.

   _____

8. The Johnsons live in the apartment upstairs. Their son goes to Stanford University.

   _____

9. Claire lives in New York. Her son goes to school in California.

   _____

10. Robert wants to go to the big game. His favorite team made the finals.

    _____

Directions: Complete the sentences with *where / in which* or *which*.

Working in the City

Example: Our city, _____*which has*_____ more than 678,000 people, has grown quickly.

The part of the city _____*where / in which*_____ I work is very busy.

1. The subway system _____ is in our city is fast and convenient.

2. The building _____ I work is only a 5-minute walk from the train station.

3. At lunchtime, there are many restaurants _____ I can enjoy tasty food.

4. After work I like to go to the gym _____ is in our building.

5. The gym _____ many employees work out has a lot of equipment.

Directions: Combine the sentences with *where / in which*. Use the second sentence as the adjective clause.

Life at the Office

Example: Our company has a large conference room. We have weekly meetings there.

_____*Our company has a large conference room where / in which we have weekly meetings.*_____

1. I have a job in the public relations department. Fourteen people work there.

_____

2. Our department is in the east wing. The advertising department is also located there.

_____

3. I share an office with another worker. We have our desks and computers there.

_____

4. My boss has a large office. She meets important clients there.

_____

5. This company is a good place. Employees are treated fairly there.

_____

Directions: Complete the sentences with *where* or *when*.

Childhood Memories

Example: Please tell me a story about the time _____*when*_____ you were a child.

1. I remember the small town in Montana _____ I grew up.

2. In the 1960s, _____ I was a kid, life was simple.

3. We lived in a wonderful neighborhood _____ there were many families.

4. The kids of all ages played games outdoors _____ there was room for everyone.

5. In the summertime, we played outside until 10:00 P.M. _____ our parents called us home.

6. One of our favorite summertime activities was to sell lemonade on hot days _____ everyone was thirsty.

7. We put up a table in front of our house _____ many people passed by.

8. On good days, _____ we sold all of our lemonade, we made several dollars.

9. After we had sold all of our lemonade, we happily walked to the neighborhood store _____ we spent our hard-earned money on ice cream, candy, and soda pop.

10. Next year _____ I go on vacation, I would like to visit my old neighborhood again.

Directions: Combine the sentences with ***where*** or ***when***. Use the second sentence as the adjective clause.

Example: My mother enjoys going to the library. She can check out many books and materials there.

My mother enjoys going to the library where she can check out many books and materials.

1. My favorite season is spring. The colorful spring flowers bloom then.

2. That is the furniture store. We bought our couch and coffee table there.

3. I last saw David on that day. David got his new car then.

4. Jim remembers a time. Gasoline cost $1.25 per gallon then.

5. The Chinese restaurant served delicious seafood. We ate dinner there.

6. Do you know the name of the city? The Olympic games will be held there.

7. Every student looks forward to the day. Summer vacation begins then.

8. A market is near our house. They sell many international products there.

9. My favorite time of year is the fall. I play soccer then.

10. That is the house. My best friend lives there.

Directions: Use an adjective clause from the list to complete each sentence. Write the letter on the line. The first one is done for you.

a. who is really famous
b. who knows the answer
c. she says
d. who get too much help from others
e. I can do to help you
f. who can repair it for him

g. that are the freshest
h. who went to the concert
✓ i. who can perform like they do
j. my husband said
k. who knew how to unlock the safe

1. My favorite rock group is The Skinks. There's nobody __i__.

2. Carl's bicycle has a flat tire. He has to find somebody _____.

3. Everyone _____ really enjoyed the music.

4. I know many interesting people, but I don't know anybody _____.

5. Mary is so funny! Everything _____ makes me laugh.

6. Students must be honest and do their own work. Those _____ don't learn as much.

7. Jerry was the only one _____. We had to wait for him to open it.

8. I'm sorry, but there's nothing _____.

9. My cell phone signal was weak. I couldn't hear anything _____.

10. I need three tomatoes. Please give me the ones _____.

11. I'm stuck on this problem. Is there anybody _____?

Directions: Choose the correct meaning for each sentence.

Example: My brother, who lives in Phoenix, works at an engineering firm.

      (a.) I have only one brother.

      b. I have more than one brother.

1. The students who were accepted into the university were very excited.

   a. All of the students were accepted into the university.

   b. Only some of the students were accepted into the university.

2. The visiting executives, who were from Okinawa and were used to a warm climate, arrived in Chicago during a snowstorm.

   a. All of the executives were from Okinawa.

   b. Only some of the executives were from Okinawa.

3. John watched a movie on the big screen TV that is in the living room.

   a. John has only one big screen TV.

   b. John has more than one big screen TV

4. The wood-burning stove, which is in the corner of our living room, keeps the first floor of the house warm.

   a. There is only one wood-burning stove in the house.

   b. There is more than one wood-burning stove in the house.

5. Conifers, which have needles instead of leaves, are plentiful in the forests of the western United States.

   a. All conifers have needles instead of leaves.

   b. Only some conifers have needles instead of leaves.

6. The bicycle that is in front of our house belongs to my brother.

   a. There is only one bicycle near the house.

   b. There is more than one bicycle near the house.

Directions: Add commas where necessary. Write *no change* if commas aren't needed in the sentence.

Example: Dr. Janice Miller who is an expert in children's health spoke at the Parents' Club meeting.

Dr. Janice Miller, who is an expert in children's health, spoke at the Parents' Club meeting.

1. The city of Dubrovnik which is on the Adriatic coast is surrounded by an ancient stone wall.

2. The instructor who teaches grammar class gives very clear explanations.

3. On our last family vacation we went to Disneyland where we shook hands with Mickey Mouse.

4. I saw Alex and Alice who are twins at the shopping center.

5. The Mississippi River which is one of the most important rivers in the United States has an interesting history.

6. Mr. Mitchell whom we saw at the flower show is a fantastic gardener.

7. People who travel and live in other countries learn to appreciate other cultures and customs.

8. *The Marriage of Figaro* which is one of Mozart's comedic operas is performed regularly on stages around the world.

9. Jason has two brothers. One brother who lives in New York is a financial advisor, and the other one is a police officer.

10. The book that I'm reading is from the Everett Public Library where you can borrow books for up to three weeks.

Directions: Combine the two sentences. Use the second sentence as the adjective clause.

At the Movies

Example: The theater is showing two movies. Both of them are comedies.

The theater is showing two movies, both of which are comedies.

1. Many people were waiting to go inside. Most of them bought their tickets online.

   _____

2. Some moviegoers went to the midnight show. Several of them looked sleepy.

   _____

3. The movie has three main characters. All of them are interesting and funny.

   _____

4. The stars in the movie are very talented. Most of them studied acting.

   _____

5. My sister saw the movies last week. She liked both of them.

   _____

6. Most people laughed a lot during the movie. Some of them had tears in their eyes.

   _____

7. There are many movie snacks to choose from. The majority of them are sweets.

   _____

8. Theater employees sell a lot of popcorn. More than half of them are college students.

   _____

9. My friends went to the theater with me. Two of them go to the movies every weekend.

   _____

10. After the movie, the building caretaker found two jackets. Neither of them was mine.

    _____

Directions: Decide if the adjective clause modifies a noun or the whole sentence.

Examples: a. Sue missed the bus, which made her late for work.   a noun   (the sentence)

          b. Sue missed the 98 bus, which she usually takes to work.   (a noun)   the sentence

1. a. The teacher assigned 20 pages of homework, which made   a noun   the sentence
   all of the students groan.

   b. The teacher gave the students a careful explanation of the   a noun   the sentence
   homework assignment, which was quite difficult.

2. a. Max lived for several years in Turkey, which was one of the   a noun   the sentence
   most interesting times in his life.

   b. He lived in Istanbul, which is a city on two continents.   a noun   the sentence

3. a. Dan thoroughly enjoyed the play, which was about an   a noun   the sentence
   American family in Berlin in the 1980s.

   b. The people behind him talked loudly during the performance,   a noun   the sentence
   which was really annoying.

Directions: Combine the two sentences. Use the second sentence as the adjective clause. Add commas where necessary.

Example: Anna burned the casserole. That made her family unhappy.

              Anna burned the casserole, which made her family unhappy.

1. Harold bought a newspaper. He read it on the train on the way to work.

   _____

2. On the way to work, Max stopped to get coffee. This was part of his morning routine.

   _____

3. After she got off the phone, Margaret typed an email. It was a message for her boss.

   _____

4. The receptionist answered the phone. It was a big part of her job.

   _____

Directions: Change the adjective clauses to adjective phrases.

Example: The woman who is sitting across the room is Jeff's aunt.

The woman sitting across the room is Jeff's aunt.

1. The police officer who is responsible for directing traffic is very helpful.

_____

2. Anyone who passes the national exam will get a diploma.

_____

3. Montana, which is the fourth largest state in the U.S., is on the border with Canada.

_____

4. The boys who are playing soccer are preparing for a big tournament.

_____

5. Instructors who attend the workshop will learn about using cell phone apps in teaching.

_____

6. How much are the tickets for the flight that leaves at 11:30 P.M.?

_____

7. The archeologists who were digging in an area in eastern China made an important discovery.

_____

8. The Olympic official who presented the medals shook hands with the athletes.

_____

9. There are more and more Americans who are driving cars that run on electricity.

_____

10. Heather is the manager who oversees the accounting department.

_____

Directions: Check (✓) the correct sentence in each pair.

Example: _____ a. My sister, who lives in Guadalajara, she comes to visit every summer.

_✓_ b. My sister, who lives in Guadalajara, comes to visit every summer.

1. _____ a. The book that we read it in class was about the history of jazz.

_____ b. The book that we read in class was about the history of jazz.

2. _____ a. My best friend went to work in Indonesia, which consists of thousands of islands.

_____ b. My best friend went to work in Indonesia, that consists of thousands of islands.

3. _____ a. I like to shop at the farmers' market on Saturdays when I have a day off.

_____ b. I like to shop at the farmers' market on Saturdays where I have a day off.

4. _____ a. Emma borrowed money from her sister whom she has to pay her back by next weekend.

_____ b. Emma borrowed money from her sister whom she has to pay back by next weekend.

5. _____ a. When the weather is nice, the children like to go to the beach which is close to their house.

_____ b. When the weather is nice, the children like to go to the beach where is close to their house.

6. _____ a. Mark doesn't get much sleep. He has a neighbor who his dog barks all night long.

_____ b. Mark doesn't get much sleep. He has a neighbor whose dog barks all night long.

7. _____ a. The manager locked the door at the back of the store, which he does every night before he goes home.

_____ b. The manager locked the door at the back of the store, where he does every night before he goes home.

8. _____ a. There were fourteen students in my grammar class, seven of them were from Korea.

_____ b. There were fourteen students in my grammar class, seven of whom were from Korea.

Part A *Directions:* Circle all the possible completions for each sentence.

1. Julia would like to know the name of the store _____ you got your leather bag.

   a. when   b. where   c. which   d. that

2. Philip will meet us at the bus stop _____ is on the corner of 23rd Avenue and Main Street.

   a. when   b. where   c. which   d. that

3. The travel agent needs to know some alternative dates _____ we can leave on vacation.

   a. when   b. where   c. on which   d. which

4. Can you run upstairs and get my green scarf? It's in the closet _____ I keep my winter coat.

   a. when   b. where   c. which   d. that

5. The apartment _____ Maria is going to rent has two bedrooms and one bathroom.

   a. when   b. where   c. which   d. that

Part B *Directions:* Complete the sentences with *who, whom,* or *whose.*

1. a. The hiring committee interviewed six applicants, only three of _____ they liked.

   b. They have decided to hire the woman _____ has excellent communication skills.

2. a. The person with _____ our boss was upset didn't come to the meeting.

   b. Tomorrow he has to talk with our boss. There is no one _____ can help him now.

3. a. The workers _____ evaluation scores were weak must attend an extra training next week.

   b. I offered to help Minna, _____ needs to learn the company rules.

Part C *Directions:* Combine the sentences. Use the second sentence as the adjective clause.

1. Connie finally finished preparing the documents. The department supervisor needs to sign them.

   _____

2. My grandmother bought a lot of clothes. The clothes were on sale.

   _____

3. The red truck was driven by a drunk driver. It caused the accident.

   _____

4. The young woman seemed intelligent and pleasant. Sam just met her.

   _____

5. Mrs. Tanaka is looking for the person. The person's car is blocking the driveway.

   _____

Part D *Directions:* Change the adjective clauses to adjective phrases.

1. *Little Women,* which was published in 1868, is my sister's favorite novel.

   _____

2. The science program that is showing on TV every night this week is a series about the brain.

   _____

3. People who visit the Taj Mahal are impressed that a man built it to honor his wife.

   _____

4. The director's new movie, which is opening in theaters this weekend, is sure to be entertaining.

   _____

5. People who are interested in French cooking often go to Paris to experience the food.

   _____

Part E *Directions:* Add commas where necessary.

1. Tom who lives in Port Hadlock is graduating from high school in June.

2. Mr. Parker collects toy trains which were manufactured in the 1940s and 50s.

3. Paul will call you at 5:30 P.M. when he will be home from work.

4. I have looked everywhere for my grammar book which I thought I had left on the table. I can't find it anywhere.

5. There isn't any reason for the actor who is playing the part of Romeo to dye his hair.

Part A *Directions:* Circle all the possible completions for each sentence.

1. The months _____ have 30 days are April, June, September, and November.

   a. when   b. where   c. which   d. that

2. I remember the time _____ Robert forgot to turn off the bathroom faucet and we came home to a house full of water.

   a. when   b. where   c. which   d. that

3. When we go to Atlanta, George wants to drive by the house _____ he grew up to see if it still looks the same.

   a. when   b. where   c. which   d. that

4. The office _____ you are going to be working in is down the hall, the second door to the left.

   a. when   b. where   c. which   d. that

5. The day _____ we got married was probably the happiest day of my life.

   a. when   b. where   c. on which   d. that

Part B *Directions:* Complete the sentences with *who*, *whom*, or *whose*.

1. I recently got the autograph of Suzanne Collins, _____ is the author of the *Hunger Games* books.

2. Mrs. Holton, _____ son is enrolled at North Coast University, tells all her friends about her son's excellent academic record.

3. To _____ did you address the letter?

4. The students _____ had received excellent marks on the exam were honored by the National Scholastic Society.

5. Ms. Morimoto would like to find someone _____ can organize and catalog her collection of Asian art.

6. The firefighters, several of _____ had worked through the night, were exhausted from battling the fire on the hills near the city.

Part C *Directions:* Combine the sentences. Use the second sentence as the adjective clause.

1. Joe's parents don't like the music. Joe listens to the music.

   _____

2. The printer is fast and dependable. Matthew bought it last week.

   _____

3. The police talked to the woman. Her car had been broken into.

   _____

4. The issue is not important to our company. Many people are talking about the issue.

   _____

5. People are in great demand in today's job market. People have advanced technology skills.

   _____

Part D *Directions:* Change the adjective clauses to adjective phrases.

1. Students who have high grades can apply for the scholarship.

   _____

2. The storms which are occurring in the eastern U.S. are the result of climate change.

   _____

3. Anyone who has information about the robbery should call the police.

   _____

4. The lecture will probably be attended by people who are interested in the Middle East.

   _____

5. The people who weren't able to see the lunar eclipse could look at photos of it online.

   _____

Part E *Directions:* Add commas where necessary.

1. We need to replace our roof which is 20 years old and is leaking badly.

2. The hunger program where Jack volunteers feeds more than 250 families each month.

3. People who work outside at night must wear reflective clothing so they can be seen.

4. Jennifer's birthday cake which had strawberries and cream on top was enjoyed by everyone at the party.

5. The Red Cross which provides humanitarian aid around the world is Michele's favorite charity.

CHAPTER 14   Gerunds and Infinitives, Part 1

QUIZ 1 Gerunds and Infinitives: Introduction   (Chart 14-1)

Directions: Check (✓) the sentences that have gerunds.

Small Town Life

Examples: _____ I am growing up in a town with 10,000 people.

     _✓_ My parents like living in our small town.

1. _____ Many adults dream of having a peaceful small town life.

2. _____ For young people, growing up in a small town is sometimes boring.

3. _____ Kids are always looking for fun things to do.

4. _____ During the week, kids spend time surfing the Internet or playing games.

5. _____ On weekends, teens are usually hanging out with their friends.

QUIZ 2 Gerunds and Infinitives: Introduction   (Chart 14-1)

Directions: Check (✓) the sentences that have infinitives.

Summer Activities

Examples. _____ Next weekend we will go to the pool.

     _✓_ I love to swim in the pool.

1. _____ During the summer, we often go to the park for picnics.

2. _____ My little sister likes to play on the playground.

3. _____ My parents usually plan to cook on the barbecue.

4. _____ They always give the biggest hamburger to me.

5. _____ For me, to spend the day at the park is heavenly!

Directions: Complete each sentence with the gerund or infinitive form of the verbs in parentheses.

Example: Chuck agreed (*visit*) _____to visit_____ his parents on Sunday.

1. The young women quit (*shop*) _____ when they had spent all their money.

2. Josef enjoys (*play*) _____ a few games of tennis on weekends.

3. Elena hopes (*celebrate*) _____ her birthday on a beach in Hawaii.

4. My dog refuses (*go*) _____ outside when it rains. He just keeps (*bark*) _____.

5. Mara needed (*call*) _____ a plumber when her sink wouldn't drain.

6. The journalist promised (*be*) _____ honest in his reporting.

7. Ann avoids (*drive*) _____ her car into the city. She doesn't like city traffic.

8. Michiko considered (*call*) _____ her friend, but she decided to text her instead.

9. London expects (*have*) _____ more than a million visitors for New Year's Eve.

10. Mrs. Alvarez mentioned (*plant*) _____ a vegetable garden next summer.

11. The insurance agent suggests (*keep*) _____ valuables in a safe.

12. Kate intended (*grow*) _____ her hair long, but it was too much trouble to take care of.

13. The president of the company just finished (*give*) _____ a speech to employees.

14. Paulo would like (*go*) _____ to Brazil for the holidays, but he doesn't have enough time.

15. I don't mind (*stop*) _____ for lunch if you are hungry.

16. Stefan plans (*study*) _____ Turkish for several more years, then he wants (*visit*) _____ Turkey.

17. We discussed (*go*) _____ out for dinner, but we decided (*eat*) _____ at home instead.

Directions: Choose the correct completions.

Example: Mr. Lee asked ((his wife to pass)/ *to pass*) him the butter.

1. Anthony is out of town this weekend, but he invited (*to come* / *us to come*) over for dinner next weekend.

2. The government needs (*to announce* / *citizens to announce*) the new tax plan soon.

3. Nora has two boys. She doesn't allow (*to play* / *them to play*) on the computer until after they do their homework.

4. My uncle plans (*to retire* / *him to retire*) in three to five years. His doctor advised (*to stop* / *him to stop*) working.

5. The firefighter warned (*to stay people* / *people to stay*) behind the barricades and away from the flames.

6. Teachers should always encourage (*to try* / *students to try*) their best in school.

7. Charles remembered (*to take* / *him to take*) his umbrella with him.

8. My sister studied very hard for her final exam. She expects (*her to pass* / *to pass*) it.

9. Jack's cell phone isn't working. I advised (*him to buy* / *to buy*) a new one.

10. Lynn was disappointed that she missed the gala. She planned (*her to attend* / *to attend*), but had to work.

11. Mrs. Murphy encouraged (*her son to audition* / *to audition*) for the school play.

12. My brother's 40th birthday is tomorrow, and I am going to surprise him. I will leave my house at 8:00 A.M. to drive to Los Angeles. I expect (*to arrive* / *him to arrive*) by noon. I'll meet my brother and his wife at a restaurant for lunch, but he doesn't expect (*to be* / *me to be*) there. I'm sure he'll be surprised to see me!

Directions: Choose the correct completions. More than one answer is possible.

Example: My sister will continue _____ at Oxford University next year.

     (a.)studying   (b.)to study

1. When my alarm clock rang at 6:30 this morning, the sky was beginning _____ light.

   a. getting   b. to get

2. I forgot _____ off the headlights on my car this morning. When I returned, my car wouldn't start.

   a. turning   b. to turn

3. I remember _____ Joe's parents at his graduation party last spring. They were very kind.

   a. meeting   b. to meet

4. Hannah regrets _____ her silver necklace. It was a gift from her grandparents.

   a. losing   b. to lose

5. Ann and Zach are trying _____ enough money to move into their own house.

   a. saving   b. to save

6. As soon as our teacher began _____ the class, the fire alarm sounded and we had to leave the building.

   a. teaching   b. to teach

7. While we were traveling through the western U.S., we stopped _____ several beautiful national parks.

   a. visiting   b. to visit

8. David can't stand _____ at his computer all day long. His eyes get tired from looking at the screen.

   a. working   b. to work

9. I'll never forget _____ the overnight train from Venice to Rome. I didn't sleep at all!

   a. taking   b. to take

10. Jay stopped _____ when he found out he had lung disease.

   a. smoking   b. to smoke

Directions: Complete each sentence with an appropriate preposition.

Example: The students are excited _____*about*_____ dissecting frogs in science class.

1. Adam and Megan are looking forward _____ going ice-skating on Saturday.

2. I'm very sorry. Will you please forgive me _____ being so rude to you?

3. Instead _____ cooking dinner last night, we went out for Mexican food.

4. Parents must stop children _____ throwing trash on the ground.

5. Most of the citizens at the meeting were opposed _____ closing city parks.

6. Students at the college should take advantage _____ the free tutoring available on campus.

7. The presidential candidate is committed _____ improving the country's economy.

8. Jacob is so stubborn! He always insists _____ doing things his way.

QUIZ 7 Using Gerunds as the Objects of Prepositions (Chart 14-6)

Directions: Complete each sentence with an appropriate preposition and *-ing* form of the verb in parentheses.

Example: Margaret forgave her sister (*break*) _____*for breaking*_____ her favorite necklace.

1. Are you interested (*come*) _____ to the Astronomy Center with us?

2. Mrs. Grant is committed (*help*) _____ students learn to read and write.

3. Larry is thinking (*take*) _____ a trip to the Grand Canyon this summer.

4. Joe always has an excuse (*come*) _____ late to meetings.

5. Sarah is not used (*wear*) _____ a school uniform.

6. Our class is responsible (*clean*) _____ up the playground once a week.

7. We are excited (*go*) _____ to Mexico during spring vacation.

8. Do you really think that Sonya is afraid (*stand*) _____ on a tall ladder?

Directions: Complete the sentences with a form of ***go*** + gerund, using the verbs in parentheses.

Example: Bowling is my favorite sport. I (*bowl*) _____*go bowling*_____ once a week.

1. Last Saturday, Louisa (*dance*) _____ with her friends. They learned how to dance the salsa.

2. In two weeks we (*sightsee*) _____ in the area near Salzburg. If we are lucky, we may (*hike*) _____ in the Austrian Alps.

3. Guido is training for a long-distance cycling trip. He (*bike*) _____ every day after work. Sometimes he (*jog*) _____ to increase strength.

4. On summer evenings, lots of people (*sail*) _____ on Lake Washington, where they can view beautiful sunsets over the city.

5. Pat caught three large trout the last time he (*fish*) _____.

6. Have you ever (*snorkel*) _____? I haven't, but I would like to.

7. I'm bored. Let's (*shop*) _____.

8. It snowed about a foot last night. The kids (*sled*) _____ as soon as they woke up this morning.

Directions: Make sentences with the given words.

Example: Claire \ spend a long time \ do homework \ usually

_____*Claire usually spends a long time doing homework.*_____

1. Ms. Spring \ sit at her desk \ pay bills \ yesterday

_____

2. Greg \ waste a lot of time \ surf the Internet \ every night

_____

3. We \ spend too much money \ eat in restaurants \ last month

_____

4. Stewart \ have a hard time \ solve physics problems \ always

_____

5. Carol \ have a good time \ travel with her sisters \ last summer

_____

Directions: Make sentences beginning with *It*. Use the given words in your sentence. Use the present tense.

Example: be enjoyable \ walk \ barefoot on the sand at the beach

It is enjoyable to walk barefoot on the sand at the beach.

1. be interesting \ read \ about scientific discoveries

_____

2. not be easy \ find \ a parking place \ downtown

_____

3. take a long time \ learn \ a foreign language well

_____

4. be impolite \ talk \ when someone else is talking

_____

5. cost a lot \ fly \ first class

_____

Directions: Rewrite the sentences you wrote for Quiz 10. Use gerund phrases for your subjects.

Example: _____ *Walking barefoot on the sand at the beach is enjoyable.* _____

1. _____

2. _____

3. _____

4. _____

5. _____

Directions: Check (✓) the correct sentence in each pair.

Example: ___✓___ a. Wendy enjoys sharing funny web videos with her friends.

_____ b. Wendy enjoys to share funny web videos with her friends.

1. _____ a. My doctor suggested exercising more often.

_____ b. My doctor suggested to exercise more often.

2. _____ a. I dislike eating cold eggs.

_____ b. I dislike to eat cold eggs.

3. _____ a. Benjamin hopes to find a good job this summer.

_____ b. Benjamin hopes finding a good job this summer.

4. _____ a. My daughter promised being home on time, but she was late.

_____ b. My daughter promised to be home on time, but she was late.

5. _____ a. Anna mentioned coming to town for a visit, but I don't know if she
was serious.

_____ b. Anna mentioned to come to town for a visit, but I don't know if she
was serious.

6. _____ a. Jan is responsible for putting together the work schedule.

_____ b. Jan is responsible to put together the work schedule.

7. _____ a. Many families can't afford paying the high cost of college tuition.

_____ b. Many families can't afford to pay the high cost of college tuition.

8. _____ a. Will's friends offered to help him find a new apartment.

_____ b. Will's friends offered helping him find a new apartment.

9. _____ a. My roommate and I are excited about to move into our new apartment.

_____ b. My roommate and I are excited about moving into our new apartment.

10. _____ a. Parents want their children being happy.

_____ b. Parents want their children to be happy.

Part A *Directions:* Check (✓) the correct sentence in each pair.

1. _____ a. Athletes can't help feeling nervous before an important sports event.

   _____ b. Athletes can't help to feel nervous before an important sports event.

2. _____ a. The race monitor instructed the runners beginning.

   _____ b. The race monitor instructed the runners to begin.

3. _____ a. We always appreciate getting help with our yard work.

   _____ b. We always appreciate to get help with our yard work.

4. _____ a. My children are responsible for putting their dirty clothes in the laundry.

   _____ b. My children are responsible to put their dirty clothes in the laundry.

5. _____ a. Hank claimed knowing the way to Mike's house, but we got lost.

   _____ b. Hank claimed to know the way to Mike's house, but we got lost.

Part B *Directions:* Complete each sentence with an appropriate preposition.

1. Maya is worried _____ getting her driver's license, but I'm not.

2. My little sister was so annoying! She insisted _____ going to a movie with us.

3. Eric has a good excuse _____ not sending the email. His computer crashed.

4. When Jan was twenty years old, she dreamt _____ living and working in Sweden.

5. The children are looking forward _____ the party on Saturday.

Part C *Directions:* Complete the sentences using a gerund or infinitive form of the verbs in parentheses. Add an appropriate preposition if needed.

1. Cynthia apologized to her sister (*borrow*) _____ her phone without asking permission. She promised not to do it again.

2. Last night Kaori was lying in bed (*study*) _____ before she went to sleep. She hopes (*get*) _____ a good grade on the next quiz.

3. Hamid remembers (*bring*) _____ his briefcase home from work, but now he can't find it.

4. (*Listen*) _____ to a friend talk when she has a problem is important.

5. Ella doesn't enjoy (*wait*) _____ in line at the supermarket. That's why she tries (*go*) _____ to the supermarket early in the afternoon or very late at night.

6. Nadia's allergies were very bad last spring, and she felt terrible. She couldn't help (*sneeze*) _____ all the time.

7. Jeff is interested (*learn*) _____ Chinese because he is going to Beijing next summer.

8. Janice never goes (*ski*) _____ because she can't stand the cold weather.

9. When Peter decided (*buy*) _____ a new car for the family, his wife suggested (*do*) _____ some research on the Internet.

10. Before a patient starts (*take*) _____ a new medicine, the doctor must prescribe the correct amount.

11. (*Take*) _____ care of two small children is a full-time job for parents.

12. Susan took a vacation to Hawaii. She spent six days (*relax*) _____ on the beach.

Part D *Directions:* Circle the correct completions. Pay careful attention to the meaning.

1. Oh, no! I forgot (*to send* / *sending*) my sister a birthday card, and her birthday is today.

2. Bruno went (*to snowboard* / *snowboarding*) for the first time last year.

3. **A:** Did you remember (*to lock* / *locking*) the door when you left?

   B: Yes, I did. I remember (*to put* / *putting*) my key in the lock and (*to hear* / *hearing*)
   it click.

4. Patricia regretted (*to tell* / *telling*) Jane about her problems because Jane told everyone else.

5. We stopped (*to buy* / *buying*) a newspaper on our way to work this morning.

Part E *Directions:* Make sentences using the given words. Use the present tense. Begin the sentence with **It** if necessary. Use a gerund or an infinitive where necessary.

1. my dad \ always \ take his time \ choose \ a new car

   _____

2. be uncomfortable \ live \ in a hot climate \ without air-conditioning

   _____

3. my sisters and I \ go \ swim \ at the neighborhood pool \ twice a month

   _____

4. Dennis \ sometimes \ have difficulty \ express \ his opinion

   _____

5. have \ a visa \ be \ necessary \ for traveling overseas

   _____

Part A *Directions:* Check (✓) the correct sentence in each pair.

1. _____ a. There seems being a problem with his student visa.

   _____ b. There seems to be a problem with his student visa.

2. _____ a. The travel agent recommended getting our passports as soon as possible.

   _____ b. The travel agent recommended to get our passports as soon as possible.

3. _____ a. Hannah managed finishing her homework before her favorite TV program started.

   _____ b. Hannah managed to finish her homework before her favorite TV program started.

4. _____ a. Video games allow players to pretend fighting monsters or other bad guys.

   _____ b. Video games allow players to pretend to fight monsters or other bad guys.

5. _____ a. My supervisor dislikes being late for work.

   _____ b. My supervisor dislikes to be late for work.

Part B *Directions:* Complete each sentence with an appropriate preposition.

1. We are looking forward _____ having grandchildren someday.

2. After practicing hard for weeks, Adam succeeded _____ winning the 500-meter race.

3. The jury found the accountant guilty _____ cheating his clients.

4. My dad always talks _____ visiting Australia. I hope he can go there some day.

5. The traffic cones prevented us _____ driving down the street.

Part C *Directions:* Complete the sentences using a gerund or infinitive form of the verbs in parentheses. Add an appropriate preposition if needed.

1. We had a great time (*visit*) _____ the pyramids in Egypt.

2. We are considering (*buy*) _____ a large-screen TV in June.

3. Peter said, "I fail (*see*) _____ any logic behind your argument."

4. Instead (*tell*) _____ the truth, Tom denied (*break*) _____ his brother's camera.

5. Mrs. Roberts taught all four of her daughters (*be*) _____ independent.

6. Do you recommend (*eat*) _____ at the Indian restaurant on the corner?

7. When Ken tasted the delicious chocolate cake, he couldn't resist
   (*have*) _____ a second piece.

8. Johnny, please stop (*bother*) _____ your dad. He's trying
   (*take*) _____ a nap.

9. We thanked our neighbors (*take*) _____ care of our cat.

10. Karen prefers (*wear*) _____ her hair short and curly.

11. My teacher told us (*go*) _____ to the computer lab to get extra language
    practice.

12. Do you anticipate (*need*) _____ more help packing? Josh has offered
    (*come*) _____ by on the weekend if you need him.

Part D *Directions:* Circle the correct completions. Pay careful attention to the meaning.

1. It is fortunate that so many people have stopped (*to smoke* / *smoking*) for health reasons.

2. I regret (*to tell* / *telling*) you that you didn't get the job. I know you were very interested in the position.

3. Helen doesn't remember (*to see* / *seeing*) *Romeo and Juliet* at the Shakespeare Festival, but I'm sure we did.

4. Kevin is trying (*to learn* / *learning*) Japanese, but he has trouble memorizing all the characters.

5. I have such a terrible memory. I sometimes do something, and then I forget
   (*to do* / *doing*) it.

6. Please remember (*to sign* / *signing*) the birthday card for Ruth. Her birthday is tomorrow.

Part E *Directions:* Make sentences using the given words. Use the present tense. Begin the sentence with *It* if necessary. Use a gerund or an infinitive where necessary.

  1. be terrible \ wake up \ with a headache

  _____

  2. live \ on their own \ be \ a good experience \ for young adults

  _____

  3. Jenny \ sometimes \ catch \ her children \ watch videos \ in the middle of the night

  _____

  4. be dangerous \ for children \ use fireworks \ without adult supervision

  _____

  5. the tourists \ stand \ on the corner \ try \ figure out \ where to go

  _____

CHAPTER 15 Gerunds and Infinitives, Part 2

QUIZ 1 Infinitives of Purpose: *In Order To*   (Chart 15-1)

Directions: Complete each sentence with **to** or **for**.

Examples: Mike went to Chuck's Auto Supply ___*to*___ get some oil for his car.

Mike went to Chuck's Auto Supply ___*for*___ some motor oil.

1. Zachary has worked hard _____ become a successful physical therapist.

2. My parents are going to Atlanta next month _____ my sister's wedding.

3. Our teacher is very patient with us. She gives us many examples _____ help us understand.

4. The women drove to Vancouver _____ see an exhibit.

5. My dentist advised me to come in twice a year _____ teeth cleaning.

6. We went to the baseball game _____ watch our favorite team.

7. Anna is studying _____ her biology exam.

QUIZ 2 Infinitives of Purpose: *In Order To*   (Chart 15-1)

Directions: Add **in order** whenever possible. If nothing should be added, write Ø.

Examples: I intended ___*Ø*___ to return my book to the library, but I forgot it at home.

Mary called me ___*in order*___ to invite me to her birthday party.

1. Jordan went to the aquarium _____ to see the new baby dolphin.

2. Wendy is planning _____ to spend next year traveling in South America.

3. Liz asked the taxi driver _____ to drop her off at her hotel on Tenth Avenue and Madison Street.

4. I am going to the doctor next week _____ to have my annual health checkup.

5. The chef brought the flaming dessert to the table _____ to impress his guests.

6. Sean is going _____ to Miami next week _____ to see his parents.

7. I wanted _____ to see my favorite band in concert, but I couldn't afford _____ to buy a ticket.

Directions: Complete the sentences with phrases from the box. More than one answer may be possible.

delighted to	embarrassed to	relieved to
determined to	fortunate to	surprised to
disappointed to	hesitant to	unlikely to
✓ eager to	proud to	

1. I am reading an exciting story. I'm _____ *eager to* _____ finish the book so I can find out what happens.

2. My brother was _____ hear his girlfriend say, "Yes!" when he asked her to marry him. It made him very happy.

3. When the students arrived at school, they were _____ find out that classes had been canceled. It was totally unexpected.

4. We were _____ hear that our boss refused to give us a day off for birthdays. We had hoped he would be more generous.

5. **A:** I know we have met before, but I am _____ admit that I can't remember your name.

    B: That's OK. I'm Julie.

6. Elizabeth's parents were _____ announce that she had been accepted to Georgetown University.

7. Jacob is very stubborn. He is _____ change his mind once he has made a decision.

8. Roy is _____ go to Europe next summer. He has been saving his money for a year and is planning his trip. Nothing will stop him from going!

9. I am very _____ have a good education. Not everyone is as lucky as I am.

10. My father is _____ let my sixteen-year-old brother drive. He is worried that my brother will have an accident.

11. Mona was _____ learn that her parents were not injured in the earthquake. She had been very worried about them.

Directions: Read the first sentence. Put a check mark (✓) next to the sentence that is closest in meaning.

Example: My coffee is too hot.

    _____ a. The coffee is hot, but I can drink it.

    __✓__ b. I can't drink the coffee.

1. I'm too tired to watch a movie tonight.

    _____ a. I want to watch a movie.

    _____ b. I don't want to watch a movie.

2. It's very sunny today.

    _____ a. The sun doesn't bother me.

    _____ b. I don't like the sun.

3. This bag of groceries isn't too heavy for me to carry.

    _____ a. I can carry it.

    _____ b. I can't carry it.

4. Melissa is too old to play with dolls.

    _____ a. Melissa probably plays with dolls.

    _____ b. Melissa probably doesn't play with dolls.

5. That problem was very difficult.

    _____ a. I was able to solve the problem.

    _____ b. I couldn't solve the problem.

6. The coffee shop closes too early for us to go there after work.

    _____ a. We can go to the coffee shop after work.

    _____ b. We can't go to the coffee shop after work.

7. That isn't too much to pay for a leather jacket.

    _____ a. The price of the jacket is reasonable.

    _____ b. The price of the jacket is not reasonable.

8. I have gained five pounds. My jeans are very tight.

    _____ a. I can still wear the jeans.

    _____ b. I can't wear the jeans.

Directions: Choose the correct completions.

Example: A child under age 16 is (*(too young)* / *young enough*) to drive.

1. My toothache has become (*too painful* / *painful enough*) for me to go to the dentist tomorrow. I hope it's nothing serious.

2. The tomatoes in my garden are (*too ripe* / *ripe enough*) to pick. I'm going to use some for a salad.

3. The sun is (*too bright* / *bright enough*) for me to see well. I need my sunglasses.

4. This soup is (*too spicy* / *spicy enough*) for Bill to eat. He will enjoy it.

5. These shoes don't fit me, but they are (*too big* / *big enough*) for my brother to wear. I'll give them to him.

6. Edward isn't (*too strong* / *strong enough*) to move the piano by himself. He has to hire a professional mover.

7. The double chocolate cookies aren't (*too sweet* / *sweet enough*) for me to eat. I ate three of them.

8. This 70-degree weather is (*too warm* / *warm enough*) for Ruth. She doesn't like it much warmer than this.

QUIZ 6 **Passive Infinitives and Gerunds: Present** (Chart 15-4)

Directions: Complete the sentences with the passive forms of the verbs in parentheses.

Examples: I didn't expect (*give*) ____*to be given*____ such a nice gift for my birthday.

Kelsey avoids (*invite*) ____*being invited*____ to parties. She hates them.

1. Jane intends (*marry*) _____ by the time she is 30.

2. Sarah was excited about (*interview*) _____ for the job.

3. Movie stars sometimes don't enjoy (*ask*) _____ questions by the public.

4. Paul hopes (*invite*) _____ to speak at the managers' meeting.

5. The weather forecast warned people (*prepare*) _____ for a terrible windstorm.

6. Stan appreciates (*drive*) _____ to work by his neighbor every day. They share the cost of gas.

7. I expect (*treat*) _____ with courtesy and respect.

8. Sometimes teenagers complain about not (*take*) _____ seriously by adults.

9. My grandfather gives a lot of money to the poor. He wants (*remember*) _____ as a caring and generous man.

10. The dedicated teacher appreciated (*recognize*) _____ for her inspiring work.

Directions: Choose the sentence that has the same meaning.

A Bank Robber's Story

Example: The bank robber was clearly upset that the police caught him.

       (a.) The bank robber was upset to have been caught.

       b. The bank robber was upset to catch the police.

1. At first, the man denied having robbed the bank.

    a. At first, the man said that he hadn't robbed the bank.

    b. At first, the man said that the bank hadn't been robbed.

2. He later admitted that he had stolen the money.

    a. He later admitted that the money was stolen from him.

    b. He later admitted having stolen the money.

3. He mentioned having been told that the bank didn't have an alarm.

    a. He said someone had told him that the bank didn't have an alarm.

    b. He said he had told someone that the bank didn't have an alarm.

4. The robber appeared to have broken the law before.

    a. It appeared that the law hadn't been broken by him before

    b. It appeared that the robber had broken the law before.

5. The police apologized for not catching the robber sooner.

    a. The police apologized that they hadn't caught the robber sooner.

    b. The robber was sorry for his crime.

Directions: Choose the correct completions.

Example: The accountants were happy (*(to have finished)*/ *having finished*) their work for the tax season.

1. I regretted (*having lent* / *to have lent*) my friend money because she didn't pay it back.

2. The disruptive group deserved (*to have asked* / *to have been asked*) to leave the restaurant.

3. The other driver appears (*to have caused* / *having been caused*) the accident.

4. Jane took advantage of (*having told* / *having been told*) the dates of the conference and made her reservations right away.

5. Sue would have preferred (*to have notified* / *to have been notified*) about the problem sooner.

Directions: Complete the sentences with an appropriate form of the verbs in parentheses. More than one answer may be possible.

Example: My car needs (*repair*) __to be repaired / repairing__ before we leave on our vacation.

The mechanic needs (*repair*) __to repair__ my car.

1. Our windows really need (*wash*) _____. They're really dirty!

2. I need (*buy*) _____ a new phone because I dropped mine in water.

3. The exams need (*correct*) _____ by Friday so the students can get their results.

4. You need (*get*) _____ a visa before you go to Canada.

5. We need (*find*) _____ the document before we can sell our house.

6. My computer needs (*repair*) _____. It isn't working right.

7. Alice needs (*fix*) _____ the hole in her sock.

8. Our house needs (*paint*) _____. We haven't painted it in years.

Directions: Complete the sentences with an appropriate form of a verb from the box. If more than one form is appropriate, write both.

burn	✓ feed	give	ring
discuss	flash	get	tell

1. I watched an old lady __feed / feeding__ ducks at the park.

2. When I heard my phone _____, I had to find it in my bag so I could answer it.

3. Kate pulled over to the side of the street when she saw the ambulance's lights _____ behind her.

4. It was exciting to hear the scientists at the conference _____ their newest discoveries.

5. Last year, I watched my son _____ an award for being the top student in his class and _____ a speech at graduation.

6. I smelled something _____ in the kitchen, so I ran in there to see what it was. I realized that I had forgotten to turn off the stove.

7. We really enjoyed hearing Michael _____ about his amazing trip to Antarctica.

Directions: Choose the correct completions. More than one answer may be possible.

Example: Sally got her sister _____ the dinner dishes.

       a. wash   ⓑ to wash   c. washed

1. The movers helped Shane and Alicia _____ into their new home.

       a. move   b. to move   c. moved

2. Pat filled out an online form to have the address on his account _____.

       a. change   b. to change   c. changed

3. The baseball players got their coach _____ practice because it was raining.

       a. cancel   b. to cancel   c. canceled

4. Mrs. McGuiness lets her children _____ up past midnight on New Year's Eve.

       a. stay   b. to stay   c. stayed

5. Charlie finally got his watch _____ after complaining about it for weeks.

       a. fix   b. to fix   c. fixed

6. The president of the company made the human resources manager _____ three people.

       a. fire   b. to fire   c. fired

7. I had my doctor _____ my blood pressure when I was in his office.

       a. check   b. to check   c. checked

8. I work Monday-Thursday from 8:00 to 6:00. This schedule lets me _____ three-day weekends.

       a. have   b. to have   c. had

9. Jane always helps her elderly parents _____ their bills.

       a. pay   b. to pay   c. paid

10. My brother had his car _____ to the mechanic's when it wouldn't start.

       a. take   b. to take   c. taken

Directions: Choose the meaning that is closest in meaning to the verb in **bold**.

Example: The teacher **made** the students turn off their cell phones.

        ⓐ gave no choice   b. requested   c. persuaded

1. Frank always **makes** his kids eat their vegetables.

     a. gives no choice   b. requests   c. persuades

2. George **got** Mary to cut his hair.

     a. gave no choice   b. requested   c. persuaded

3. Mrs. Mikkelson always **has** her son take out the garbage.

     a. gives no choice   b. requests   c. persuades

4. The boys didn't want to clean up the backyard, so they **got** their little brother to do it by paying him $5.00.

     a. gave no choice   b. requested   c. persuaded

5. We were looking for someone to track our company's recycling practices, and we finally **had** the director of maintenance do it.

     a. gave no choice   b. requested   c. persuaded

6. When I was a teenager, my parents always **made** me finish my homework before I could call my friends.

     a. gave no choice   b. requested   c. persuaded

Directions: Complete the sentences with the correct form of the pronoun in parentheses.

Examples: (you) a. *Formal:*   I don't understand ___*your*___ not liking to travel.

  b. *Informal:* I don't understand ___*you*___ not liking to travel.

1. (we) a. *Formal:*   The neighbors are accustomed to _____ going on a trip for two weeks every summer.

  b. *Informal:* The neighbors are accustomed to _____ going on a trip for two weeks every summer.

2. (I) a. *Formal:*   My husband always worries about _____ taking too many suitcases.

  b. *Informal:* My husband always worries about _____ taking too many suitcases.

3. (he) a. *Formal:*   Our taxi driver was helpful. I appreciated _____ making suggestions for restaurants.

  b. *Informal:* Our taxi driver was helpful. I appreciated _____ making suggestions for good restaurants.

4. (they) a. *Formal:*   Taxis are sometimes expensive. Many people complain about _____ charging too much.

  b. *Informal:* Taxis are sometimes expensive. Many people complain about _____ charging too much.

5. (she) a. *Formal:*   My daughter often goes on trips by herself, but I dislike _____ traveling alone.

  b. *Informal:* My daughter often goes on trips by herself, but I dislike _____ traveling alone.

Directions: Choose the correct completions.

Example: Margaret went shopping (*(to get)* / *for getting*) some new shoes.

1. I heard the ship's horn (*to ring* / *ring*) out across the water.

2. Alan is (*very tall* / *tall enough*) to reach the top shelf.

3. The kids were (*very* / *too*) excited to sit still.

4. Chris let his little brother (*borrow* / *to borrow*) his books.

5. Eddie was surprised (*to hear* / *hearing*) that he hadn't passed his final exam in biology.

6. Ms. Williams was relieved (*to have been told* / *to have told*) good news by her doctor.

7. It has been a long time since I've cleaned. My room really needs (*dusted* / *to be dusted*).

8. I am pleased (*introduce* / *to introduce*) you to my parents, Carol and Bob Matthews.

9. Teresa saw her best friend (*to wave* / *waving*) at her from across the street.

10. Toshiko got her brother-in-law (*to pick* / *picking*) her up at the airport.

11. Sharon is looking forward (*to be sent* / *to being sent*) on a business trip to Hawaii.

12. My cousin moved to Alaska (*for working* / *to work*) in the tourist industry.

13. Mark's parents let him (*to have* / *have*) a barbeque on his birthday.

14. Karen insists on (*I* / *my*) telling her all of the family news.

15. John had his roommate (*stop* / *stopping*) for groceries on the way home from work.

Part A *Directions:* Add *in order* whenever possible to express purpose. If nothing should be added, write Ø.

    1. The office staff decided _____ to have a retirement party for Norma.

    2. Janice called the airport _____ to see whether her flight had been delayed.

    3. Susan takes good care of her teeth _____ to keep them healthy.

    4. Please remember _____ to raise your hand if you have a question during the test.

    5. Sometimes children lie to their parents _____ to avoid getting in trouble.

Part B *Directions:* Read the first sentence. Put a check mark (✓) next to the sentence that is closest in meaning.

    1. Kathy is old enough to get her driver's license.

        _____ a. Kathy can get her driver's license.

        _____ b. Kathy can't get her driver's license.

    2. The music is too loud.

        _____ a. I like this music.

        _____ b. I don't like this music.

    3. The chocolate that Ari bought was very expensive.

        _____ a. Ari spent a lot of money, but that's OK.

        _____ b. Ari shouldn't have spent so much money.

    4. Mitch is too young to babysit his little sisters.

        _____ a. Mitch can babysit his little sisters.

        _____ b. Mitch can't babysit his little sisters.

    5. Jack isn't fast enough to play basketball well.

        _____ a. Jack can play basketball well.

        _____ b. Jack can't play basketball well.

Part C *Directions:* Use the passive to complete the sentences with an appropriate form of the verbs in parentheses.

1. Bill's car is really dirty. He hasn't washed it in three weeks. It needs

    (*wash*) _____ soon!

2. My co-worker really cares about (*see*) _____ by the "right" people at

    social events.

3. Ann didn't want (*ask*) _____ a question, so she didn't look at the teacher.

4. Mary was delighted (*introduce*) _____ to her son's fiancée.

5. I don't enjoy (*laugh*) _____ at or made fun of.

Part D *Directions:* Complete the sentences with an appropriate form of a verb from the box. If more than one form is appropriate, write both.

brush	burn	cry	fly	hide

1. The little boy noticed someone _____ in the bushes in front of the

    house, so he ran inside to tell his father.

2. Polly smelled something _____ and realized that she had forgotten that

    rice was cooking on the stove.

3. Ivan watched the other boys _____ their kites and wished that his kite

    were still in one piece.

4. Jake was eating dinner at his friend's house when he felt something _____

    against his leg. He looked down and saw his friend's cat.

5. When I take my little daughter to the doctor, I have to wait outside because I hate to hear

    her _____ when the doctor gives her a shot.

Part E *Directions:* Choose the correct completions.

1. My parents let me (*stay / staying*) up late on weekends.

2. I'm not very strong. I always have my older brother (*move / to move*) my furniture for me.

3. I don't understand this assignment. Can you help me (*figure / figuring*) it out?

4. At the wedding, the bride even got my father (*dance / to dance*).

5. Because the jeans were too expensive, Carol's mother made her (*return / to return*) them.

Part F *Directions:* Check (✓) the correct sentence in each pair.

1. _____ a. Pete is going to graduate school for getting a master's degree.

   _____ b. Pete is going to graduate school to get a master's degree.

2. _____ a. Our house needs to be painted before we can sell it.

   _____ b. Our house needs to paint before we can sell it.

3. _____ a. Our boss was unhappy about we not finishing all of the reports by Friday.

   _____ b. Our boss was unhappy about our not finishing all of the reports by Friday.

4. _____ a. Tanya was sorry being late, and she apologized to miss part of the presentation.

   _____ b. Tanya was sorry to be late, and she apologized for missing part of the presentation.

5. _____ a. Chuck is excited to move out of his parents' house and find a job.

   _____ b. Chuck is excited moving out of his parents' house and finding a job.

Part A *Directions:* Add *in order* whenever possible to express purpose. If nothing should be added, write Ø.

1. Rick closed the door to his office _____ to have privacy during the phone call with his boss.

2. Cathy offered _____ to take care of my cats while I was out of town.

3. It is important _____ to take care of your health.

4. My teacher quizzed us often _____ to help us prepare for the advanced placement exam.

5. Children should be encouraged _____ to develop their individual interests.

Part B *Directions:* Read the first sentence. Put a check mark (✓) next to the sentence that is closest in meaning.

1. Bradley is too nervous to sit still because he is waiting for the test results.

_____ a. Bradley can sit calmly while he waits.

_____ b. Bradley can't sit calmly while he waits.

2. Our children are old enough to stay home alone.

_____ a. The parents can leave the children home alone.

_____ b. The parents can't leave the children home alone.

3. English grammar is very confusing for me.

_____ a. English grammar is confusing, but I can understand it.

_____ b. English grammar is confusing, and I can't understand it at all.

4. The sofa Diana wants to buy is too expensive.

_____ a. Diana will buy the sofa.

_____ b. Diana won't buy the sofa.

5. Pat doesn't speak enough German to have a simple conversation.

_____ a. Pat can talk to others in German.

_____ b. Pat can't talk to others in German.

Part C *Directions:* Use the passive to complete the sentences with an appropriate form of the verbs in parentheses.

1. Instead of (*worry*) _____ about her grade on the test, Maria doesn't care about it.

2. I expected (*invite*) _____ to Tina's wedding and was disappointed when I didn't get an invitation.

3. The children were excited about (*allow*) _____ to spend the night at their friend's house.

4. These socks are so old. They have holes in both the toes and the heels. They need (*throw*) _____ away.

5. Just because he's the oldest, John expects (*treat*) _____ like a king.

Part D *Directions:* Complete the sentences with an appropriate form of a verb from the box. If more than one form is appropriate, write both.

beep   blow   report   stand   take

1. Carlos looked at the elephant _____ _____ in the middle of the street. He couldn't believe his eyes!

2. When I watched my baby _____ her first steps, I clapped and smiled.

3. We were listening to the news when we heard the announcer _____ that some valuable artwork had been stolen from the museum.

4. The teenagers were safe from the storm, but they could feel the wind _____ outside.

5. When Helen's food is ready, she hears the microwave oven _____ .

Part E *Directions:* Choose the correct completions.

1. If you get lost, a policeman can help you (*find / finding*) your way.

2. Do you think the teacher will let us (*use / to use*) our dictionaries during the test?

3. After three hours, Sheila finally got her computer (*to open / opening*) the document she was trying to access.

4. The coach had all of the players (*stretch / to stretch*) well before the game.

5. The bad weather might make the airline (*postpone / postponing*) our flight. We should call the airport.

Part F *Directions:* Check (✓) the correct sentence in each pair.

1. _____ a. I heard the rain fell on the roof and realized that I needed to bring an umbrella with me.

   _____ b. I heard the rain fall on the roof and realized that I needed to bring an umbrella with me.

2. _____ a. My doctor made me wait 45 minutes before he would see me.

   _____ b. My doctor made me to wait 45 minutes before he would see me.

3. _____ a. Mrs. Won wouldn't let her son play football because she was worried about his getting hurt.

   _____ b. Mrs. Won wouldn't let her son to play football because she was worried about him getting hurt.

4. _____ a. These shoes are tight enough for me. I can't wear them anymore.

   _____ b. These shoes are too tight for me. I can't wear them anymore.

5. _____ a. John appeared to have forgotten his glasses. He was squinting in order to see.

   _____ b. John appeared to forget his glasses. He was squinting in order to see.

CHAPTER 16

Coordinating Conjunctions

QUIZ 1 Parallel Structure (Chart 16-1)

Directions: Choose the correct completions.

Example: George is a strong and (*health* / (*healthy*)) man.

1. Caitlin turned on her music and (*begins* / *began*) to dance.

2. My father is old but (*fit* / *fits*).

3. The kids were chasing each other around the field and (*tried* / *trying*) to catch one another.

4. Trust and (*forgives* / *forgiveness*) are necessary for a successful relationship.

5. He has difficulty understanding both (*spoken* / *speaking*) and written English.

6. My dog likes to jump up and (*catches* / *catch*) sticks in his mouth.

7. Talking on a cell phone and (*to send* / *sending*) text messages are inappropriate in class.

8. My teacher was shocked and (*disappointed* / *disappointing*) when she caught students cheating on the test.

QUIZ 2 Parallel Structure: Using Commas (Chart 16-2)

Directions: Add commas as necessary.

High School Graduation

Example: Carrie Claire and Jordan are all graduating from high school this June.

Carrie, Claire, and Jordan are all graduating from high school this June.

1. High school graduation is an exciting fun and rewarding time for most students and their families.

2. Students are tired of high school are ready for something new and are looking forward to college or work.

3. Parents feel proud satisfied and relieved that their children have reached this milestone in their lives.

4. There are many events leading up to graduation day. For example, most graduates get their picture taken send out graduation announcements and invite friends and family to celebrate with them.

5. On graduation day there is a ceremony that includes speeches awards and music.

6. Parents siblings and friends look on as students receive their diplomas.

7. High school graduation is a sort of "coming of age" into the adult world of opportunity independence and responsibility.

Directions: Combine the sentences into one concise sentence that contains parallel structure. Punctuate carefully.

Example: The food was tasty.

The food was cheap.

The food was plentiful.

The food was tasty, cheap, and plentiful.

1. Vienna, Austria, is famous for classical music.

    Vienna, Austria, is famous for opera.

    Vienna, Austria, is famous for the waltz.

    _____

2. The new magazine was colorful.

    The new magazine was glossy.

    The new magazine had lots of photographs.

    The new magazine had lots of advertising.

    _____

3. The fireman put out a fire.

    The fireman rescued a cat stuck in a tree.

    The fireman helped a man who had had a heart attack.

    _____

4. In Brazil, I saw white sand beaches.

    In Brazil, I saw beautiful young women.

    In Brazil, I saw beautiful young men.

    In Brazil, I saw crystal clear blue water.

    _____

5. When Jane got home from work, she took off her suit.

    She took off her high-heeled shoes.

    She put on an old pair of jeans.

    She put on an old pair of slippers.

    She put on a warm wool sweater.

    _____

Directions: Punctuate the sentences by adding commas and periods. Do not add any words. Capitalize as necessary.

Example: Sarah Lucy and Brian are making a cross-country road trip they will come to visit us in two weeks.

> Sarah, Lucy, and Brian are making a cross-country road trip. ᵀthey will come to visit us in two weeks.

1. My brother is an accountant he can help us with our income taxes.

2. An Australian swimmer was attacked by a shark but he scared the animal away by poking it in the eye.

3. Denny's computer stopped working while he was working on his college application fortunately he had saved his documents so he didn't lose any data.

4. A woman in Michigan got a $1 parking ticket in 1976 she finally paid it in 2008 by sending a twenty-dollar bill to the local police station she also sent a note explaining the money but she told the police not to try to find her.

5. People have been playing soccer since ancient times the first soccer clubs were formed in England in the 1850s but official soccer rules were not written until 1863 many of those same rules still govern soccer today.

Directions: Complete the sentences with *is* or *are*.

Example: Not only my parents but also my grandparents _____are_____ here for my birthday.

1. Both Liz and Margaret _____ teaching English at the university.

2. Neither talking nor looking around _____ acceptable during exams.

3. Not only the children but also their mother _____ looking forward to going on a picnic.

4. Either chips or cookies _____ an appropriate snack for the meeting.

5. Not only Cathy but also Jan _____ taking a day off tomorrow.

6. Both rats and mice _____ rodents with long thin tails.

7. Either English 101 or English 115 _____ required for graduation.

8. Not only governments but also individuals _____ responsible for taking care of the environment.

Directions: Combine each pair of sentences into one new sentence with parallel structure. Use the conjunctions given in parentheses.

Example: Coffee contains caffeine. Tea contains caffeine. (*both … and*)

_____ *Both coffee and tea contain caffeine.* _____

1. Janice doesn't have any brothers or sisters. Erica doesn't have any brothers or sisters. (*neither … nor*)

   _____

2. Greg is interested in studying medicine. His twin brother is interested in studying medicine. (*both … and*)

   _____

3. We can have broccoli for dinner. We can have cauliflower for dinner. (*either … or*)

   _____

4. I don't have a passport. I don't have money for travel. (*neither … nor*)

   _____

5. The New York Yankees is a great baseball team. The Tokyo Giants is a great baseball team. (*both … and*)

   _____

6. My husband and I will go to a movie tonight. My daughter and I will go to a movie tonight. (*either … or*)

   _____

7. My English teacher hadn't graded our essays. My English teacher hadn't returned our vocabulary quizzes. (*neither … nor*)

   _____

8. During her speech, Lina spoke loudly. During her speech, Lina spoke clearly. (*both … and*)

   _____

Directions: Choose the correct completions.

Example: George is a strong and (*health* / (*healthy*)) man.

1. The students' presentation was thoughtful, (*intelligent* / *intelligence*), and interesting.

2. I'm sorry, but I can't help you right now. Please ask (*either John or Linda* / *neither John nor Linda*) to help you.

3. Anna has traveled by car, bus, ship, and (*took a plane* / *plane*).

4. Our English teacher speaks (*slow* / *slowly*) and carefully so we can understand what she says.

5. Teresa (*likes* / *doesn't like*) neither spinach nor beets.

6. I took out my wallet and (*payment* / *paid*) for dinner.

7. Both the neighborhood committee and the city parks department (*works* / *work*) to keep Echo Lake Park clean.

8. The documentary gave interesting (*factual* / *facts*) and surprising statistics on honeybees.

9. Neither cows nor horses (*eats* / *eat*) meat. They are herbivores.

10. Not only a movie studio but also a famous director (*is* / *are*) interested in making a movie about Cuba.

Part A *Directions:* Choose the correct completions.

1. Both Anita and Sandra (*loves / love*) to play volleyball, but neither Betty nor Jackie (*likes / like*) sports.

2. Not only the athlete but also the spectators (*was / were*) angry about the referee's decision.

3. Either the meatballs or the chicken (*is / are*) what I will order for dinner.

4. Not only students but also their teacher (*appreciates / appreciate*) holidays.

Part B *Directions:* Punctuate the sentences by adding commas and periods. Do not add or delete any words. Add capitalization as necessary.

1. Polly was looking for a new tablet computer for her brother's birthday she wanted a large selection and good prices so she used the Internet to do her shopping.

2. Both Silvia and her husband love the rock band Wind Tunnel but they refuse to pay $125 a ticket to attend a concert.

3. Myron has written short stories and poems for the school literary magazine and sports and feature articles for the school newspaper.

4. Acme Toy Company continues to produce dolls metal cars construction sets and action figures but it no longer makes bicycles or board games.

5. Flights 2058 and 2065 to Los Angeles have been delayed but Flight 2061 is departing on time I can get you a seat on Flight 2061.

Part C *Directions:* Combine the sentences into one concise sentence that contains parallel structure. You may add *and, but,* and *or* where appropriate.

1. Linda has traveled by car. Linda has traveled by bus. Linda has traveled by train. Linda has not traveled by ship. Linda has not traveled by plane. Linda has not traveled by balloon.

   _____

   _____

   _____

2. Thomas has read about computers. Thomas has read about the Internet. Thomas has taken classes in computer programming. Thomas has taken classes in computer applications.

   _____

   _____

   _____

3. Next weekend, Shirley wants to visit her grandmother. She wants to spend time with friends. She has to do her laundry. She has to clean the bathroom, too.

   _____

   _____

   _____

4. Last year, I traveled to Germany on business. I traveled to France on business. This year I hope to find a new job. I hope to stop traveling so much.

   _____

   _____

   _____

5. At her surprise birthday party, Gloria was surprised to see her high school friends. Gloria was surprised to see her aunt and uncle from New York City. Gloria was surprised to see her old college roommate. She was disappointed not to see her sister. She was disappointed not to see her niece.

   _____

   _____

   _____

Part D *Directions:* Combine the sentences into one concise sentence that contains parallel structure. Use paired conjunctions (**both ... and; either ... or;** or **neither ... nor**).

1. The terrible rainstorm flooded basements and sewers. The terrible rainstorm caused mudslides.

   _____

   _____

2. Cindy will babysit the kids this evening. Mrs. Smith will babysit the kids this evening.

   _____

   _____

3. Arthur has never been to Disneyland. His cousins have never been to Disneyland.

   _____

   _____

4. During the holiday weekend, the parking lots at San Francisco International Airport were full. During the holiday weekend, the parking lots at San Jose Airport were full.

   _____

   _____

5. Bread should be stored in the freezer instead of the refrigerator. Flour should be stored in the freezer instead of the refrigerator.

   _____

   _____

Part A *Directions:* Choose the correct completions.

1. Both doctors and nurses (*saves / save*) people's lives every day.

2. Not only my brother but also my cousins (*lives / live*) in Orlando.

3. Neither James' new boss nor his co-workers (*has / have*) met James' wife.

4. Either texting or emailing (*is / are*) a convenient way for most people to contact relatives who live out of town.

5. Not only the sales team but also the company's chief administrator (*wants / want*) to improve communication with customers.

Part B *Directions:* Punctuate the sentences by adding commas and periods. Do not add or delete any words. Add capitalization as necessary.

1. I have tried the low fat diet the low sugar diet and the protein diet too but none of them worked.

2. The weather forecaster predicts heavy fog and light drizzle for the morning but clear skies and sunshine for the late afternoon.

3. Mary doesn't like to drink tea or decaffeinated coffee so we need to pick up some regular coffee for her.

4. Bicycles motorcycles and handicapped drivers' cars can be parked in Lot A but everyone else needs to park in Lots B or C.

5. Barbara has had many different jobs she has been a flight attendant a salesclerk a waitress and a receptionist but now she has her MBA and is the regional manager for a large multinational corporation.

Part C *Directions:* Combine the sentences into one concise sentence that contains parallel structure. You may add *and, but,* and *or* where appropriate.

1. Last night, Larry watched some TV. Larry surfed the Internet. Larry listened to some music. Larry read the newspaper. Today, Larry has to do some serious work.

   _____

   _____

   _____

2. Mr. Kincaid owns real estate. Mr. Kincaid owns stocks. Mr. Kincaid owns bonds. Mr. Kincaid has to sell some stocks to pay his taxes. Mr. Kincaid has to sell some bonds to pay his taxes.

   _____

   _____

   _____

3. Craig has good computer skills and can type 70 words a minute. Jean has good computer skills and can type 70 words a minute. They both got jobs as executive assistants.

   _____

   _____

   _____

4. French is an Indo-European language. German is an Indo-European language. Chinese is not an Indo-European language. Korean is not an Indo-European language.

   _____

   _____

   _____

5. Because it was an extremely cold day, Mark put on a heavy sweater. Mark put on a warm jacket. Mark didn't wear a hat. Mark didn't wear a scarf.

   _____

   _____

   _____

Part D *Directions:* Combine the sentences into one concise sentence that contains parallel structure. Use *both ... and; either ... or;* or *neither ... nor*.

1. The earthquake knocked down several freeways. The earthquake broke gas and water lines.

   _____

   _____

2. Philip doesn't want to go to college. Philip doesn't want to find a job.

   _____

   _____

3. Oranges are a good source of vitamin C. Cabbage is a good source of vitamin C.

   _____

   _____

4. The contractor will try to repair the broken fence. She will tear down the fence and replace it. (choice)

   _____

   _____

5. Mayoral candidate Jim Brown did not talk about the homeless problem. Mayoral candidate Alicia Taylor did not talk about the homeless problem.

   _____

   _____

CHAPTER 17   Adverb Clauses

Introduction to Adverb Clauses   (Chart 17-1)

Directions: Add a comma to the appropriate place in each sentence.

1. As soon as I finish my report I will email you.

2. Since it was hot today Claire went swimming.

3. By the time I graduate I will be 18 years old.

4. When Robert went to the game he saw Marie.

5. As soon as I get home I'm going to make dinner.

6. Just as I was about to leave my sister called me.

QUIZ 2 **Identifying Adverb Clauses of Time**   (Charts 17-1 and 17-2)

Directions: Underline the adverb clause in each sentence.

Example: When Alexa came home from work, she took off her shoes.

1. Bryan and Cathy went to Rome after they visited Florence.

2. As soon as my plane arrives in Jakarta, I will call you.

3. Just as Ciela finished loading the game on her phone, the phone battery died.

4. Max was watching a video on his computer while he was folding his laundry.

5. By the time we see you next summer, you will have graduated from high school.

6. The police won't leave until the accident is cleared from the highway.

7. The first time Kevin tried to ride a motorcycle, he crashed into a fence.

8. I have been a *Star Wars* fan ever since I was a child.

9. Carol will return to her office once the meeting ends.

10. Since the 3M Company first made Post-It Notes, they have been sold in many sizes, shapes, and colors.

Directions: Choose the best completions.

Example: As soon as the experiment was completed, the scientists _____ their findings.

      a. analyze   b. will analyze   ⓒ analyzed   d. have analyzed

1. When James finishes washing the windows today, he _____ the fence.

      a. paint   b. paints   c. has painted   d. will paint

2. Until my brother went to Brazil last year, he _____ outside of the United States.

      a. has never been   b. wasn't   c. had never been   d. won't be

3. Ever since Nina moved to Nebraska, she _____ a lot of problems with allergies.

      a. had   b. has had   c. is having   d. has

4. Podcasts on the Internet allow people to listen to their favorite programs whenever they _____ to.

      a. want   b. wanted   c. are wanting   d. will want

5. We missed our bus. By the time we arrived at the bus station, the bus _____.

      a. left   b. had left   c. will have left   d. leaves

6. Someone's cell phone rang just as the musicians _____ to play.

      a. begin   b. are beginning   c. were beginning   d. will begin

7. After the magician finishes his show, he _____ the children some simple magic tricks.

      a. will teach   b. has taught   c. had taught   d. taught

8. Big tears filled my father's eyes as he _____ his only daughter get married.

      a. watches   b. watched   c. has watched   d. will watch

9. By the time Lisa graduates from high school, her oldest brother _____ his master's degree.

      a. is getting   b. gets   c. will have gotten   d. had gotten

10. The last time we _____ online, the cost of airline tickets had gone up.

      a. checks   b. checked   c. has checked   d. had checked

Directions: Combine each pair of sentences with the words in parentheses. Add commas where necessary.

Example: Jennifer checked her bank account online. She ordered a book from Books.com. (*before*)

_____ *Before Jennifer ordered a book from Books.com, she checked her bank account online.* _____

1. Sue comes home late. Her parents are upset. (*whenever*)

_____

2. The chef heated up the barbecue. He grilled the steaks. (*before*)

_____

3. I showed my passport. The customs officer let me pass into the terminal. (*after*)

_____

4. Shelley works out at the gym. She needs to drink a lot of water. (*every time*)

_____

5. Mr. Arnold turns off the lights. We will be able to see the screen better. (*as soon as*)

_____

6. The crowd cheered. They saw the baseball fly over the stadium wall. (*when*)

_____

7. I finish my homework. It will be midnight. (*by the time*)

_____

8. The pilot got a message from the control tower. Then the plane landed. (*just before*)

_____

9. Karen was shutting down her computer. The computer made a strange noise. (*while*)

_____

10. Brad and Martha got married in 2012. They have played Scrabble once a week. (*since*)

_____

Directions: Combine each pair of sentences with the words in parentheses. Add commas where necessary.

Example: Ellen took a nap when she got home from work. Ellen had had a very difficult day. (*because*)

Ellen took a nap when she got home from work because she had had a very difficult day.

1. John arrived at the airport just ten minutes before his flight's departure time. John nearly missed his plane. (*because*)

   _____

2. We did a lot of research about Scotland before our trip. We had never been to Scotland. (*because*)

   _____

3. The rain has stopped. We can open the windows and get some fresh air. (*now that*)

   _____

4. We will have to call or email Mr. Adams. Mr. Adams doesn't like to text. (*since*)

   _____

5. Sue did not enjoy going to the movies. Sue had left her eyeglasses at home. (*because*)

   _____

6. Larry has to do a lot of traveling. Larry is the senior manager for his company. (*now that*)

   _____

7. We can stay up late and talk. We don't have to go to work tomorrow. (*since*)

   _____

8. I need to find a new place to get my hair cut. My barber has retired after 25 years. (*now that*)

   _____

9. Last week I didn't pay my phone bill. Today, the phone company sent me a notice. (*because*)

   _____

10. Rosa didn't have any cash. She paid for her groceries with a credit card. (*since*)

    _____

Directions: Complete the sentences with ***even though*** or ***because***.

Examples: Mark has a good job and makes a lot of money _____*even though*_____ he didn't graduate from college.

_____*Because*_____ Sue has to catch the bus at 4:59, she has to leave the meeting early.

1. Joshua is very thin _____ he eats lots of fattening junk food.

2. My husband yells at the computer _____ he gets frustrated with it.

3. _____ I have enjoyed many movies with that actor, I didn't enjoy this one.

4. Ann gives her children their own spending money _____ she wants them to learn to be responsible.

5. _____ the weather was so terrible, the soccer game was canceled.

6. Emma moved to New York _____ she was afraid of living in such a big city.

7. Meghan passed the test _____ she studied all week.

_____ she had to miss tennis practice, it was worth it.

8. Bryan had fun at the basketball game _____ his team lost. He had a great time _____ it was a really exciting game.

9. _____ John enjoys working with people, he still works part-time at the coffee shop _____ he retired from his full-time job years ago.

10. _____ my car wouldn't start, I got to work on time _____ my neighbor gave me a ride.

Directions: Choose the best completions.

Example: While most children in the U.S. start school at age five, Charles _____.

　　　　　a. has a late birthday　　　　　c. went to school in Texas

　　　　　(b.) started school at age six　　　d. had a nice teacher

1. Americans celebrate their Independence Day on July 4th, while Canadians _____.

　　a. speak both French and English　　c. are proud of their country

　　b. celebrate theirs on July 1st　　　　d. gained independence from Britain

2. George drives an old Honda, while Bill drives _____.

　　a. his boss crazy　　　　　　　　　　c. a new Mercedes

　　b. an old Honda too　　　　　　　　　d. too fast

3. While some older people have difficulty with text messaging, most young people _____.

　　a. call their friends often　　　　　　c. can't read their email

　　b. do math　　　　　　　　　　　　　d. send texts quickly and easily

4. While my younger sister _____, my older sister doesn't have any children.

　　a. has two daughters　　　　　　　　c. takes her kids swimming on weekends

　　b. loves children　　　　　　　　　　d. is a college student

5. A gas-powered car uses only gasoline to run the engine, while a hybrid car runs on _____.

　　a. four wheels　　　　　　　　　　　c. cheaper prices

　　b. both gasoline and electric power　　d. freeways

6. One of our new co-workers is from Hawaii, while the other _____.

　　a. doesn't like his job　　　　　　　c. has three children

　　b. is a female　　　　　　　　　　　d. is from Texas

Directions: Match the first half of each sentence to the clause that best completes it.
The first one is done for you as an example.

1. __e__ If Joe's boss doesn't give him a raise,

2. ____ Did you bring your camera? If not,

3. ____ Christine might be late for class

4. ____ If Daniel has to have knee surgery,

5. ____ Are you going to the movies tonight?
   If you are,

6. ____ You should study at the Art Institute

7. ____ If the bank doesn't correct the error
   in my account,

8. ____ If the students have time,

9. ____ Are you going to bring your camera?
   If so,

10. ____ My brother says he will never get
    married. If he does,

11. ____ If we don't leave soon,

12. ____ If Jana does well on the exam,

a. if she forgets to set her phone alarm.

b. she will get into a top university.

c. Bob can take some pictures instead.

d. if you want to learn graphic design.

e. he will look for a new job.

f. I'm going to change banks.

g. please take some pictures of us.

h. he will be in the hospital for a few days.

i. they want to get some coffee before
   class starts.

j. my parents will be very happy.

k. I can give you a ride to the theater.

l. we will be late for the concert.

Directions: Complete each sentence in two ways:

a. Use *so* or *not*.

b. Use a helping verb or main verb *be*.

Examples: Do Erin and Meg like to hike?

a. If __so__ , you should invite them to go hiking with us.

b. If they __do__ , you should invite them to go hiking with us.

1. Does Tom have a car?

   a. If _____ , maybe he can give us a ride.

   b. If he _____ , maybe he can give us a ride.

2. Are you hungry?

   a. If _____ , let's stop for lunch.

   b. If you _____ , let's stop for lunch.

3. Did the kids clean up their room?

   a. If _____ , they should do it before they go outside.

   b. If they _____ , they should do it before they go outside.

4. Is Sam going to the beach tomorrow?

   a. If _____ , he had better be careful that he doesn't get sunburned.

   b. If he _____ , he had better be careful that he doesn't get sunburned.

5. Do Sara and Martin need help with their garden?

   a. If _____ , I can help them next weekend.

   b. If they _____ , I can help them next weekend.

6. Was Yang a good student in high school?

   a. If _____ , he probably didn't like school.

   b. If he _____ , he probably didn't like school.

Directions: Use the given information to complete the sentences.

Examples: Maybe Andy likes his teacher, or maybe he doesn't. It doesn't matter. He has to pass the class.

    a. Andy has to pass the class even if _____*he doesn't like his teacher*_____.

    b. Andy has to pass the class whether or not _____*he likes his teacher*_____.

You probably won't need to get into the house, but maybe you will. If so, I'll give you a key.

    a. I'll give you a house key in case _____*you need to get into the house*_____.

1. Sometimes my four-year-old sister cries a lot. It doesn't matter. My sister is really sweet.

    a. My four-year-old sister is really sweet, even if _____.

2. There might be a traffic jam on the freeway. If there is, you can take Evergreen Way instead.

    a. In case _____,

    you can take Evergreen Way instead.

3. Sometimes the boys have a soccer game three times a week, and sometimes they don't. It doesn't matter. They never get bored.

    a. The boys never get bored playing soccer whether or not _____

    _____.

4. I might not see you tomorrow. If I don't, I'm going to send you an email to remind you about the meeting.

    a. I'm going to send you an email to remind you about the meeting in case _____

    _____.

5. Steve usually gets nine hours of sleep a night. It doesn't matter. He is always tired.

    a. Whether or not _____,

    he is always tired.

6. Maybe they will lower the price, and maybe they won't. I still can't afford a big screen TV.

    a. I can't afford a big screen TV even if _____.

7. Your support doesn't matter to me.

    a. I'm going to move to New York whether _____ or not.

    b. I'm going to move to New York even if _____.

Directions: Complete the sentences with **unless** or **only if**.

Examples: You won't pass the driving test _____*unless*_____ you practice parallel parking.

You will pass the driving test _____*only if*_____ you practice parallel parking.

1. I brush my teeth every morning _____ I get up late. Then I don't have time.

2. _____ you have a passport can you travel to foreign countries.

3. My parents will help me pay my cell phone bill _____ I promise to pay them back later.

4. Students aren't allowed to work in the art studio _____ an instructor is with them.

5. _____ John calls us soon, we'll assume he isn't coming.

6. Faisal can improve his English pronunciation _____ he speaks English often.

7. Our office assistant won't interrupt a manager's meeting _____ he has a good reason.

8. Pat thinks movies are worth watching _____ they have a lot of action.

9. You can have this weekend off _____ you agree to work next weekend.

10. Jim can't buy a new car _____ he gets a loan from the bank.

11. _____ you pass the test will you be able to graduate.

12. You can go to the basketball game _____ you clean your room before you go.

13. I'm going to go to the movies with my sister _____ I have to work late.

14. He can buy a new car _____ he has enough money.

15. My brother is going to run the NYC marathon _____ he trains for it.

Directions: Choose the correct completions.

Example: _____ the experiment was completed, the scientists analyzed their findings.

       a. Now that   b. While   ⓒ As soon as   d. Unless

1. _____ the doctor discovers that the cancer has returned, I will have to have more treatment.

    a. Since   b. If   c. Even though   d. Until

2. We will have to cancel the hike _____ the weather improves by tomorrow.

    a. while   b. because   c. unless   d. as soon as

3. _____ you aren't sure about the correct answer, you should make your best guess.

    a. After   b. Only if   c. Before   d. Even if

4. Lisa can't drive us to the airport _____ her car is in the repair shop.

    a. in case   b. because   c. until   d. by the time

5. My neighbor continues to use a lot of water in her garden _____ there is a water shortage.

    a. even though   b. after   c. as soon as   d. because

6. You have to attend the department meeting _____ you want to. It's important for you to be there.

    a. while   b. in case   c. whether or not   d. after

7. The last day of school is next week. _____ school is out, I won't have to get up early every morning.

    a. Before   b. Even though   c. Unless   d. Once

8. _____ you need to contact me, here is my cell phone number.

    a. In case   b. After   c. While   d. Even if

9. My father will lend me the money for a new car _____ I promise to drive carefully.

    a. unless   b. in case   c. only if   d. though

10. _____ Bob plans to retire next year, his wife doesn't want to retire yet. She will keep working.

    a. When   b. After   c. Only if   d. While

Part A *Directions:* Choose the best completions.

1. If it rains tomorrow, _____.

    a. we don't go to the baseball game

    b. we won't go to the baseball game

2. Are you going to the library? _____, will you please return this book for me?

    a. If so

    b. If not

3. James will be very happy if _____.

    a. he will get a promotion at work

    b. he gets a promotion at work

4. Do you have a flashlight? _____, you can borrow mine.

    a. If you do

    b. If you don't

5. If _____, you can call me tomorrow.

    a. you have any other questions

    b. you didn't have any other questions

Part B *Directions:* Match the first half of each sentence to the clause that best completes it. Write the letter on the line.

1. _____ The flight has been delayed because

2. _____ Even though the tuition is very low,

3. _____ John's flight has been delayed, while

4. _____ I finished reading the book although

5. _____ Kate decided to watch the movie since

a. the quality of the classes and teaching is good.

b. I thought it was poorly written.

c. there is heavy fog at the San Francisco airport.

d. her friends recommended it.

e. Mary's flight is going to leave on time.

Part C *Directions:* Complete the sentences with **whether or not**, **even if**, or **in case**.

1. Joan hangs her coat near the door just _____ she has to leave in a hurry.

2. _____ you don't like her, Margaret is the new club president.

3. I always carry bottled water in my car _____ there's an emergency.

4. John always drives his car to work _____ parking costs a lot.

5. I'm going to the midnight movie _____ my parents don't approve.

Part D *Directions:* Complete the sentences with **unless** or **only if**.

1. _____ the meeting goes late, we will meet you at the restaurant at 6:30 P.M.

2. I won't let you borrow my laptop _____ you promise to delete your files when you are finished.

3. _____ I have problems with my homework will I call you.

4. The project will be completed on time _____ there are no problems with the new design.

5. _____ your library books are returned on time, you will need to pay a fine.

Part E *Directions:* Combine each pair of sentences with the words in parentheses. Add commas where necessary.

1. The term is almost over. Students can look forward to vacation. (*now that*)

   _____

   _____

2. Shelley forgot her sister's birthday. Shelley felt terrible. (*because*)

   _____

   _____

3. We need to repair our tent. If we don't, we can't go camping. (*unless*)

   _____

   _____

4. I may win the lottery. I won't quit my job. (*even if*)

   _____

   _____

5. The workers refused to work on New Year's Eve. The company promised to pay them double their usual wage. (*even though*)

   _____

   _____

Part F *Directions:* Combine each pair of sentences with the words in parentheses. Add commas where necessary.

1. Teresa looked at a lot of college Web sites. Teresa chose the college that she wants to attend. (*after*)

   _____

   _____

2. We were working on the new project. Our boss returned from his vacation on Monday. (*when*)

   _____

   _____

3. Joe gets up tomorrow at 6:00 A.M. Joe will do his exercises. (*as soon as*)

   _____

   _____

4. For her birthday, Martina is going to go out to dinner with her friends. Martina and her friends go dancing at a nightclub. (*before*)

   _____

   _____

5. Kathy will have moved to Texas next week. Kathy's husband returns from his job in South America next month. (*by the time*)

   _____

   _____

Part A *Directions:* Choose the best completions.

1. If my neighbors don't turn down their music, _____.

   a. I'm going to complain to the building manager

   b. I complained to the building manager

2. Do we have any bananas? _____, can you get some when you go to the market?

   a. If so

   b. If not

3. If _____, our boss will be extremely proud.

   a. our department will win an award

   b. our department wins an award

4. Mr. Roddy will come to the sales meeting if _____.

   a. we invited him

   b. we invite him

5. Is Julie driving to Seattle? _____, I will ask her for a ride.

   a. If she is

   b. If she does

Part B *Directions:* Match the first half of each sentence to the clause that best completes it. Write the letter on the line.

1. _____ I think this book is quite interesting, while

2. _____ The flight has been delayed even though

3. _____ The weather this month has been terrible because

4. _____ While the weather this month has been rainy and cold,

5. _____ Since cost at the school is very low,

a. last month it was warm and sunny.

b. more people can take advantage of the class offerings.

c. my brother refused to read it.

d. a wet weather system has moved down from Alaska.

e. there doesn't seem to be any problem with the weather.

Part C *Directions:* Complete the sentences with **whether or not, even if,** or **in case**.

1. Chinese is a fascinating language. _____ I never go to China, I love studying Chinese.

2. _____ you need to call me, here's my number.

3. Susan will leave work at 4:00 P.M. _____ she hasn't finished the product inventory.

4. We will have a picnic in the park _____ it rains.

5. _____ Hiromi gets a low score on the next quiz, she will pass the class.

Part D *Directions:* Complete the sentences with **unless** or **only if**.

1. Christopher likes almost all kinds of ice cream. He dislikes ice cream _____ it contains walnuts.

2. _____ the store accepts credit cards, I will need to borrow some money from you.

3. I will have to retype the entire report _____ I can find the original file on my computer.

4. _____ your shoes are clean can you come into the house.

5. I forgot my key, but my sister can let us into the house _____ she is out with her friends.

Part E *Directions:* Combine each pair of sentences with the words in parentheses. Add commas where necessary.

1. The accountant will re-calculate the taxes. The accountant found an error in the calculations. (*since*)

   _____

   _____

2. The cake recipe was very easy. Patricia read it over three times to make sure that she didn't make any mistakes. (*even though*)

   _____

   _____

3. Maria is going to marry Harry. Maria doesn't really love Harry. (*even if*)

   _____

   _____

4. Sam needs to improve his grades in math and chemistry. If he doesn't, he won't get accepted to medical school. (*unless*)

   _____

   _____

5. Some people enjoy cycling for exercise. Other people enjoy walking briskly for exercise. (*while*)

   _____

   _____

Part F *Directions:* Combine each pair of sentences with the words in parentheses. Add commas where necessary.

1. I pick up my cousin at the airport. I am going to show him the Golden Gate Bridge. *(after)*

_____

_____

2. Maurice was eating lunch in a restaurant. Maurice dropped his napkin on the floor. *(when)*

_____

_____

3. Ann gets over her bad cold. Ann will return to work. *(as soon as)*

_____

_____

4. Mary rinses the food off the dishes. Mary puts the dishes in the dishwasher. *(before)*

_____

_____

5. Ali will have graduated from high school in June. Ali's brother gets married in July. *(by the time)*

_____

_____

Reduction of Adverb Clauses to Modifying Adverbial Phrases

QUIZ 1 **Reducing Time Clauses**   (Charts 18-1 and 18-2)

Directions: Check (✓) the sentences that are grammatically correct.

Examples: _____ Before playing her piano solo, the piano had to be moved to the center of the stage.

_✓_ Before playing her piano solo, Carolyn bowed to the audience.

1. _____ While playing online games, Mike never answers his phone.

2. _____ Meg decided to write a letter to the newspaper after publishing her picture without permission.

3. _____ Before calling the police, Jason's parents tried to reach him on his cell phone.

4. _____ After waiting for the bus in the rain for 30 minutes, it finally arrived.

5. _____ Since embarrassing me in public, I haven't spoken to my ex-boyfriend.

6. _____ After arriving at the scene of the accident, the reporters began asking questions.

7. _____ Beverly learned the truth about Tony's unusual family before agreeing to marry him.

8. _____ While visiting the Statue of Liberty, the wind was blowing hard.

9. _____ Since going on vacation two weeks ago, I haven't checked my email.

10. _____ Before ordering dinner at the restaurant, the waiter asked Maggie if she wanted something to drink.

11. _____ While jogging in the park, it was raining.

12. _____ I went to the movies after I finished cleaning up the house.

13. _____ Since working out, I've lost almost ten pounds!

14. _____ Before leaving for work, I ate breakfast and read the newspaper.

15. _____ After studying for over a week, the test was hard.

Directions: Change the adverb clauses to modifying adverbial phrases if possible.
Write *no change* if it's not possible to reduce the adverb clause.

Examples: While Nathan was chopping wood yesterday, he broke his axe.

While chopping wood yesterday, Nathan broke his axe.

While Nathan was chopping wood yesterday, his mom called him for supper.

no change

1. Since he moved to California a year ago, Harry has been to Disneyland five times.

_____

2. Before Calum left Milwaukee for Toronto, he filled up the gas tank.

_____

3. While I was driving to Boston from New York, my parents were flying to Boston
   from Seattle.

_____

4. Usually after Katherine works an eight-hour shift at the busy department store, she is
   exhausted.

_____

5. While Mary was living in Los Angeles, she often ran into famous people.

_____

6. George has quit his job and started traveling around the world since he won $1,000,000
   on a TV game show.

_____

7. Before Derek picked up his sister at the airport, she called to let him know that she
   had arrived.

_____

8. Mark used to watch videos on his phone while he was waiting for the bus.

_____

9. Jason will do his laundry after he finishes his accounting homework.

_____

10. Before Julie and Jay go to a new restaurant, they always read reviews and look at a
    sample menu online.

_____

Directions: Read each sentence. What is the meaning of the adverbial phrase? Write *because* or *while*.

Example: Flying in economy class, Paul finds it difficult to get comfortable because of his long legs. _____*while*_____

1. Having received Alan's marriage proposal, Sue told all her friends that she was getting married. _____

2. Standing in a long line at the post office, Betty surfed the Web on her phone to pass the time. _____

3. Working on his quiz, Ken found that his pen had run out of ink. He had to borrow one from a classmate. _____

4. Being over six feet tall, Sam is always asked to try out for the basketball team.

_____

5. Knowing the basics of plumbing and electrical wiring, Carla saves a lot of money by doing her own home repairs. _____

QUIZ 4 **Reducing Clauses with *While* and *Because*** (Charts 18-3 and 18-4)

Directions: Combine each pair of sentences. Change the first sentence to a modifying phrase if possible. Use *because* or *while* where needed.

Example: Henry was studying at the library. He turned off his cell phone.
_____*While studying at the library, Henry turned off his cell phone.*_____

1. Phoebe is a talented singer. She often sings in local coffee houses on weekends.

_____

2. Christine was ice-skating with her son. She fell and broke her ankle.

_____

3. Andy was unable to finish writing his report at the office. He took it home with him.

_____

4. Fighting fires is a very demanding job. Firefighters have to be in excellent physical condition.

_____

5. The college administrators were attending a seminar on Friday. They discussed goals for the coming year.

_____

Directions: Combine these sentences using ***upon + -ing***.

Example: Jeff received the good news about his new job. Jeff immediately called his family.

Upon receiving the good news about his new job, Jeff immediately called his family.

1. The teachers heard that the meeting was canceled. They were very happy.

   _____

2. Maya passed her driving test. She breathed a sigh of relief.

   _____

3. The actor received an award for her performance. She gave a brief acceptance speech.

   _____

4. Tom found a gold coin in the sand at the beach. He couldn't believe his good luck.

   _____

5. Margaret Peters was elected mayor of the city. She set up a committee to study the traffic problems.

   _____

6. Tina had her sixth baby. She said, "I think this will be my last one."

   _____

7. The plumber was fired from his job. He filed a complaint with his workers' union.

   _____

8. Mrs. Alexander returned from a trip to Ecuador. She started a small business that sold Ecuadorean handicrafts.

   _____

Directions: Change the adverb clauses into modifying adverbial phrases.

Example: After James lost his wallet, he was much more careful with his things.

After losing his wallet, James was much more careful with his things.

1. While Joe was lying in bed feeling depressed, he wondered what he should do about his problems.

   _____

2. When Jane arrives in London, she will have afternoon tea at the Ritz Hotel.

   _____

3. Because Billy had no money to buy a present for his mother, he made her a birthday card.

   _____

4. After the research scientists test the drug on mice, they will test the drug on monkeys.

   _____

5. Since Alex took a course in public speaking, he has developed more self-confidence.

   _____

6. While Susan was working in her garden, she disturbed a wasp's nest and was stung several times.

   _____

7. Because Carol was confused about the directions to the party, she had to stop at a gas station to ask for help.

   _____

8. Before Brian left for India, he had to get several shots to protect him from tropical diseases.

   _____

9. While Omar was talking with his accountant, he realized that starting his own business would be quite complicated.

   _____

10. When Louis tasted Mrs. Wilson's blueberry pie, he said that it was the most delicious pie he had ever eaten.

    _____

CHAPTER 18 – TEST 1

Part A *Directions:* Change the adverb clauses to modifying adverbial phrases if possible. If not possible, write *no change*.

Cleaning

1. While John was cleaning out his garage, he found some old photos.

   _____

   _____

2. After John cleaned out the garage, Mary reorganized the shelves and cabinets.

   _____

   _____

3. Before Mary threw anything away, she consulted with John to make sure it was OK.

   _____

   _____

4. Since they moved into their house in 2010, Mary and John have gotten a lot of furniture.

   _____

   _____

5. After John and Mary finished their work in the garage, they drank some cold sodas.

   _____

   _____

Part B *Directions:* Check (✓) the sentences that are grammatically correct.

1. _____ Upon hearing about the earthquake in Japan, everyone turned on the international news channel.

2. _____ Needing money to pay the rent, Scott asked his brother for a loan.

3. _____ Before making coffee in the morning, the beans must be ground.

4. _____ Not trusting her children at home alone, Mrs. Jones hired a babysitter to stay with them.

5. _____ After having sung the baby a lullaby, she finally fell asleep in my arms.

6. _____ Jesse has been working hard since starting his new job last month.

Part C *Directions:* Combine each pair of sentences. Change the first sentence to a modifying phrase if possible.

1. I didn't want to interrupt your meeting. I left a message with your secretary.

   _____

   _____

2. Mr. Santos became a citizen. Afterward, he registered to vote.

   _____

   _____

3. George was on a ladder changing a light bulb. Suddenly, his dog ran by and knocked the ladder over.

   _____

   _____

4. First the doctor explained the medical procedure. Then the doctor asked if the patient had any questions.

   _____

   _____

5. Mrs. Nguyen was a single mom with three children. She had to work at two jobs to support her family.

   _____

   _____

Part A *Directions:* Change the adverb clauses to modifying adverbial phrases if possible. If not possible, write *no change*.

Joe's Car

1. Since Joe had a car accident last summer, he had to ride his bike to work.

_____

_____

2. While Joe was riding to work every day, he was dreaming about buying a new car.

_____

_____

3. Before Joe bought a new car, his sister helped him do some research on the Internet.

_____

_____

4. While Joe's sister was searching for information, she found two cars that she thought would interest him.

_____

_____

5. After Joe read all the articles that his sister had found for him, he chose which car he wanted.

_____

_____

Part B *Directions:* Check (✓) the sentences that are grammatically correct.

1. _____ Unable to eat the large hamburger, it got cold on my plate.

2. _____ Being interested in psychology, my sister subscribes to three psychology magazines.

3. _____ After receiving an award for his writing, the novelist signed copies of his newest book.

4. _____ Listening to the governor's speech, she impressed us with her energy and intelligence.

5. _____ Upon hearing about her husband's death in battle, the young soldier's wife began to sob.

6. _____ After giving the interesting lecture, the students thanked the visiting professor.

Part C *Directions:* Combine each pair of sentences. Change the first sentence to a modifying phrase if possible.

  1. My brother was playing basketball with his friends. He fell and sprained his ankle.

  _____

  _____

  2. Sam read a book about sharks. Since then, he has been afraid to swim in the ocean.

  _____

  _____

  3. First, Paul finished his homework assignment. Then he was free to watch TV for the rest of the evening.

  _____

  _____

  4. Luisa didn't receive a package that her brother sent. She contacted the post office about tracking it.

  _____

  _____

  5. George graduated from the university with a degree in French history. He has been looking for a job in education.

  _____

  _____

CHAPTER 19

Connectives That Express Cause and Effect, Contrast, and Condition

QUIZ 1 Identifying Connecting Words for Cause/Effect, Contrast and Condition   (Chart 19-1)

Directions: Underline the connecting words in each sentence. Then choose what type of connecting words they are.

Example: Julian spends a lot of time practicing guitar <u>because</u> he wants to play in a band.

          (a.) adverb clause   b. transition   c. conjunction   d. preposition

1. Carmen was worried about poor children in her city, so she started an after-school program to help them.

   a. adverb clause   b. transition   c. conjunction   d. preposition

2. Carmen was worried about poor children in her city. Therefore, she started an after-school program to help them.

   a. adverb clause   b. transition   c. conjunction   d. preposition

3. Due to his illness, Bernard has missed almost three weeks of work.

   a. adverb clause   b. transition   c. conjunction   d. preposition

4. Bernard has been sick, so he has missed almost three weeks of work.

   a. adverb clause   b. transition   c. conjunction   d. preposition

5. Even though I don't like to exercise, I try to go to the gym regularly.

   a. adverb clause   b. transition   c. conjunction   d. preposition

6. I don't like to exercise, but I try to go to the gym regularly anyway.

   a. adverb clause   b. transition   c. conjunction   d. preposition

7. Since my brother really likes art, he goes to the art museum at least once a year.

   a. adverb clause   b. transition   c. conjunction   d. preposition

8. Because of his love of art, my brother goes to the art museum at least once a year.

   a. adverb clause   b. transition   c. conjunction   d. preposition

9. My niece couldn't get a visa to work in Italy. Consequently, she went to Korea to teach English.

   a. adverb clause   b. transition   c. conjunction   d. preposition

10. Because my niece couldn't get a visa to work in Italy, she went to Korea to teach English.

    a. adverb clause   b. transition   c. conjunction   d. preposition

Directions: Complete the sentences with either *because* or *because of*.

Examples: Sam is excited _____*because*_____ he has been accepted to Colorado

State University. Marcia decided not to send the package express mail

_____*because of*_____ the high cost of postage.

1. _____ its favorable climate, southeast Washington is a rich agricultural area.

2. It takes Peter two hours to get home from work _____ he lives on Staten Island.

3. I am looking for a new job _____ changes in leadership at my workplace.

4. _____ our apartment is on the fourth floor of the building, we get a lot of exercise going up and down the stairs.

5. Alexa can go online almost anywhere _____ the wireless capabilities of her smartphone.

6. Some types of animals are dying out _____ changes in the environment.

7. Mr. Anderson worries about his elderly neighbor _____ she lives alone.

8. _____ the lack of parking at my job, I have to arrive at work early to find a place to park.

9. Chuck is curious about Olivia's family _____ she talks about them all the time.

10. Josh dislikes most Mexican food _____ it's too spicy and upsets his stomach.

11. Janet took some cough medicine _____ her cold.

12. Carlos is upset _____ he lost his cell phone on vacation.

13. _____ the main highway is closed, we're going to take another road.

14. School is canceled today _____ the snow.

15. _____ Robert is overweight, his doctor told him he should exercise regularly.

Directions: Complete the sentences with the ideas in parentheses.

Example: (*The wind was blowing hard.*) Our plane couldn't take off due to

_____ *the strong wind* _____ .

1. (*The weather was bad.*) The Wilsons had to cancel the picnic because of _____

_____ .

2. (*Sarah had a fever.*) Due to _____ ,

Sarah stayed home from school yesterday.

3. (*Marie has car problems.*) Marie had to take the bus to work today due to _____

_____ .

4. (*My mother is very ill.*) Because of _____ ,

I have to fly home tonight.

5. (*The snow was deep.*) Due to the fact that _____ ,

many roads were closed.

6. (*I have an 8:00 A.M. appointment tomorrow.*) Due to _____

_____ , I am going to bed early tonight.

7. (*Mark has a toothache.*) Mark is going to the dentist tomorrow because of _____

_____ .

8. (*Caffeine bothers Shelley.*) Shelley has stopped drinking coffee due to _____

_____ .

9. (*Carl is lazy.*) I am not very patient with Carl due to the fact that _____ .

10. (*There have been many advances in medicine.*) Because of

_____ , new treatments for a variety of diseases

have been developed.

Directions: Punctuate the sentences. Add capital letters if necessary.

Example: Jerry wants to go to medical school so he is studying hard for entrance exams.

Jerry wants to go to medical school, so he is studying hard for entrance exams.

1. My coffee got cold so I reheated it in the microwave.

2. Fish was on sale at the market therefore Pat bought three fillets to have for dinner.

3. Andrea was upset that her favorite team was losing the match so she turned off the TV.

4. The regular radio announcer had a sore throat consequently another announcer was on the program.

5. Electricity, water, and gas are getting more expensive people therefore are trying to conserve energy.

6. My little sister dropped my glasses and cracked a lens so I had to replace it.

7. Jason really enjoyed reading stories by Tom Miller consequently he was excited when one of them was made into a movie.

8. Khanh speaks English every day therefore his pronunciation is improving.

9. The supervisor gave her employees a lot of freedom in doing their work consequently they liked working for her.

10. My doctor didn't have the right equipment for the medical test I needed he therefore sent me to a specialist.

Directions: Combine the ideas by using the words in parentheses.

Example: The spring weather was too cold. My tomato plants didn't grow. (*because of*)

_____ *Because of the cold spring weather, my tomato plants didn't grow.* _____ OR

_____ *My tomato plants didn't grow because of the cold spring weather.* _____

1. The chicken was left in the oven too long. The meat was dry and chewy. (*so*)

   _____

2. My husband doesn't like lima beans. We never eat them. (*because*)

   _____

3. The economy is weak. Many citizens are unhappy with the government. (*due to*)

   _____

4. A new book by Maggie's favorite author was just published. Maggie bought it
   immediately. (*consequently*)

   _____

5. The manager has a cold. The meeting is canceled. (*therefore*)

   _____

6. There is damage from the windstorm. Many people have joined in the cleanup. (*because of*)

   _____

7. Hannah loves sweets. She has gained back all the weight she lost. (*consequently*)

   _____

8. Jason dropped his cell phone in the swimming pool. His cell phone stopped working.
   (*therefore*)

   _____

9. It was very late. We decided not to go out for coffee after the play. (*due to*)

   _____

10. We didn't have any milk. We used ice cream in our coffee instead. (*because*)

    _____

Directions: Complete the sentences with **such** or **so**.

Example: Adam was ___*so*___ hungry that he ate four pieces of pizza.

1. My desk is _____ a mess that I can't find anything!

2. Christopher laughed _____ hard that he got tears in his eyes.

3. Harry has _____ little money that he can't buy groceries until he gets paid.

4. It was _____ a crazy idea that we wanted to try it.

5. James ate _____ much cake that his stomach hurt.

6. Mr. Schafer is _____ forgetful that he often leaves his glasses at home.

7. The salesclerk brought out _____ an ugly dress that I didn't even want to try it on.

8. My neighbor has _____ a big dog that small children are afraid of it at first.

QUIZ 7 Cause and Effect: *Such … That* and *So … That*   (Chart 19-5)

Directions: Make new sentences using **such … that** or **so … that** by combining the ideas. Make all necessary changes.

Example: David was very tired. He fell asleep immediately after he went to bed.

_____*David was so tired that he fell asleep immediately after he went to bed.*_____

1. Mike's motorcycle is loud. The neighbors have complained about the noise.

   _____

2. It was a heavy desk. We needed three people to move it.

   _____

3. The weather in June was cold. We had to wear our winter sweaters.

   _____

4. The store has dirty windows. We can hardly see inside.

   _____

5. The Sunday paper has great comics. Nick reads them every week.

   _____

6. Patrick ate too much chocolate ice cream. He got a stomachache.

   _____

Directions: Combine the ideas by using *so that*.

Example: Max bought a bicycle. He wanted to be able to have cheap transportation.

Max bought a bicycle so that he would have cheap transportation.

1. I have a part-time job. I want to be able to afford to go to college.

_____

2. Jim will take the bus to the airport. He wants to make sure he doesn't have to pay for parking.

_____

3. The mechanics at Sam's Garage do careful work. They want to make sure their customers come again.

_____

4. Frank and Joan took a parenting class. They wanted to learn more about children.

_____

5. The music director stood on a podium. He wanted to be able to see all of the musicians.

_____

Directions: Add *that* to the sentence if *so* means *in order that*. If *so* means *therefore*, add a comma.

Examples: I set my alarm clock for 6:30 so I wouldn't oversleep.

I set my alarm clock for 6:30 so⌃ I wouldn't oversleep.
that

James didn't know the person on the phone so he hung up.
James didn't know the person on the phone, so he hung up.

1. Fahad doesn't enjoy video games so he rarely plays them.

2. Rob practices kung fu three times a week so he can stay in shape.

3. I need to use the spelling checker so I don't have spelling mistakes in my emails.

4. Meg is going to be gone on vacation for three months so a temporary worker will replace her.

5. Miki texts her parents in Japan almost every day so they won't worry about her while she's in the U.S.

Directions: Complete the sentences with *but, even though, nevertheless,* or *despite*. Pay close attention to the given punctuation and capitalization.

Examples: The children are very tired, _____*but*_____ they don't want to go to bed.

The children don't want to go to bed _____*even though*_____ they are very tired.

The children are very tired. _____*Nevertheless*_____, they don't want to go to bed.

The children don't want to go to bed _____*despite*_____ the fact that they are very tired.

1. The sun is shining, _____ it is still cold outside.

2. Ken studies English hard. _____, he has weak English conversation skills.

3. The chocolate cake tasted terrible _____ it looked delicious.

4. Mark had to work until he finished the report _____ he was tired and wanted to go home.

5. _____ the fact that Roberto had his car repaired last week, it is still not running smoothly.

6. The University of Washington offered Greg a great scholarship. _____, he decided to go to a different university.

7. _____ I am interested in the space program, I was bored by the astronaut's speech.

8. The vacation was more expensive than we had planned, _____ we decided to go anyway.

9. _____ his busy schedule, Ali still found time to coach his son's baseball team.

10. Millions of dollars have been spent on cancer research. _____, scientists have not found a cure for the disease.

Directions: Add commas, periods, and capital letters as necessary. Do not add, omit, or change any words.

Example: In spite of the terrible weather Mark went for a three-mile run.

In spite of the terrible weather, Mark went for a three-mile run.

1. I wasn't really hungry but I ate lunch anyway.

2. Even though Emily skipped breakfast she still has a lot of energy.

3. Mr. Kwan is a rich man nevertheless he refuses to buy his daughter a new car.

4. In spite of the high cost of postage Omar sends a package overseas every week.

5. Rosanne really wanted to learn to drive yet she was too young to get a driver's license.

6. Helen always talks about losing weight she constantly snacks however.

7. Although Jamaal grew up in San Francisco he prefers living in Oakland.

8. Despite the fact that Anthony had already lost two cell phones his parents gave him another one.

9. Edward doesn't like to smoke nonetheless he sometimes smokes a cigar with his business partners.

10. Pat was the most qualified person for the job however the company hired someone else.

11. Despite the fact that she studied for hours Monica failed the exam.

12. Sean has a fear of heights nevertheless he enjoys skydiving.

13. Although it's the middle of December it's very warm today.

14. In spite of the storm that was approaching we still started our morning jog.

15. Even though I don't like to swim I love going to the beach in the summer.

Directions: Read the information about car camping and backpacking. Using that information, write sentences with the given words to show direct contrast. Pay attention to punctuation and capitalization. Answers will vary.

People who car camp ...	People who backpack ...
can take whatever they want with them.	have to pack light.
pack everything into their cars.	carry everything on their backs.
usually camp in a campground they can drive to.	have to hike into the camp area.
often like meeting other campers.	often enjoy getting away from crowds.
can enjoy fresh food prepared in camp.	eat dried and canned foods in camp.
often take their pets along.	rarely take their pets with them.

Example: (*while*) _____ People who car camp can take whatever they want with them, while people who backpack have to pack light._

1. (*but*) _____

_____

2. (*on the other hand*) _____

_____

3. (*while*) _____

_____

4. (*however*) _____

_____

5. (*on the other hand*) _____

_____

Directions: Make sentences with the same meaning by using ***otherwise***.

Example: If we don't turn on the heat, we'll get cold.

We should turn on the heat. Otherwise, we'll get cold.

1. If Maria doesn't study for her quiz, she won't get a good grade.

   _____

2. If I don't find my passport, I won't be able to cross the border.

   _____

3. Unless you have a reservation, you can't get a table for dinner.

   _____

4. If Kathleen's flight from the Philippines doesn't arrive on time, she will miss her connecting flight to Boston.

   _____

Directions: Create sentences with the same meaning by using ***or (else)***.

Example: If I don't eat more fresh vegetables, I will get sick.

I had better eat more fresh vegetables, or else I will get sick.

1. If our teacher doesn't remember students' names, the whole class laughs.

   _____

2. If Dan doesn't work hard, the repairs on the house won't get finished by winter.

   _____

3. Mark can't afford a car unless he saves money every month.

   _____

4. If Beth doesn't get a new car license, she'll get a ticket.

   _____

Part A *Directions:* Combine ideas by using the words in parentheses.

1. The sweater Jane bought has a hole in it. She needs to return it to the store. (*so*)

_____

_____

2. The traffic on Highway 101 was jammed. We took Highway 280 instead. (*therefore*)

_____

_____

3. Ron was late for work for the third time. He was fired from his job. (*because*)

_____

_____

4. Bill injured his lower back. He can't lift heavy objects. (*due to*)

_____

_____

5. The Mars *Rover* has many cameras. Scientists on Earth can see photos of Mars. (*consequently*)

_____

_____

Part B *Directions:* Complete each sentence with a word or expression from the box. Pay attention to punctuation and capitalization. Use each word or expression one time only. More than one answer may be possible.

but	even though	nevertheless
despite	in spite of the fact that	

1. Jack had planned to go to the theater, _____ he got sick and had to go to the hospital.

2. _____ I don't eat much meat at home, I enjoy going out for burgers occasionally.

3. I'm going out tonight _____ I'm exhausted.

4. Sue promised she could keep a secret. _____, she told everyone about my problems.

5. _____ being in a wheelchair, Jerry was a fantastic basketball player.

Part C *Directions:* Complete the sentences with *such* or *so*.

1. Mary was _____ late that she missed the first half hour of the movie.

2. James is _____ a liar that no one believes anything he says.

3. Many people in the world are _____ poor that they don't get enough to eat.

4. Tom always checks his dictionary _____ that he spells words correctly.

5. This is _____ a good book that I can't put it down!

Part D *Directions:* Complete each sentence with a word or expression from the list. Pay attention to punctuation and capitalization. Use each word or expression one time only. More than one answer may be possible.

| although | because of | even though | otherwise | such |
| because | despite the fact | nevertheless | so | while |

1. I like to cook, but I hate cleaning up because I always make _____ a mess in the kitchen.

2. _____ my mother doesn't understand Italian, she loves listening to Italian opera, especially when the singer is Luciano Pavarotti.

3. The typhoon caused some damage to our house _____ that we boarded up the windows and doors.

4. Lina had to retire from her job as a medical technologist _____ problems with her hips.

5. _____ most students are motivated and care about their grades, there are others who are lazy and don't care at all.

6. The archeologist's primary research took place in Nepal _____ he doesn't like being in the mountains.

7. The thunder during last night's storm was _____ loud that my children got really scared.

8. _____ Jordan is interested in sea animals, he got a part-time job at the Monterey Aquarium.

9. Tim's boss had warned him that he might lose his job. _____, Tim was shocked when he got fired.

10. We had better get a new car soon. _____, we'll get stuck somewhere when this one breaks down.

Part E *Directions:* Combine ideas by using the words in parentheses.

1. Mary speaks Chinese and Japanese. Her sister Linda speaks Spanish and French.

   (*while*) _____

   _____

2. Botanists study plants and plant life. Zoologists study the animal kingdom.

   (*on the other hand*) _____

   _____

3. I really wanted to go to New York. I decided that the trip would be too expensive.

   (*but*) _____

   _____

4. My wife is always telling me we need to save money. She spends as much money as she
   wants. (*however*) _____

   _____

Part A *Directions:* Combine ideas by using the words in parentheses.

1. Sally doesn't like the crowds at the shopping center. She usually shops online.

   (*because*) _____

   _____

2. I am an optimist, and my husband is a pessimist. We sometimes disagree.

   (*therefore*) _____

   _____

3. The house is now in bad condition. The previous owners never took care of it.

   (*consequently*) _____

   _____

4. There have been many construction delays. The subway line will not open on time.

   (*because of*) _____

   _____

5. Isaac majored in engineering. His father pressured him to do so

   (*due to*) _____

   _____

Part B *Directions:* Complete each sentence with a word or expression from the box. Pay attention to punctuation and capitalization. Use each word or expression one time only. More than one answer may be possible.

although	however	yet
despite the fact that	in spite of	

1. _____ it's raining, we're going out for a walk.

2. Elvira has a high-stress job, _____ she still likes it a lot.

3. My boss told me I was going to get a raise this year. _____, when I asked him about it, he didn't remember saying that.

4. Murray has a very loud voice. I like spending time with him _____ his annoying voice.

5. Playing games on a computer by myself is entertaining. _____ it's not as much fun as playing online with other people.

Part C *Directions:* Complete the sentences with *such* or *so*.

1. Last term I had _____ little time between classes that I never had time for lunch.

2. Our restaurant is doing _____ well that we need to hire another waiter.

3. We had a big meeting last week. It was _____ an important meeting that the entire staff attended.

4. Robert bought a new car _____ that he would get better gas mileage.

5. Tom has _____ poor keyboarding skills that it takes him a long time to type anything on the computer.

Part D *Directions:* Complete each sentence with a word or expression from the box. Pay attention to punctuation and capitalization. Use each word or expression one time only. More than one answer may possible.

| because | even though | in spite of | on the other hand | so |
| due to | however | nonetheless | otherwise | such |

1. Amy had two cups of coffee this morning. _____, she is still sleepy and is almost falling asleep at her desk.

2. School has been canceled today _____ the extremely hot weather.

3. I am _____ angry that I feel like steam is coming out of my ears.

4. _____ Lynn has to finish her research paper this weekend, she can't go out with her friends.

5. Many American high school students plan to study at a university _____ high tuition costs.

6. The swimmer had tried to make the Olympic team before. On his third attempt, _____, he finally succeeded.

7. My psychology professor was _____ a boring teacher that I often skipped class.

8. Teenagers should listen to music at a reasonable volume. _____, they might have some hearing loss.

9. _____ the government has been studying nuclear power for years, no one has discovered a way to make it completely safe.

10. My neighbor has two dogs and a canary. _____, I don't have any pets.

Part E *Directions:* Combine ideas by using the words in parentheses.

1. Terry is very shy and quiet in class. Hannah is outgoing and very talkative with classmates. (*on the other hand*) _____

_____

2. Jan is interested in current events and listens to the news every day. Art never listens to the news and doesn't care much about what's happening in the world.

(*however*) _____

_____

3. Mount McKinley, in Alaska, is the highest peak in North America. Aconcagua, in Argentina, is the highest mountain in South America and the Western Hemisphere.

(*while*) _____

_____

4. Coffee is made from roasted and ground beans that grow on bushes. Tea is made from the leaves and flowers of a variety of plants.

(*but*) _____

_____

CHAPTER 20

Conditional Sentences and Wishes

Real Conditionals in the Present or Future   (Chart 20-2)

Directions: Decide if the sentence expresses a habitual activity, a fact / general truth, or a future activity / situation.

Examples: If we have time, we will go to the bookstore.

   a. a habitual activity   b. a fact / general truth   ⓒ a future activity / situation

   If we have time, we go to the bookstore.

   a. a habitual activity   ⓑ a fact / general truth   c. a future activity / situation

1. If Melissa passes a shoe store, she usually stops to look at shoes.

   a. a habitual activity   b. a fact / general truth   c. a future activity / situation

2. In most countries, if you are 18, you can get a driver's license.

   a. a habitual activity   b. a fact / general truth   c. a future activity / situation

3. If my parents visit this weekend, we are going to go to the rose garden in the park.

   a. a habitual activity   b. a fact / general truth   c. a future activity / situation

4. If I see a car accident, I always call the police right away.

   a. a habitual activity   b. a fact / general truth   c. a future activity / situation

5. Children are more successful in school if they learn to read at an early age.

   a. a habitual activity   b. a fact / general truth   c. a future activity / situation

6. If clothes fit well, they look good on the person wearing them.

   a. a habitual activity   b. a fact / general truth   c. a future activity / situation

7. Chris will be pleased if he finds a good job in Shanghai.

   a. a habitual activity   b. a fact / general truth   c. a future activity / situation

8. Jenny takes a nap in the afternoon if she's tired.

   a. a habitual activity   b. a fact / general truth   c. a future activity / situation

9. If the plane arrives on time, I will be amazed.

   a. a habitual activity   b. a fact / general truth   c. a future activity / situation

10. My brother usually gets upset if someone interrupts him.

   a. a habitual activity   b. a fact / general truth   c. a future activity / situation

Directions: Choose the correct verb for the result clause. Both answers may be correct.

Example: If Ann is late for work, she ((feels) / (will feel)) embarrassed and upset.

1. If Jill is hungry after school, she usually (*eats* / *will eat*) some cheese and crackers.

2. If you exercise regularly, you (*don't gain* / *won't gain*) weight.

3. If Jack needs money for college next year, he (*borrows* / *will borrow*) some from his aunt.

4. If my bills are due, I always (*pay* / *will pay*) them on time.

5. If it's cloudy and rainy tomorrow, I (*feel* / *will feel*) depressed.

Directions: Complete the sentences with the verbs in parentheses to express a future or habitual meaning.

Example: If the weather is good next Saturday, we (*go*) _____*will go*_____ shopping at the flea market.

1. In Seattle, if the sun is shining, most people usually (*wear*) _____ sunglasses.

2. If I should see you after I get home from work tomorrow, I (*pay*) _____ you the money I owe you.

3. If Sarah isn't feeling well, she always (*stay*) _____ home from work.

4. If children are late for school every day, the teacher (*call*) _____ their parents.

5. If I have enough time, I (*wash*) _____ my clothes later tonight.

Directions: Complete the sentences with present unreal conditionals using the verbs in parentheses.

Examples: If my mother (*know*) _____knew_____ the truth, she would be upset.

If Philip were here, he (*enjoy*) _____would enjoy_____ this program very much.

1. If Jack (*be*) _____ a lawyer, he would be in court every week.

2. If I could fly, I (*enjoy*) _____ seeing the world from above.

3. I would go to the beach, if I (*have, not*) _____ to work today.

4. If my computer stopped working, I (*be, not*) _____ able to finish my essay.

5. If we (*understand*) _____ our teacher better, studying would be easier.

6. Rush-hour traffic (*be*) _____ terrible if the city were bigger.

7. If eating in restaurants (*be, not*) _____ so expensive, Sarah and

   Nick (*eat*) _____ out more often.

8. If Paul (*live*) _____ far away, we (*see, not*) _____

   each other so often.

Directions: Complete the sentences with present or future conditionals using the verbs in parentheses. Some are real and some are unreal.

Examples: If Richard goes to the hardware store, he (*buy*) _____will buy_____ some
   light bulbs.

If Richard went to the hardware store, he (*buy*) _____would buy_____ some
   light bulbs.

1. My car is low on gas. If I run out of gas on the way to the gas station,

   I (*call*) _____ you.

2. Jim is moving to a new apartment. He would tell us if he

   (*need*) _____ help.

3. If the repairman (*come, not*) _____ this afternoon, I'll call the electric

   company again.

4. I'm worried about Sue. She's not usually late. If she called,

   I (*feel*) _____ better.

5. If Marie (*receive*) _____ an email, she always answers it promptly.

6. If I (*be*) _____ you, I (*be*) _____ angry about

   the broken window.

Directions: Underline the clause that expresses a condition. Write "R" (real conditional) next to statements that express a true idea or "U" (unreal conditional) next to statements that express an untrue idea. Then decide if the verb has a present / future or past meaning.

1. _____R_____ <u>If the coffee is ready</u>, we will drink it.   ⟨present / future⟩   past

2. _____U_____ <u>If the car had started</u>, I would have driven.   present / future   ⟨past⟩

3. _____ If children are scared, they cry.   present / future   past

4. _____ The police would have come if we had called.   present / future   past

5. _____ If Rebecca is tired, she goes to bed early.   present / future   past

6. _____ If the dogs had stopped barking, I would have slept.   present / future   past

---

Directions: Answer the questions.

Example: If I had been hungry, I would have eaten breakfast.

      a. Was I hungry? _____no_____

      b. Did I eat breakfast? _____no_____

1. If I were rich, I would quit my job and move to an island in the Caribbean.

    a. Am I rich? _____

    b. Have I quit my job? _____

    c. Have I moved to an island in the Caribbean? _____

2. Susan wouldn't listen to country and western music if she didn't like it.

    a. Does Susan like country and western music? _____

    b. Does Susan listen to country and western music? _____

3. If Javier had thought carefully about the assignment, he wouldn't have had trouble with it.

    a. Did Javier think carefully about the assignment? _____

    b. Did Javier have trouble with the assignment? _____

4. Alicia would have avoided the traffic jam if she had listened to the traffic report before leaving home.

    a. Did Alicia get stuck in a traffic jam? _____

    b. Did Alicia listen to the traffic report? _____

5. If I didn't have a job, I would be poor.

    a. Do I have a job? _____

    b. Am I poor? _____

Directions: Complete the sentences with past conditionals using the verbs in parentheses.

Examples: If my mother (*know*) _____*had known*_____ the truth, she would have been upset.

If Philip had been there, he (*enjoy*) _____*would have enjoyed*_____ the program very much.

1. If the doctors (*find*) _____ the problem sooner, Marie wouldn't have gotten so sick.

2. If our team hadn't won the championship game, we (*be*) _____ disappointed.

3. The runner (*win*) _____ the race if she hadn't hurt her foot.

4. If Joseph (*bring, not*) _____ his guitar, he would have played the piano instead.

5. If Jorge had been honest with me before, I (*trust*) _____ him.

6. My cell phone battery (*die, not*) _____ if I had brought my charger with me.

7. If Maya (*want*) _____ to call you last night, I (*give*) _____ her your number.

8. Ahmed (*drive, not*) _____ so fast yesterday if it (*be, not*) _____ an emergency.

9. When we were at the party last weekend, if I (*be*) _____ in your situation, I don't know what I (*do*) _____.

10. I bought a motorcycle. If I (*have*) _____ more money, I (*buy*) _____ a car instead.

Directions: Complete the sentences with conditionals using the verbs in parentheses. Pay attention to the tense.

Examples: If it (*be*) _____*is*_____ windy this weekend, we (*go*) _____*will go*_____ sailing.

If it (*be*) _____*were*_____ windy now, we (*go*) _____*would go*_____ sailing.

If it (*be*) _____*had been*_____ windy yesterday, we (*go*) _____*would have gone*_____ sailing.

1. It's a beautiful day. If the weather (*stay*) _____ warm,

   I (*work*) _____ in my garden later this afternoon.

2. I'm not invisible. If I (*be*) _____ invisible, I (*enjoy*) _____

   surprising people.

3. If William (*stay, not*) _____ up so late last night,

   he (*be, not*) _____ late for class this morning.

4. You are so unhappy at work. I (*quit*) _____ my job if

   I (*hate*) _____ mine as much as you hate yours.

5. I fell down and hurt my knee. It got really swollen. My knee

   (*get, not*) _____ so swollen if I (*put*) _____ ice on it

   right away.

6. If we (*have, not*) _____ cell phones, communication

   (*be, not*) _____ so easy.

7. If Mika (*need*) _____ a ride to the gym tomorrow, she

   (*call*) _____ me.

8. I always carry my umbrella, so if it (*rain*) _____,

   I (*get, not*) _____ wet.

9. If Ron (*send*) _____ an email to all employees last week, they

   (*know*) _____ that the corporate executives were coming.

10. I'm exhausted. If I (*be, not*) _____ so tired, I (*watch*) _____

    a movie.

Directions: Complete each sentence with an appropriate auxiliary verb.

Examples: Sue doesn't live in New York, but if she _____*did*_____, she would see Broadway shows often.

We already ate dinner, but if we _____*hadn't*_____, we would have asked you for a snack.

1. I don't have a pair of scissors with me, but if I _____, I would cut the label off my jeans.

2. Alexander already finished his homework, but if he _____, he wouldn't have gone to his friend's house.

3. I have to go to an appointment at 3:00, but if I _____, I'd have coffee with you.

4. Paul doesn't like classical music, but if he _____, he would go to the symphony.

5. My brother is already married, but if he _____, I would try to find him a wife.

6. We didn't go to Las Vegas, but if we _____, I'm sure we would have loved it.

7. I haven't finished that book yet, but if I _____, I would lend it to you.

8. We aren't vegetarians, but if we _____, we wouldn't eat meat.

9. Mr. Lee is a good salesman, but if he _____, his sales numbers wouldn't be so high.

10. Ted and Nadia don't have any kids, but if they _____, they wouldn't be able to travel so much.

Directions: Complete the sentences with the correct form of the verbs. Make conditional statements.

Example: It's raining. I can't hang the laundry outside to dry.

If it _____*weren't raining*_____, I could hang the laundry outside to dry.

1. Shhh! The baby is sleeping. We have to be quiet.

   If the baby _____, we wouldn't have to be quiet.

2. Since Hank isn't using his tablet computer, I'll borrow it.

   If Hank _____ his tablet computer, I wouldn't borrow it.

3. Chieko's mom was talking on the phone. She didn't smell the pizza burning.

   If Chieko's mom _____ on the phone, she would have smelled the pizza burning.

4. Clara graduated from the university two months ago, but she isn't looking for a job yet.

   Clara's parents would be happy if she _____ for a job.

5. Fatima went to the museum last weekend, but she left after 30 minutes. She wasn't enjoying the exhibit.

   If Fatima _____ the exhibit, she wouldn't have left so soon.

6. You were sleeping, so you didn't hear the news about the big fire downtown.

   If you _____, you would have heard about the fire.

7. The wind is blowing so hard. We can't go skiing.

   If the wind _____ so hard, we could go skiing.

8. I was studying late last night. I overslept this morning.

   If I _____ late last night, I wouldn't have overslept this morning.

Directions: Restate the sentences as conditional statements.

Example: I didn't eat breakfast this morning, so I'm very hungry now.

_____*If I had eaten breakfast this morning, I wouldn't be so hungry now.*_____

1. I didn't feed the cats, so now they are hungry.

_____

_____

2. The children have practiced a lot, so they can sing the song by heart.

_____

_____

3. John didn't pay his bills because he doesn't have enough money.

_____

_____

4. The house is too hot inside because the heat was left on.

_____

_____

5. I didn't buy stamps yesterday, so I can't mail these letters today.

_____

_____

6. Paulo hasn't contacted his parents for two weeks, so his parents are worried about him.

_____

_____

7. Martha can't check her online account because she forgot her password.

_____

_____

8. Mark is tired because he flew in from Hong Kong late last night.

_____

_____

Directions: Make sentences with the same meaning by omitting *if*.

Example: If I had known the address, I would have written it down for you.

Had I known the address, I would have written it down for you.

1. If Pat were lazy, he wouldn't be so successful.

_____

2. If the phone should ring, please answer it.

_____

3. I would have come sooner if someone had told me about the accident.

_____

4. If I were you, I would look for a new hair stylist.

_____

5. If Abdul had wanted to join us for dinner, he would have been welcome.

_____

Directions: Identify the implied conditions by making sentences using *if*-clauses.

Example: Marcia would have called, but she didn't know my phone number.

If she had known my phone number, Marcia would have called.

1. I would have done the dishes last night, but I was too tired.

_____

2. Bob would have bought concert tickets, but the show was sold out.

_____

3. Julio lent me $500. Otherwise, I wouldn't have been able to buy a plane ticket home.

_____

4. It wouldn't have been as much fun without Talia.

_____

5. Kate would have played the piano for us, but she has a broken finger.

_____

Directions: Choose the correct completions.

Example: I'm sorry I missed your birthday. I wish I (*remembered* / *had remembered*) it.

1. I've never been to Thailand. I wish I (*went* / *could go*) there to see all the old temples.

2. It's too bad Henry can't go to the zoo with us next weekend. I really wish he (*will be going* / *were going*) with us.

3. Olga loves her parents, but she wishes they (*aren't* / *weren't*) so conservative.

4. I can't speak Chinese, but I wish I (*could* / *could have*).

5. I don't like it when people tell lies. I wish everyone (*will* / *would*) just be honest.

6. James didn't get accepted to the university he wanted to go to. Now he wishes he (*had studied* / *would have studied*) harder in high school.

7. Wow! That was such a close game. I wish our team (*would win* / *had won*). It's disappointing.

8. We used to shoot off fireworks on Independence Day, but now they are illegal. I wish fireworks (*were* / *will be*) legal again.

9. Nikolai has gained a lot of weight, but he wishes he (*hadn't* / *wouldn't*).

10. Mrs. Archibald wishes her students (*do* / *did*) all of their assignments and (*turn* / *turned*) them in on time.

Directions: Complete the sentences with an appropriate verb form. You may need to add "not."

Example: I didn't buy gas before I left, but I wish I _____*had bought*_____ some.

1. We don't have time to stop for lunch. I wish we _____ time. I'm really hungry.

2. It's too cold today. My hands and feet are frozen! I wish it _____ so cold.

3. Susan can't speak Italian. She wishes she _____ Italian because she loves visiting Italy.

4. Mr. Babcock wasn't my teacher last year. I wish he _____ my teacher because I heard he was really nice.

5. James couldn't come hiking with us. He wishes he _____, but he already had plans.

6. My sister forgot to tell me about her doctor's appointment. She wishes she _____ to tell me about it because she wanted me to babysit her kids.

7. I wasn't listening carefully when Pat told me where he was going. I wish I _____ because now I don't know where he is.

8. Max won't call his parents. I wish he _____ them, but he won't.

9. I am not going to the party tonight. I wish I _____, but I have to work.

10. My son can't find a job. He wishes he _____ one because he needs money.

Directions: Answer the questions with your own ideas. Write complete conditional sentences.

Example: What would you do if you were a movie star?

If I were a movie star, I would sign many autographs.

1. If you could live anywhere in the world, where would you live?

   _____

   _____

2. What would you have done if you hadn't learned English?

   _____

   _____

3. What will you do if you don't understand your next English assignment?

   _____

   _____

4. What do you wish would happen in the future?

   _____

   _____

5. What do you wish had happened in the past, but didn't?

   _____

   _____

6. If you were not taking this quiz, what would you be doing?

   _____

   _____

7. What would you be doing if you were ten years older?

   _____

   _____

8. What would you change about your past life if you could? What would you have done differently?

   _____

   _____

Part A *Directions:* Complete the sentences with conditionals using the verbs in parentheses. Pay attention to the tense.

1. I (*be*) _____ very surprised if I didn't do well on my exams.

2. If babies cry, their parents usually (*pick*) _____ them up.

3. If Benjamin (*study, not*) _____ in the U.S. now, he would be studying in France.

4. George (*catch, not*) _____ a cold if he
(*wear*) _____ a jacket last night.

5. If James always (*pay*) _____ his bills on time, he wouldn't be so worried about them.

6. If the price of gasoline (*go*) _____ up much more, I will start taking the bus.

7. Leila (*visit*) _____ her grandchildren last summer if they
(*visit, not*) _____ her.

8. If Byoung wins the lottery next week, he (*buy*) _____ a new car.

Part B *Directions:* Restate the sentences as conditional statements.

1. Madeleine missed her flight, so she is feeling angry and frustrated.

_____

_____

2. Saya can't play the music for her piano lesson because she hasn't practiced all week.

_____

_____

3. Michael got three traffic tickets last year, so now his auto insurance costs more.

_____

_____

4. Tomás doesn't want to move to a different city, so he didn't accept the job offer.

_____

_____

5. Stacy Smith is the new mayor because she won the election.

_____

_____

Part C *Directions:* Identify the implied conditions by creating sentences using *if*-clauses.

1. I would stop to chat with you, but I'm in a hurry.

   _____

   _____

2. Fred had to work late. Otherwise, he would have met us for dinner.

   _____

   _____

3. I would never have completed this project on time without your help.

   _____

   _____

Part D *Directions:* Choose the correct completions.

1. Elena wishes she (*had gone* / *went*) to the concert last weekend. She heard it was amazing.

2. I wish my son (*wasn't* / *weren't*) going to move to Australia.

3. Mrs. Miyagaki doesn't speak Japanese very well. She wishes she (*spoke* / *speaks*) it better.

4. Brian wants to ride on the roller coaster, but he's too little. He wishes he (*was* / *were*) tall enough.

5. I'm not a good cook. I wish I (*could* / *were going to*) cook better.

6. Sam is so lazy! I wish he (*would* / *were*) help me.

7. Khalid's hair is turning gray, but he wishes it (*weren't* / *isn't*). He's only 30.

8. Sarah wishes she (*hadn't gone* / *didn't go*) on a date with Marsha's brother.

Part A *Directions:* Complete the sentences with conditionals using the verbs in parentheses. Pay attention to the tense.

1. If Geoffrey (*lose*) _____ his job, he will look for a new job.

2. We (*go*) _____ for a hike yesterday if the weather

   (*be, not*) _____ so bad.

3. Leo (*visit*) _____ us more often if he had time.

4. If Lara goes to Paris for vacation this summer, she (*see*) _____ the Eiffel Tower.

5. If Tanya (*get*) _____ more exercise, she could lose weight.

6. Mr. Martinez (*pull, not*) _____ a muscle in his back if he

   (*be*) _____ more careful moving the sofa.

7. If I finish a good book, I always (*feel*) _____ satisfied.

8. My dad would answer the phone if he (*cook, not*) _____ dinner right now.

Part B *Directions:* Change the statements into conditional sentences.

1. Wendy didn't work hard in high school, so she isn't going to college.

   _____

   _____

2. Paula can't ride her bike to work because she damaged the front wheel on it.

   _____

   _____

3. The children are running and yelling, so they can't hear their teacher calling them.

   _____

   _____

4. I didn't finish the report because my computer isn't working.

   _____

   _____

5. Roberta doesn't like cheese, so she didn't eat any pizza last night.

   _____

   _____

Part C *Directions:* Identify the implied conditions by creating sentences using *if*-clauses.

1. I would have answered the door, but I was in the shower.

   _____

   _____

2. Lisa has a doctor's appointment. Otherwise, she wouldn't have left work early.

   _____

   _____

3. The team couldn't have won the championship without their coach's leadership.

   _____

   _____

Part D *Directions:* Choose the correct completions.

1. The mayor wishes the city (*can* / *could*) help homeless people find places to live.

2. I don't live in California any more, but I wish I still (*live* / *lived*) there.

3. Amy wishes she (*didn't* / *wouldn't*) have such a terrible headache right now.

4. This blouse is kind of expensive. I wish it (*was* / *were*) on sale.

5. It's too bad Aunt Rose couldn't come to my birthday party. We all wish she (*had* / *could*) come.

6. These vegetables aren't fresh. I wish this supermarket (*had* / *will have*) fresher vegetables.

7. The Marshalls wish they (*were* / *could*) going on a vacation this year, but they won't have any time off.

8. Sam got another parking ticket yesterday, but he wishes he (*didn't* / *hadn't*).

Directions: Choose the correct completions.

1. Bruce was 20 minutes late for this morning's meeting. He _____ stuck in traffic.

   a. might be   c. had to be
   b. must be   d. must have been

2. The teacher was surprised that the students needed more time. They _____ finish the quiz in 30 minutes.

   a. should have could   c. should be
   b. should have been able to   d. had better

3. When the famous actress entered the room, everyone turned and looked at _____.

   a. herself   c. her
   b. she   d. hers

4. Dogs make excellent pets. _____ provide good companionship and even protection.

   a. They   c. It
   b. Its   d. It's

5. By the time Brian _____ a parking space, he was late for the movie.

   a. was finding   c. had found
   b. was found   d. finds

6. While John _____ for his glasses, he had difficulty seeing things clearly.

   a. was looking   c. is looking
   b. looked   d. has looked

7. Shirley wasn't able to concentrate all morning. She _____ at all the night before and was very sleepy.

   a. wasn't sleeping   c. sleeps
   b. hadn't slept   d. hasn't been sleeping

8. Peter rarely _____ a promotion at work. He is sometimes lazy and never does more than he has to.

   a. got   c. will get
   b. is getting   d. gets

9. Mrs. Taylor is worried about the children. They _____ come home two hours ago.

   a. have got to   c. should have
   b. had better   d. didn't have to

10. _____ please turn down the volume on your game? It's too loud.

    a. Would you   c. May you

    b. Would you mind   d. You must

11. Can I borrow _____? I must have left mine at home.

    a. one of your pen   c. one of those pen

    b. one of your pens   d. those pen

12. Maria has invited all of the students and all of the _____ parents to her birthday party.

    a. students'   c. student's

    b. students   d. students their

13. By the time William is forty years old, he _____ fifteen novels and two collections of short stories.

    a. wrote   c. has written

    b. will have written   d. will be writing

14. I'm not sure where Rob is, but he _____ to music in his room.

    a. might be listening   c. might have listened

    b. might listen   d. must have been listening

15. I need to buy _____ meat for Sunday dinner. What should I get?

    a. a   c. some

    b. an   d. one

16. _____ not smoking? I'm allergic to cigarette smoke.

    a. Would you mind   c. Can you

    b. Would you   d. Will you

17. The Chinese _____ the oldest calendar of any culture in the world today.

    a. have had   c. have

    b. has had   d. has

18. Each of _____ graduated from school and found a good job.

    a. their children has   c. their children have

    b. their child has   d. their child is

19. Mario _____ for four hours straight. He had better take a break to stretch and eat something.

    a. is studying   c. studied

    b. was studying   d. has been studying

20. Janice _____ a koala bear before she went to Australia last November.

    a. had never seen   c. had ever seen

    b. has never seen   d. doesn't see

21. The employees at Matrix Motors get paid _____ week.

    a. every other   c. one after the other

    b. each other   d. another

22. It looks like your cup is empty. Would you like _____ cup of coffee?

    a. other   c. one another

    b. another   d. the other

23. Babies like to talk to _____ in order to practice the sounds of a language.

    a. itself   c. herself

    b. ourselves   d. themselves

24. Oh, no! _____ is missing! We have to call the police!

    a. All of the stamps   c. All of the computers

    b. All of the jewelry   d. All of the children

25. _____ a different topic. We will study Chapters 1 through 10 this semester.

    a. Every chapter is covered   c. Each of the chapters covers

    b. Each of the chapters cover d. All of the chapter covers

26. I don't think we'll need an umbrella this afternoon. The forecast is for _____ late tonight.

    a. a little rain   c. a few rain

    b. little rain   d. few rain

27. This chemical is very dangerous. You _____ handle it without gloves and goggles.

    a. don't have to   c. could not

    b. have to   d. must not

28. Philip usually cleans up the kitchen while his roommate _____ the dishes.

    a. will wash   c. is going to wash

    b. is washing   d. was washing

29. I'm amazed! No one _____ any problems with the equipment since we bought it.

    a. have   c. have had

    b. has   d. has had

30. One hour may be enough for the midterm test, but two hours _____ necessary for the final exam.

   a. was   c. are

   b. were   d. is

31. We enjoyed our trip to Yellowstone National Park. We saw _____ and even a black bear.

   a. several deers   c. severals deers

   b. several deer   d. severals deer

32. When I _____ to my country next year, I am going to visit all my friends.

   a. will return   c. return

   b. returns   d. am going to return

33. Rosie needs _____ money to pay her rent, so she's working extra hours.

   a. a   c. the

   b. an   d. Ø

34. After the hurricane has passed, people _____ to their homes to check on the damage.

   a. will be able to return   c. will have returned

   b. could have returned   d. return

35. Jay won't hear from the doctor again until he _____ the test results.

   a. has   c. will have had

   b. is going to have   d. had

36. While the children are watching a movie later this afternoon, I _____ a nap.

   a. am taking   c. was taking

   b. take   d. will be taking

37. I'm not sure what I'm going to do this afternoon. I might go for a walk or do _____ shopping.

   a. few   c. little

   b. a few   d. a little

38. By this December, we _____ in this city for more than twenty years.

   a. will live   c. will have been living

   b. had lived   d. are going to be living

39. When Christopher went to the refrigerator for a snack, _____ many things to eat.

   a. there isn't   c. there wasn't

   b. there aren't   d. there weren't

40. Please don't bother me right now. I _____ to finish the last page of this report.

    a. try   c. will try

    b. am trying   d. have tried

41. Nora isn't sure, but she thinks she _____ her purse in the restaurant.

    a. might leave   c. might have left

    b. might have been left   d. might be leaving

42. I take medicine for high blood pressure. _____ medicine keeps my blood pressure low.

    a. A   c. The

    b. An   d. Ø

43. If a person _____ one foreign language, it is usually easier to learn a second one.

    a. has studied   c. was studied

    b. will study   d. studied

44. Don't worry. We _____ the reports by the time you get here tomorrow morning.

    a. complete   c. completed

    b. will be completed   d. will have completed

45. Here are _____ keys you were looking for. I found them in your pants pocket.

    a. some   c. the

    b. Ø   d. a

46. We have two problems. One is lack of time, and _____ is lack of money.

    a. another   c. other

    b. the other   d. Ø

47. Kevin didn't finish watching _____ movie. It was boring.

    a. a   c. some

    b. the   d. Ø

48. You _____ hungry already! You just ate a big lunch and a dish of ice cream.

    a. must not be   c. could have been

    b. can't be   d. might not be

49. The city of Milwaukee, Wisconsin is on the shore of _____ Lake Michigan.

    a. a   c. the

    b. an   d. Ø

50. After he retired, Mr. Patterson bought _____ a new set of golf clubs. Now he plays golf every week.

    a. him   c. himself

    b. he   d. his

Part A *Directions:* Complete the sentences. Use an appropriate form of the verbs in parentheses.

1. Some people (*be*) _____ very afraid of spiders. They have arachnophobia.

2. As soon as the TV program is over, Martha (*make*) _____ a salad for dinner.

3. My grandmother (*work*) _____ in the garden when we arrived at her house.

4. Do you need help with your homework? I (*help*) _____ you after lunch.

5. I have so much laundry to do. I just (*have, not*) _____ time to do it lately.

6. After I lost my third cell phone, I (*buy*) _____ a cheap one.

7. When she returns from her trip to Ecuador, Carrie (*speak*) _____ Spanish fluently.

8. Last summer, it (*rain*) _____ almost every afternoon. The weather was terrible!

9. Don't call me tomorrow night at 8:00 because I won't be able to answer my phone. I (*attend*) _____ a town council meeting.

10. Right now my cousin (*study*) _____ his astronomy notes. He has a test tomorrow.

11. By this time next year, Chris (*finish*) _____ his training and will be an electrician.

12. Steve (*surf*) _____ the Internet for three hours. He needs to take a break.

13. Josef often (*have*) _____ trouble with English verbs. He gets really confused.

14. It was good to talk to Maggie yesterday. Before that, I (*talk, not*) _____ to her for months.

15. The entire family (*celebrate*) _____ my parents' 50th wedding anniversary next month.

Part B *Directions:* Choose the correct sentence in each pair.

1. a. The number of employees on the project are increasing weekly.

   b. The number of employees on the project is increasing weekly.

2. a. We took a two week vacation to Hawaii last January.

   b. We took a two-week vacation to Hawaii last January.

3. a. I read a book about the life of Nelson Mandela. He was a courageous man.

   b. I read a book about life of Nelson Mandela. He was a courageous man.

4. a. Todays' lunch special is Spaghetti Bolognese with green salad for $7.95.

   b. Today's lunch special is Spaghetti Bolognese with green salad for $7.95.

5. a. My soda is on a table. Where is yours?

   b. My soda is on the table. Where is yours?

6. a. Each of the stars from the movie has a fan club.

   b. Each of the stars from the movie have a fan club.

7. a. Suzanne speaks three languages, but she wants to learn the other one.

   b. Suzanne speaks three languages, but she wants to learn another one.

8. a. Joshua had too much homework last weekend. He didn't have much time to relax.

   b. Joshua had too many homeworks last weekend. He didn't have much time to relax.

9. a. Maddy memorized the whole poem all by herself!

   b. Maddy memorized the whole poem all by myself!

10. a. One of the student in my writing class studies at the library every night.

    b. One of the students in my writing class studies at the library every night.

11. a. It was an honor to meet the president and his wife.

    b. It was a honor to meet the president and his wife.

12. a. The children made the peanut butter and jelly sandwiches for lunch.

    b. The children made peanut butter and jelly sandwiches for lunch.

13. a. Let's go get some coffee. I have little time before my next appointment.

    b. Let's go get some coffee. I have a little time before my next appointment.

14. a. The *New York Times* is among the top newspapers in the U.S.

    b. The *New York Times* are among the top newspapers in the U.S.

15. a. The cucumbers at the market were reasonably priced, so I bought two of they.

    b. The cucumbers at the market were reasonably priced, so I bought two of them.

Part C *Directions:* Read each paragraph. Then complete the statements about it with an appropriate modal (***must, may, might, could, should,*** etc.) and the given verb. More than one answer may be possible.

1. Adam and his friend stayed up late watching a movie. The next morning, Adam fell asleep on the bus to work. When he woke up, he had already passed his stop. By the time he caught the next bus back, he was late for work.

   a. Adam (*stay, not*) _____ up so late.

   b. Adam's boss (*be*) _____ upset about Adam's late arrival.

   c. Adam (*be*) _____ more careful about arriving at work on time,

      or he will lose his job.

2. You call your friend Susan, but her mother tells you that she isn't home. You have some important news for Susan and you want to leave a message.

   a. (*leave*) _____ I please _____ a message for Susan?

   b. (*ask*) _____ you please _____ her to call me?

Part D *Directions:* Using the information about each situation, complete the sentences.

SITUATION 1: Hannah, James, and Will work for the same company. They start work at 8:30 AM. Who do you expect to be on time for work today?

INFORMATION: **Hannah** almost always arrives a few minutes late for work because she can't find a parking place.
James takes the bus to work and usually arrives by 8:20.
Will has to drop off his kids at school on the way to work. He occasionally gets to work late.

   a. _____ might be on time for work today.

   b. _____ won't be on time today.

   c. _____ should be on time for work today.

SITUATION 2: The final paper for the English 105 class is due tomorrow. Who has already completed the assignment?

INFORMATION: **Ken** hates writing assignments. He said he'd be up late tonight.
Max has already left for a semester break trip to California.
David said last night that he had almost finished writing his paper.

   a. _____ must have finished his paper already.

   b. _____ may have finished his paper by now.

   c. _____ must not have finished writing his paper yet.

Part E *Directions:* Complete the conversations with *must, have to, must not, don't have to, could,* or *couldn't.* Use each modal one time only.

1. **A:** Why didn't Karen go out for Chinese food with you last night?

   B: She hardly ever eats Chinese food. She _____ like it much.

2. **A:** What time does your flight leave?

   B: It leaves at 4:00. I _____ be at the airport by 2:00.

3. **A:** When Paul was young, he _____ run a 10K race in about 50 minutes.

   B: Really? That's pretty good. I'm sure he's much slower now, though.

4. **A:** It's nice to be on vacation. I _____ think about work for two weeks!

   B: That's wonderful!

5. **A:** Are you sure Jason is out of town this week? I thought I saw him at the soccer game today.

   B: That _____ have been Jason! He's in the Bahamas right now. It _____ have been somebody else.

Directions: Choose the correct completions.

1. Our city _____ a record number of traffic accidents last year, so the city has worked to make streets safer.

   a. has

   b. had

   c. is having

   d. was having

2. Carlos _____ in the United States since he enrolled in art school three years ago.

   a. lived

   b. lives

   c. has been living

   d. living

3. When Linda _____ to Los Angeles next month, she will stay with her sister until she finds her own apartment.

   a. moves

   b. will move

   c. has moved

   d. is going to move

4. Please keep your voice down in this section of the library. If you _____ to talk loudly, I will have to ask you to leave.

   a. continued

   b. could continue

   c. will continue

   d. continue

5. I bought the red leather bag because it was well made, stylish, and _____.

   a. inexpensively

   b. inexpensive

   c. less expensive than

   d. no expense

6. The chemistry book _____ was a little expensive.

   a. that I bought it

   b. I bought that

   c. what I bought

   d. I bought

7. Why did Beth ask you _____ a bicycle?

   a. that if you had

   b. do you have

   c. that you had

   d. if you had

8. Eighty-five percent of the students in the class _____ brothers and sisters.

   a. has

   b. are having

   c. have

   d. is having

9. I got Barbara _____ her car for the weekend.

    a. to let me borrow   c. to let me to borrow

    b. let me borrow   d. let me to borrow

10. If I _____ you, I would get some rest before the game tomorrow.

    a. am   c. were

    b. could be   d. had been

11. Frank's parents recommended that he _____ in Spain next year. They think it will be a good experience for him.

    a. studies   c. will study

    b. study   d. studied

12. Emily is motivated to study _____ she knows that a good education can improve her life.

    a. therefore   c. because

    b. because of   d. so

13. Ms. Moore, the school counselor, has had years of experience dealing with student problems. _____, sometimes she asks for assistance with unusual cases.

    a. Therefore   c. Otherwise

    b. Nevertheless   d. On the other hand

14. I have always wanted to visit Paris, _____ of France.

    a. is the capital   c. that is the capital

    b. which the capital is   d. the capital

15. When I went on a business trip to China last September, I had _____ time for sightseeing because of work. I would like to go there again so I can see more of the country.

    a. little   c. few

    b. a little   d. a few

16. Gloria never seems to get tired. I sure wish I _____ her energy.

    a. would have   c. have had

    b. have   d. had

17. After getting home from elementary school, _____.

    a. our house is busy with the children's many activities

    b. the dog greets the children at the front door with a wagging tail

    c. the children have an hour to play before they begin their homework

    d. the school bus drops the children at the corner near their house

18. Jack offered to take care of my garden and _____ my mail while I was out of town.

    a. gets   c. got

    b. getting   d. get

19. Sonia broke her leg in two places. _____, she had to wear a cast and use crutches for three months.

    a. Nevertheless   c. For that

    b. Consequently   d. Because

20. Next year Nathan will attend _____ university in Germany. He's looking forward to it.

    a. a   c. the

    b. an   d. Ø

21. Even though a duck lives on water, it stays dry _____ the oil on its feathers, which prevents water from reaching its skin.

    a. because of   c. because

    b. since   d. for

22. One of the funniest _____ I saw last year was *Agent 13*. It had a crazy plot and hilarious actors.

    a. movie   c. movies

    b. a movie   d. the movies

23. I talked to Bob two weeks ago. I thought he wanted to know about my cat, but I misunderstood him. He asked me where _____, not my cat.

    a. is my hat   c. my hat is

    b. my hat was   d. was my hat

24. I am tired of my neighbors _____ dogs are always barking.

    a. who their   c. their

    b. whose   d. which

25. _____ go to the beach this weekend. The weather is supposed to be hot.

    a. Let's   c. Why don't

    b. Could we   d. Lets

26. Please remember _____ your hand during the test if you have a question.

    a. raising   c. having raised

    b. to raise   d. to have raised

27. I have to go to our monthly sales meeting _____ I want to or not.

    a. because   c. even though

    b. whether   d. only if

28. The painting was beautiful. I stood there _____ it for a long time.

    a. for admiring   c. admire

    b. being admired   d. admiring

29. Would you mind _____ me your email address? I'd like to get that recipe from you.

    a. to give   c. giving

    b. if I gave   d. give

30. My mouth is burning! This is _____ spicy food that I don't think I can finish it.

    a. such   c. very

    b. so   d. too

31. The customs officer opened the suitcase _____ if anything illegal was being brought into the country.

    a. seeing   c. see

    b. for seeing   d. to see

32. That man _____ looked before he stepped into the street. He almost got hit by a truck!

    a. should   c. shouldn't

    b. should have   d. shouldn't have

33. Sometimes very young children have trouble _____ what's real and what's imaginary, so they may believe that dragons are real.

    a. to know   c. to be known

    b. knowing   d. for knowing

34. I have to eat breakfast in the morning. _____, I get grouchy and hungry before my lunch break.

    a. Consequently   c. Otherwise

    b. And   d. However

35. Tony spent _____ money buying movie tickets that he didn't have enough left to buy a soft drink or candy bar.

    a. so many   c. too much

    b. a lot of   d. so much

36. Not wanting to be late my first day of class, _____ to school after I missed my bus.

    a. so I ran   c. I ran

    b. because I ran   d. therefore, I ran

37. Christopher was wet and muddy when he came home from playing soccer. It _____ during the game.

    a. must rain   c. had to rain

    b. must not rain   d. must have rained

38. Yesterday, Mary left _____ backpack on the school bus.

    a. her   c. hers

    b. she   d. his

39. There _____ ten students from Korea in my English class.

    a. is   c. are

    b. be   d. being

40. The city of Seattle has changed a lot over the past 30 years _____ growth in job opportunities.

    a. due to   c. therefore

    b. because   d. so

41. The police _____ when there is a traffic accident.

    a. calls   c. called

    b. is called   d. are called

42. When I saw my classmates at our ten-year reunion last month, I _____ most of them since graduation.

    a. didn't see   c. hadn't seen

    b. haven't seen   d. won't see

43. More than 50 buildings in the downtown area _____ in the earthquake.

    a. destroyed   c. were destroying

    b. were destroyed   d. was destroyed

44. I think I did OK on my speech last night _____ I'd had almost no sleep for 24 hours.

    a. despite the fact that   c. so that

    b. unless   d. in spite of

45. While I _____ for the train, I sent several texts and checked my email on my cell phone.

   a. wait   c. waited
   b. am waiting   d. was waiting

46. The _____ news about robberies in the neighborhood caused everyone to be sure to lock their doors.

   a. disturbed   c. disturbs
   b. disturbing   d. disturb

47. The scientists explained how _____ insects breathe underwater.

   a. the   c. Ø
   b. an   d. a

48. Jim should have asked for help instead _____ to do it himself.

   a. of trying   c. try
   b. to try   d. from trying

49. If I _____ following that other car too closely, I would have been able to stop in time instead of running into it.

   a. wasn't   c. was
   b. would have been   d. hadn't been

50. **A:** Is it true that you fell asleep in class yesterday and began to snore?

   B: Unfortunately, yes. _____ is unbelievable! I'm very embarrassed.

   a. That I could do such a thing it   c. I could do such a thing it
   b. That I could do such a thing   d. I could do such a thing

Part A *Directions:* Complete the sentences. Use the appropriate form of the verbs in parentheses. More than one answer may be possible.

1. Next week, my whole family (*go*) _____ on a trip to the Grand Canyon.

2. Last year, Tim (*study, not*) _____ enough, so his grades weren't very good.

3. While Fatima (*wait*) _____ in the doctor's office, the doctor suddenly had to leave for an emergency.

4. By the time we arrived at the hotel, the wedding reception (*start, already*) _____.

5. The college entrance exam (*give*) _____ next Saturday in the high school auditorium.

6. I'm almost ready for my trip to Kenya. I have my plane ticket, but my new passport (*arrive, not*) _____ yet. I should get it soon.

7. We (*stay*) _____ in our tent until it stops raining. Otherwise, we'll get soaking wet!

8. Every girl, boy, woman, and man on earth (*be*) _____ affected by global warming.

9. One fourth of the students in the class (*plan, not*) _____ to go to college.

10. Thirty minutes (*be*) _____ too long to wait for a taxi!

Part B *Directions:* Choose the correct sentence in each pair.

1. a. You don't have to leave a candle burning when you leave the house. It could cause a fire.

    b. You must not leave a candle burning when you leave the house. It could cause a fire.

2. a. Ninety-five percent of the professors at the university have a PhD.

    b. Ninety-five percent of the professors at the university has a PhD.

3. a. My aunt and uncle's new baby is a sweet little girl. She's my newest cousin.

    b. My aunt's and uncle's new baby is a sweet little girl. She's my newest cousin.

4. a. There are two major hypotheses about why the dinosaurs died.

    b. There are two major hypothesis about why the dinosaurs died.

5. a. The middle-school teachers always give students too many homework.

    b. The middle-school teachers always give students too much homework.

6. a. I'm not sure when the bus is supposed to come. It should be here soon.

    b. I'm not sure when the bus is supposed to come. It must be here soon.

7. a. Max is worried about his daughter. She should call him by now.

    b. Max is worried about his daughter. She should have called him by now.

8. a. Even though Carol is only seven years old, she can read some novels by herself.

    b. Even though Carol is only seven years old, she can't read some novels by herself.

9. a. John may have given his paycheck at work today. I'm not sure.

    b. John may have been given his paycheck at work today. I'm not sure.

10. a. I'm almost sure that story was made up. It couldn't be true!

    b. I'm almost sure that story was made up. It may not be true!

Part C *Directions:* Combine each pair of sentences into one new sentence with parallel structure. Use the conjunctions given in parentheses.

1. Mary got 100% on her last grammar test. John got 100% on his last grammar test. (*both … and*)

   _____

2. Barbara can't attend the meeting on Monday. Steven can't attend the meeting on Monday. (*neither … nor*)

   _____

3. Stewart's team won the city championship. Stewart's team won the regional championship. (*not only … but also*)

   _____

4. We can watch a comedy film. We can watch a drama. (*either … or*)

   _____

Part D *Directions:* Complete the sentences. Either change the questions or rewrite the speaker's words to make noun clauses.

1. (*What time does the train for Edinburgh leave?*)

   Can you tell me _____?

2. (*"Did Kevin get his driver's license?" asked Cathy.*)

   Cathy wanted to know _____.

3. (*"Whose car is that?" asked Pat.*)

   Pat asked me _____.

4. (*How does that machine work?*)

   _____ is explained in the instructions.

Part E *Directions:* Combine the two sentences. Use the second sentence as the adjective clause.

1. Barbara wants to go to an island for her vacation. The island has warm sandy beaches and lots of sunshine.

   _____

   _____

2. Anne and Emily like to go shopping at the mall. Their mom also shops there.

   _____

   _____

3. The police are trying to find the man. Someone found his car near the scene of the crime.

   _____

   _____

Part F *Directions:* Match the first half of each sentence to the clause that best completes it.

1. _____ Michael needs to buy a new suit

2. _____ Maya didn't have enough money,

3. _____ After reading many reviews and articles on the Internet,

4. _____ We could go to the museum

5. _____ While Mark loves science,

6. _____ The movie was so funny that

7. _____ I ate too much, so I have a stomachache,

8. _____ Students may not go on the class trip

9. _____ William still goes to that restaurant

10. _____ If I hadn't forgotten my phone at home,

a. even though the waiter was rude and made a mistake on the bill.

b. I would have gotten your message sooner.

c. but I wish I didn't.

d. everyone in the audience was laughing.

e. because he has a job interview next Monday.

f. if it were open today.

g. so she couldn't go on a vacation with her friends.

h. Lori hates it.

i. unless they have permission from their parents.

j. Barry chose a movie to watch.

Part G *Directions:* Complete the sentences with the gerund or infinitive form of the verbs in parentheses. More than one answer may be possible.

1. My friends and I are interested in (*study*) _____ abroad during college.

2. My cat enjoys (*play*) _____ with her mouse toy.

3. We agreed (*meet*) _____ Karen and Heather for coffee at 3:00 P.M.

4. I forgot (*get*) _____ my co-workers cell phone numbers. Now I can't call them.

5. Last summer was so hot that we went (*swim*) _____ almost every day.

6. Lynne was embarrassed (*admit*) _____ that she had forgotten her teacher's name.

7. I'm too tired (*go*) _____ out of town this weekend. I just want to rest.

8. Jan and Maria had a good time (*travel*) _____ together last year.

9. Julie got her sister (*drive*) _____ most of the way because she doesn't like to drive.

10. Paul can't stand (*get*) _____ home from work late.

ANSWER KEY

CHAPTER 1

Quiz 1, p. 1
1. stand
2. departs
3. is not running
4. are trying
5. are still waiting
6. takes
7. works
8. is sitting
9. is tapping
10. is calling

Quiz 2, p. 1
A.
2. are playing
3. is swimming
4. is enjoying

B.
1. is
2. does
3. cleans
4. rides
5. plays
6. is talking
7. are using

Quiz 3, p. 2
1. gives
2. study
3. am taking, am not relaxing
4. worry
5. are, make

Quiz 4, p. 2
1. Do
2. Is
3. Does
4. Do
5. Are

Quiz 5, p. 2
1. is appearing
2. smells
3. is thinking
4. is tasting
5. love

Quiz 6, p. 3
1. don't care
2. are seeing
3. do you think
4. isn't feeling
5. dislikes

Quiz 7, p. 3
1. stopped
2. made
3. caught
4. met
5. stood
6. drove
7. read
8. drank
9. wrote
10. slept
11. cost
12. studied
13. found
14. rang
15. spoke
16. heard
17. wore
18. quit
19. played
20. chose

Quiz 8, p. 4
1. had
2. were
3. didn't drive, crashed
4. spilled, got
5. came, didn't catch
6. flew
7. killed

Quiz 9, p. 4
1. Did
2. Was
3. Did
4. Were
5. Did
6. Did
7. Was
8. Were
9. Did
10. Did

Quiz 10, p. 5
1. was listening
2. lost
3. was driving
4. heard
5. was eating
6. was watching
7. was cleaning
8. ran
9. played
10. was traveling

Quiz 11, p. 5
A.
2. fell
3. broke
4. took
5. was not

B.
1. took
2. stayed
3. spent
4. ate
5. were having
6. was playing
7. were dancing
8. walked

Quiz 12, p. 6
1. Michiko was chopping some vegetables when she cut her finger with the knife.
2. While Travis was working on his homework, he was listening to the radio.
3. When Fatima woke up, she made a cup of tea for herself.
4. When Janice broke her leg, she was skiing.
5. Geoff worked on his report while he was riding the train.
6. While Faruz was shopping for a new computer, he ran into an old friend.
7. When Ana was in Orlando, she went to Disney World every day.
8. When Carrie dropped her tablet computer, she started to cry.

Quiz 13, p. 6
1. No
2. Yes
3. Yes
4. No
5. Yes
6. No
7. Yes
8. Yes

Test 1, p. 7
A.
1. b, c
2. c, a
3. c, b
4. c, b

B.
1. had
2. stopped
3. is calling
4. usually goes
5. were visiting

C.
1. finds
2. is
3. reports
4. was reading OR read
5. has OR had
6. bought

D.

1. Every summer Sarah's cousin from England visits her.
2. Ibrahim was very upset when he heard the news.
3. You can't talk to Mr. James right now because he is talking to another student.
4. While I was writing my essay, I was also surfing the Internet.
5. Karen is very kind and always helps the teachers with their work.

E.

1. No, he didn't help me fix my car yesterday.
2. Yes, it was working OK last night.
3. Yes, she spends a lot of time on her phone.
4. Yes, they finished putting in the new window.
5. No, they aren't planning to go on a vacation this summer.

Test 2, p. 9

A.

1. a, b
2. c
3. b, a
4. a, c

B.

1. wakes
2. worked OR were working
3. was waiting
4. am taking
5. was discussing

C.

1. swim
2. live
3. move
4. is
5. is studying
6. goes
7. migrate OR are migrating

D.

1. The workers were very tired and forgot to lock the door when they left for the day.
2. I didn't know about the party for my birthday. It was a surprise.
3. David was very busy yesterday, so he is taking the day off.
4. Steven is in the library. He is reading a book.
5. The little boy bought another toy because he broke the first one.

E.

1. No, she didn't leave her keys on the hall table.
2. Yes, I was sleeping at ten o'clock last night.
3. Yes, the kids liked the movie.
4. No, Jun isn't cooking dinner.
5. Yes, he usually watches the evening news on TV.

CHAPTER 2

Quiz 1, p. 11

2. saw, seen
3. took, taken
4. bought, bought
5. taught, taught
6. flew, flown
7. made, made
8. ate, eaten
9. won, won
10. stole, stolen
11. fell, fallen
12. built, built
13. fed, fed
14. rode, ridden
15. lost, lost
16. gave, given
17. forgot, forgotten (*British: forgot*)
18. held, held
19. sang, sung
20. told, told
21. shook, shaken
22. studied, studied
23. wrote, written
24. drank, drunk

Quiz 2, p. 11

1. for
2. for
3. since
4. since
5. since
6. for
7. since
8. for
9. since
10. since

Quiz 3, p. 12

1. never
2. since
3. yet
4. already
5. ever
6. still
7. for
8. so far
9. since
10. recently

Quiz 4, p. 12

1. has won
2. has already gotten
3. have you called
4. has promised
5. have never eaten
6. haven't learned
7. has tried
8. has driven
9. hasn't been
10. has given

Quiz 5, p. 13

1. b
2. a
3. a
4. b
5. b
6. a
7. b
8. a
9. b
10. a

Quiz 6, p. 14

1. has caught
2. texted, haven't texted
3. has given
4. met, haven't known
5. worked
6. have changed, saw, has grown

Quiz 7, p. 14

1. has worked OR has been working
2. has gone
3. has been taking
4. have worked OR have been working
5. has seemed
6. has read
7. have lived OR have been living
8. have known
9. has not visited
10. has chatted OR has been chatting

Quiz 8, p. 15

1. have been waiting
2. is taking, has been taking
3. is starting
4. haven't been sleeping
5. have been planning
6. is raining, is blowing

Quiz 9, p. 15

1. had not finished
2. had put
3. had forgotten
4. had broken
5. had lost
6. had had
7. had become
8. had bought
9. had never seen

Quiz 10, p. 16

1. had already finished
2. hadn't finished
3. had died, came
4. had been
5. arrived
6. hadn't called
7. had already left
8. played
9. had never visited
10. wanted, had forgotten, was

Quiz 11, p. 17

1. had been sleeping
2. had forgotten
3. had already left
4. had been waiting
5. had not saved
6. had been trying
7. had lost
8. had gotten
9. had not stopped
10. had never had

Quiz 12, p. 18

1. has seen
2. had just begun
3. have never been
4. had told
5. have been seeing
6. has been sitting
7. had won
8. had been talking

Test 1, p. 19

A.

1. b
2. a
3. b
4. a
5. b
6. b
7. a
8. b
9. b
10. a

B.

1. has visited
2. has enjoyed
3. has learned / has been learning
4. had never seen
5. had been looking

C.

1. for
2. since
3. yet
4. already
5. just

D.

1. has been playing OR has played
2. had been playing OR had played
3. had been studying OR had studied
4. had been traveling
5. has performed OR has been performing
6. has caused
7. has encouraged
8. have watched
9. has become
10. has won

Test 2, p. 22

A.

1. b
2. b
3. a
4. a
5. b
6. a
7. b
8. a
9. a
10. a

B.

a. 1. has become
2. has made
3. have been

b. 1. have been
2. had read
3. had been studying OR had studied

C.

1. already
2. for
3. just
4. since
5. yet

D.

1. has been building
2. has been working OR has worked
3. has been
4. had already learned
5. had won
6. had become
7. had led
8. had been working OR had worked
9. has designed OR has been designing
10. have given

CHAPTER 3

Quiz 1, p. 25

1. a. will graduate   b. am going to graduate
2. a. will have   b. is going to have
3. a. will take   b. are going to take
4. a. will fly   b. are going to fly
5. a. will live   b. are going to live

Quiz 2, p. 25

1. plan
2. prediction
3. willingness
4. prediction
5. prediction
6. plan
7. willingness
8. plan
9. prediction
10. plan

Quiz 3, p. 26

1. will get
2. am going to take
3. are going to go
4. will meet
5. is going to work
6. will work
7. will probably clean, am going to go
8. will get
9. are going to come

Quiz 4, p. 27

1. My parents won't let me drive on the freeway.
2. Teri and George aren't going to come to the wedding.
3. That dog won't stop barking.

4. Luigi isn't going to pass / won't pass his math class this semester.
5. Nathan and Lucy are not going to live in Bellingham after this year.
6. You will never get / are never going to get to the airport in this traffic jam.
7. My neighbor won't turn down his music at night.
8. I won't win a prize at the carnival.
9. My sister won't let me borrow her clothes.
10. We won't see a movie tonight.

Quiz 5, p. 28

1. ends, will receive
2. finishes, is going to iron
3. will wait, park
4. arrives, is going to rent
5. boils, will make
6. get, am going to travel
7. finds, will be
8. will go, finish
9. will stop, tells
10. are going to love, hear

Quiz 6, p. 28

1. celebrate, am going to have
2. will wait, comes
3. arrives, will pay
4. will be, starts
5. buys, is going to give
6. is going to watch, goes

Quiz 7, p. 29

1. in the future
2. habitually
3. now
4. in the future
5. habitually
6. in the future
7. in the future
8. habitually
9. in the future
10. now

Quiz 8, p. 29

1. opens OR is opening
2. is coming
3. leaves OR is leaving
4. are visiting
5. is leaving
6. begins OR is beginning
7. are going
8. are buying
9. closes OR is closing
10. am meeting

Quiz 9, p. 30

1. will be taking, will be worrying
2. will be graduating, will be looking, will be working
3. will be traveling, will be taking
4. will be cleaning, will be washing, will be relaxing

Quiz 10, p. 30

1. will have eaten
2. will have finished
3. will have won
4. will have been
5. will have played

Quiz 11, p. 31

1. will have been playing
2. will have been talking
3. will have been raining
4. will have been living
5. will have been learning

Quiz 12, p. 31

1. At noon tomorrow, he is going to attend a luncheon at the Hilton Hotel.
2. As soon as the program ends, I'm going to bed.
3. By the time Mr. Wilcox reads my email, I will have left the office.
4. I am going to finish my homework after school.
5. After the baby stops crying, she will fall asleep.
6. Will English be an international language in 25 years?
7. The swimmers will have been training for several years by the time the Olympics begin next summer.
8. In six months, I am going to be living in a new apartment.
9. Benjamin is playing at a new golf club this weekend.
10. We have tickets to a play tomorrow night. We are going to see "The Mongol Horseman."

Quiz 13, p. 32

1. When my brother comes home from school, he will have two cookies and a glass of milk.
2. The builders will have been making a lot of progress since early morning.
3. At 10:00, I will be teaching my physics class.
4. By 3:00, Junichi will have finished his essay on studying in the U.S.
5. After we eat dinner at the Ethiopian restaurant, we are going to go to a movie.
6. Carl will be really tired. By the time the movie ends, he will be falling asleep.
7. As soon as I finish my homework, I am going to call my best friend.
8. After the music stops, everyone will be waiting for the next song.
9. When the fireworks start, people will clap / are going to clap excitedly.
10. Dr. Solack is going to be seeing patients all day. She is going to be very busy.

Test 1, p. 33

A.
1. in the future
2. in the future
3. in the future
4. now
5. habitually

B.
1. a, b
2. b, a
3. a, c
4. a, b
5. c, a

C.
1. is going to rain OR will rain
2. is going to give
3. will make
4. will go
5. aren't going to be

D.
1. Barbara will be working at the computer until she goes out with her friends.
2. By the time Carol goes to bed, she will have finished correcting all her students' papers.
3. In the morning we will go to the zoo, and then we will eat lunch in the park.
4. When my daughter graduates from the university, I will be so proud.
5. Jason will have never met his girlfriends' parents.

E.
1. The movie is going to start at 7:45 P.M. and will end around 10:00 P.M.
2. As soon as I find my key, I will open the door.
3. The book sale tomorrow will help the students raise money for their trip.
4. By the time he arrives in Boston, Bert will have spent three weeks cycling across the U.S.
5. I won't lend my brother any money. He will never pay it back!

Test 2, p. 35

A.
1. now
2. now
3. in the future
4. in the future
5. habitually

B.
1. c, a
2. a, b
3. a, b
4. b, a
5. a, c

C.
1. will get OR am going to get
2. are going to go
3. will help
4. is going to have
5. will be OR are going to be

D.
1. Chuck will be giving a lecture in his history class.
2. She will throw her old shoes away and (will) buy some new ones.
3. By 4:00 we will have been sitting on the runway for an hour. Bad weather will have delayed our flight.
4. I will study until it is time to go to my appointment with my lawyer.
5. Michelle will have travelled to Spain three times.

E.
1. Tommy will have lost 20 pounds by December.
2. The radio station will announce the name of the prizewinner at 4:30. We have to listen!
3. My cousins are sending me a postcard from Bali when they get there.
4. By the time my mom comes home, I will have cleaned up the kitchen.
5. Mr. Ballard will be a very good principal for our school.

CHAPTER 4

Test 1, p. 37

1. c	6. a	11. a	16. c	21. b
2. a	7. c	12. b	17. a	22. c
3. b	8. c	13. a	18. c	23. a
4. a	9. a	14. c	19. a	24. c
5. b	10. c	15. a	20. c	25. c

Test 2, p. 39

1. a	6. b	11. b	16. b	21. a
2. b	7. b	12. c	17. a	22. c
3. c	8. c	13. a	18. b	23. a
4. b	9. a	14. c	19. c	24. c
5. c	10. c	15. a	20. b	25. b

CHAPTER 5

Quiz 1, p. 41
1. churches
2. boys
3. chickens
4. boxes
5. kisses
6. lands
7. months
8. taxes
9. ladies
10. coughs
11. buzzes
12. salaries
13. lists
14. languages
15. friends
16. dishes
17. businesses
18. minutes
19. valleys
20. families

Quiz 2, p. 41
1. a. come
   b. needs
   c. is
2. a. has
   b. is
   c. aren't
   d. has
3. a. leave
   b. require
   c. is

Quiz 3, p. 42
1. a. are
   b. do
   c. go
2. a. likes
   b. have
   c. plays
3. a. watch
   b. are
   c. screams
   d. requires

Quiz 4, p. 42
1. Ø
2. Ø
3. members
4. Ø
5. members
6. Ø
7. Ø
8. members

Quiz 5, p. 43
1. was
2. is
3. were
4. was
5. Do
6. last
7. looks
8. was
9. Is
10. don't

Quiz 6, p. 43
1. Every one of the children needs love and affection.
2. Seventy-five percent of the teachers in our school speak Spanish
3. A number of volunteers are needed to finish this cleaning project.
4. A lot of my friends recommend this apartment complex.
5. None of my friends thinks I should sell my car.
6. The number of restaurants in San Francisco exceeds 2,000.

7. Each of these photographs is worth more than $150.
8. All of the money really belongs to that man over there.
9. One of my pencils needs to be sharpened.
10. Half of the airplanes leave on time.

Quiz 7, p. 44

1. are
2. have been
3. aren't
4. are
5. was
6. Were
7. isn't
8. Is
9. has been
10. are

Quiz 8, p. 44

1. is
2. are
3. was
4. isn't
5. are
6. is
7. have been
8. is
9. has been
10. is

Quiz 9, p. 45

1. is
2. is
3. includes
4. are
5. have
6. is
7. live
8. is
9. have
10. reports

Quiz 10, p. 45

1. takes
2. come
3. are
4. is
5. have
6. is
7. are
8. is
9. discusses
10. help

Quiz 11, p. 46

1. rides
2. requires
3. have
4. don't remember
5. is
6. are
7. knows
8. uses
9. take
10. has
11. needs
12. works
13. is
14. has
15. is

Test 1, p. 47

A.

2. I
3. C
4. I
5. I
6. I
7. C
8. I
9. I
10. C
11. I

B.

1. are
2. is
3. are
4. is
5. is
6. are
7. is
8. is

C.

1. is
2. is
3. has
4. helps
5. tell
6. is
7. affects

D.

is ... is ... are ... are ... help ... have ... is ... buys ... spend ... comes

Test 2, p. 49

A.

2. I
3. I
4. I
5. C
6. C
7. I
8. C
9. I
10. I
11. C

B.

1. Are
2. is
3. are
4. are
5. is
6. are
7. is
8. are

C.

1. is
2. like
3. is
4. sounds
5. is
6. are
7. consists

D.

happens ... take ... leave ... ride ... are ... serve ... ride ... make ... increases ... is

C H A P T E R 6

Quiz 1, p. 51

-s	-es	-ves	no change
beliefs	bushes	lives	deer
cliffs	echoes	loaves	sheep
kilos	foxes	shelves	species
memos	heroes	wolves	
pianos	tomatoes		
solos			

Quiz 2, p. 51

1. ladies, men
2. bacteria, teeth
3. hypotheses
4. tickets
5. mice
6. phenomena

Quiz 3, p. 52

1. tomato, tomatoes
2. storms, storm
3. two hours, two-hour
4. peas, pea
5. three weeks, three-week
6. eighteen years old, eighteen-year-old
7. flower, flowers
8. hotels, hotel

Quiz 4, p. 53

1. Mr. Jones' OR Mr. Jones's
2. Marissa and George's
3. group's
4. children's
5. boss' OR boss's
6. Andrea's
7. baby's
8. cousins'
9. building's
10. month's

Quiz 5, p. 53

1. boys'
2. knife's
3. Rhonda, Mick's
4. movie's
5. woman's
6. parents'
7. brother's
8. phone's
9. Tom's, Jerry's
10. company's

Quiz 6, p. 54

1. The United Nations' headquarters is located in New York City.
2. The roof of the house collapsed under the heavy snow.
3. Today's news was mostly about forest fires in our state.
4. People in my country usually drive small cars.
5. I waited for 1-1/2 hours at the doctor's. / I waited for 1-1/2 hours at the doctor's office.
6. My sister's hair is short, so it's easy to care for.
7. My friend's bike is red and yellow.
8. The manager of the coffee shop wants the customers to be happy. / The coffee shop manager wants the customers to be happy.

Quiz 7, p. 55

1. Our teacher gave us *suggestions* on how to be successful students. We appreciated her *advice*.
2. My dad bought new *luggage* for his trip. He got three large *suitcases* and a small duffle bag.
3. I just got today's *mail*. There are *bills* and a magazine.
4. no change
5. Pat always puts *pepper* on his food. He likes spicy *dishes*.
6. David bought *coffee, butter,* and *apples* at the grocery store yesterday.
7. The queen's necklace was made of *gold* and *diamonds*.
8. Many Chinese meals include *rice, meat,* and *vegetables*.
9. Lee received twenty *dollars* for his birthday. Now he has enough *money* to buy a new game.
10. no change

Quiz 8, p. 55

1. chickens
2. luck
3. chess
4. lights
5. oranges
6. beef
7. coffee
8. hair
9. homework
10. trips

Quiz 9, p. 56

1. many years
2. much time
3. many questions
4. much stuff
5. many photos
6. much patience
7. many reasons
8. many varieties
9. many sheep
10. much information

Quiz 10, p. 56

1. little
2. a few
3. a little
4. few
5. a little

Quiz 11, p. 57

1. a few
2. (very) few
3. little
4. a few
5. a little

Quiz 12, p. 57

1. Every
2. Many
3. Each
4. The majority of
5. One of
6. Most
7. Seventy-five percent of
8. Some
9. Many of
10. Some of

Quiz 13, p. 58

1. a
2. b
3. b
4. a
5. a
6. b
7. a
8. b
9. a
10. b

Quiz 14, p. 59

1. I found several new movies to watch online.
2. When Greg was a college student, he didn't have much money for going out.
3. My mom set the table with knives, forks, salad forks, and spoons.
4. The flower shop across the street has the biggest sunflowers I've ever seen.
5. My boss gave me some good advice.
6. Fifty percent of my classmates are from Asia.
7. Maurice doesn't eat many vegetables, but he loves fruit.
8. I have a twelve-year-old sister.
9. Two deer were standing near the lake in the early morning.
10. English is an international language.
11. Joan needs more bookshelves in her room. She has lots of books.
12. Steve loves basketball. He plays on a ten-man team.

Test 1, p. 60

A.

1. potatoes
2. feet
3. pianos
4. knives
5. roofs

B.

1. students'
2. friend's
3. Doris' OR Doris's
4. men's
5. patients'

C.
1. I love *snow* in the winter, especially when it falls in big *flakes*.
2. The *information* on the Internet is much more current than in printed *articles*.
3. Grace has had some good *jobs*. She really enjoys her *work* as a customer service representative.
4. *Life* is an adventure full of interesting *experiences*.
5. Baxter bought a lot of *stamps*. He was unsure about how much *postage* he needed.

D.
1. office
2. sixteen years old
3. bicycle
4. doctor's office
5. baby

E.
1. When Gloria went to the zoo yesterday, she took few pictures because it was raining.
2. One of the problems facing big cities is homelessness.
3. Brian was late for work because of so much traffic on the road.
4. Every child needs to play outdoors to be healthy.
5. Most stores in that mall close at 9:30 P.M.

Test 2, p. 62

A.
1. sheep
2. thieves
3. mice
4. crises
5. teeth

B.
1. this morning's
2. ladies'
3. Louis' OR Louis's
4. city's
5. Patty and Mike's

C.
1. Tim spent a lot of time on his *homework*. He had to finish *assignments* in chemistry and math.
2. Nina has fun trying on *dresses* and *shoes*. She loves to shop for *clothing*.
3. no change
4. The police found several *hairs* at the crime scene while they were gathering *evidence*.
5. It was difficult to lose *weight*, but I lost thirty *pounds*.

D.
1. six-page
2. orange
3. vegetable
4. eighteen-year-old
5. view of the city

E.
1. When I asked Adam for advice, he didn't have many suggestions.
2. When I got to the train station, there was plenty of room in the parking lot.
3. I have a few minutes to finish writing this report before the meeting.
4. One of the actors in the play forgot his lines.
5. The store accepts both credit cards and electronic payments.

CHAPTER 7

Quiz 1, p. 64
1. a
2. b
3. b
4. c
5. b
6. a
7. c
8. c
9. a
10. c

Quiz 2, p. 65
1. the
2. Ø
3. Ø
4. the
5. the
6. Ø
7. Ø
8. the
9. Ø
10. the

Quiz 3, p. 65
1. An
2. Ø Leather
3. A
4. A
5. Ø Smart phones
6. Ø Baseball
7. A
8. Ø Oranges
9. An
10. Ø Children

Quiz 4, p. 66
1. Ø Teachers
2. a
3. The
4. Ø
5. a
6. The
7. Ø
8. The

Quiz 5, p. 66
1. an, the
2. a, the, the
3. Ø
4. Ø
5. the

Quiz 6, p. 67
2. Ø
3. Ø
4. the
5. Ø
6. the
7. the
8. Ø
9. the
10. Ø
11. Ø

Quiz 7, p. 67
1. Salt Lake City, Utah is named after the Great Salt Lake, which is nearby.
2. Please lock the door when you leave the house.
3. Christine often wears earrings made of silver.
4. There was a fire in Bev's apartment last night. The smoke was terrible.
5. Josh works at a movie theater where all tickets cost $4.00.
6. Seattle has many beautiful mountains nearby. My favorite is Mount Baker.
7. Cathy often has fresh flowers on her kitchen table.
8. Visitors to Yellowstone National Park often get too close to the wild animals there.
9. Who invented the cellphone? I want to thank him or her!

Test 1, p. 68

A.
1. a, the
2. the, a
3. a, Ø, an
4. a, a, The

B.
1. Ø, some, the, the
2. the, the, a
3. the, some, an

C.
1. b
2. c
3. a
4. c
5. c

D.
1. I'd like a hamburger from Burger Hut for lunch.
2. People who want to become accountants have to pass a certification exam.
3. The people on the bus weren't hurt in the accident.
4. Did you get the text message I sent earlier today?
5. There are stamps for your letter in the desk drawer.

E.
1. the
2. Ø, the
3. Ø
4. Ø

Test 2, p. 70

A.
1. a, the
2. a, Ø, the
3. Ø, Ø, a
4. an, Ø, Ø, a

B.
1. Ø, a, Ø, a
2. an, The, a
3. an, a, some

C.
1. a
2. c
3. c
4. b
5. c

D.
1. There is a black sock under the bed.
2. Jorge wants to borrow the new headphones that I bought.
3. It's starting to rain. Do you have an umbrella that I can borrow?
4. The movie that I saw last night was really scary!
5. Most cars have electronic keys that are expensive to replace.

E.
1. Ø
2. Ø
3. the, the
4. The

CHAPTER 8

Quiz 1, p. 72
1. Angelo
2. my sister
3. cats
4. the championship game
5. my parents and I
6. caffeine
7. coffee, tea, and cola
8. the point of the lecture OR the lecture
9. Rita
10. Sean and Adam

Quiz 2, p. 73
1. She, her
2. they, them
3. it, He, us
4. he, him
5. we

Quiz 3, p. 73
1. mine, yours
2. Their, ours
3. her
4. His
5. Your, my
6. Their, It's
7. Her, their
8. Our, its

Quiz 4, p. 74
1. Its
2. My
3. her
4. yours
5. Their
6. Our
7. her
8. His

Quiz 5, p. 74
1. his / her / his or her
2. They *are*
3. his / her / his or her; their (informal)
4. his / her / his or her
5. he / she *practices*; they *practice* (informal)
6. his / her / his or her; their (informal)
7. It *has* / They *have*
8. *forgets* his / her / his or her; *forgets* their (informal)

Quiz 6, p. 75
1. yourself
2. themselves
3. himself
4. myself
5. themselves
6. ourselves
7. herself
8. itself

Quiz 7, p. 75
1. themselves
2. herself
3. himself
4. myself
5. yourself
6. ourselves
7. himself
8. themselves

Quiz 8, p. 76
1. others
2. another
3. the other
4. others
5. another
6. another, the others
7. the others
8. other

Quiz 9, p. 76
2. one after the other
3. every other
4. another
5. one another
6. the other
7. In other words
8. other than

Quiz 10, p. 77
1. his or her
2. I
3. her
4. myself
5. the other
6. others, the others
7. her
8. his
9. other
10. is
11. themselves
12. consists
13. We
14. your
15. himself

Test 1, p. 78

A.
1. I, my, he, me
2. her, she
3. her, She, him, his
4. their, They, him
5. his, hers

B.
1. class
2. people
3. bus driver
4. couple
5. committee
6. somebody

C.
1. himself
2. myself
3. herself
4. themselves
5. yourself
6. ourselves
7. itself

D.
1. others, the others, other
2. another, the other

E.
1. every other
2. one another
3. the other
4. Other than
5. one after the other
6. another
7. In other words

F.
1. he, He, his
2. they, their
3. We, our
4. his / her, He / She
5. they, they, them

Test 2, p. 81

A.
1. We, our, us
2. her, She, him, hers
3. her, them
4. you, your, you
5. I, our, They

B.
1. parents
2. dentist
3. people
4. everyone
5. team
6. faculty

C.
1. myself
2. ourselves
3. himself
4. themselves
5. herself
6. itself
7. yourself

D.
1. The other
2. the others
3. others, other, another

E.
1. another
2. each other
3. one after the other
4. the other
5. other than
6. In other words
7. every other

F.
1. they, them, they
2. it, It
3. They, they, their
4. it, It
5. he / she / he or she, he / she / he or she, his / her / his or her

CHAPTER 9

Quiz 1, p. 84
1. a
2. b
3. c
4. a
5. b
6. a
7. c
8. a
9. b
10. c

Quiz 2, p. 85
1. must OR has to go
2. must OR have to study
3. don't have to go
4. must OR has to take
5. must not smoke
6. must OR have to do
7. doesn't have to worry
8. must OR has to pay

Quiz 3, p. 85
2. duty
3. warning
4. suggestion
5. advice
6. duty

Quiz 4, p. 86
1. had better OR must
2. must / have to OR should
3. have to
4. should
5. should OR must / has to
6. must / have to
7. should OR had better
8. had better OR have to / must

Quiz 5, p. 87
1. could
2. could, should
3. should
4. could
5. should
6. should
7. could, could, should

Quiz 6, p. 88
2. Travelers are supposed to bring a passport or ID.
3. You are supposed to turn off your phone.
4. People are supposed to exercise regularly.
5. A driver is supposed to call the police.

Quiz 7, p. 88
1. John should call soon.
2. Your parents should be here soon.
3. You should pass the test.
4. The bus should come in a few minutes.
5. The weekend should be warm and sunny.

Quiz 8, p. 89
1. Josh is able to eat a whole pizza at one meal.
2. Are you able to carry my bag, please?
3. I am able to see really well in the dark.

Quiz 9, p. 89
1. Misty knows how to make her own yogurt.
2. My brother knows how to ride a motorcycle.
3. Do you know how to speak Spanish as well as English?

Quiz 10, p. 89
1. Ms. Wilson isn't able / is unable to play tennis for hours at a time.
2. Jessie doesn't know how to iron shirts perfectly.
3. I can't send you a text message later today.

Quiz 11, p. 90
1. can / may / might
2. can
3. may / might
4. can
5. can / may / might
6. may / might
7. may / might
8. can
9. can / may / might
10. can

Quiz 12, p. 90
1. request
2. permission
3. permission
4. request
5. permission
6. request
7. request
8. request
9. permission
10. permission

Quiz 13, p. 91
1. you
2. I
3. I
4. you
5. you
6. I
7. you
8. you
9. you
10. I

Quiz 14, p. 91
1. helping me with my homework?
2. if I went to a café?
3. if I took a nap?
4. carrying the box for me?
5. waiting for me?

Quiz 15, p. 92
1. Ø, we
2. I
3. you
4. Ø, we
5. you
6. we
7. you
8. I

Quiz 16, p. 93
1. May
2. Could
3. doesn't have to
4. should
5. Why don't
6. can
7. must
8. ought
9. might
10. Let's

Test 1, p. 94
A.
1. must
2. do (we) have to
3. must not
4. have to OR must
5. don't have to

B.
1. should
2. could
3. ought to
4. should
5. had better

C.
1. ought, can, should, may, be able to
2. don't have to, Why don't, have to, would, have to

D.
1. if I opened the window?
2. you help me wash the dishes?
3. taking me to the airport?
4. I go to a movie tonight?
5. you please vacuum the carpet?

E.
1. Would you mind if I used your pen?
2. In the United States, children are supposed to go to school until age sixteen.
3. Could you please help me move this table?
4. Silvia must send out her thank-you notes soon.
5. Would you mind calling me tomorrow?

Test 2, p. 96
A.
1. have to OR must
2. must not
3. have to OR must, have to
4. don't have to, don't have to

B.
1. ought to
2. had better
3. could
4. should
5. could

C.
1. could, Should, Let's, would, had better
2. have to, should, Why don't, Would, have to

D.
1. you put the laundry away?
2. if I got a drink of water?
3. you tell me what time it is?
4. I go shopping?
5. emptying the garbage?

E.
1. Matthew should not fall asleep at work.
2. I must help my parents in their store after school, so I can't play basketball.
3. Lindsay had better call me tonight.
4. Would you mind if I left work early today?
5. When does Ben have to be at the train station?

CHAPTER 10

Quiz 1, p. 99
1. both are correct
2. Alex used to work for Microsoft, but now he is working for Apple Computer.
3. I used to study at Kirk College before I transferred to the University of Georgia.
4. both are correct
5. In 2012, Mary used to live in a chic apartment in midtown Manhattan.

Quiz 2, p. 99

1. would be
2. used to be
3. would take
4. would work
5. used to be

Quiz 3, p. 100

1. had to talk
2. ought to have given
3. had to buy
4. didn't have to pay
5. shouldn't have left
6. were supposed to be
7. had to finish
8. should have listened
9. wasn't supposed to arrive
10. had to take

Quiz 4, p. 101

1. should have
2. shouldn't have
3. shouldn't have
4. should have
5. shouldn't have
6. should have
7. shouldn't have
8. should have
9. shouldn't have
10. should have
11. should have
12. shouldn't have

Quiz 5, p. 102

1. My mother could tap dance when she was 12 years old.
2. no change
3. The baby horse could stand up immediately after being born.
4. Eddie could walk when he was only ten months old.
5. no change

Quiz 6, p. 102

2. a and b
3. b
4. a and b
5. a and b
6. b

Quiz 7, p. 103

1. must
2. may
3. couldn't
4. may
5. might not
6. might
7. must
8. must not
9. could, might
10. mustn't

Quiz 8, p. 104

1. must
2. may OR might OR could
3. must
4. may OR might OR could
5. must
6. could OR must
7. may OR might OR could
8. may OR might OR could, may OR might
9. must

Quiz 9, p. 105

1. may OR might OR could have gone
2. can't OR couldn't have gotten
3. may OR might OR could have had
4. must have been
5. must not have slept
6. may OR might OR could have hit
7. may OR might OR could have come
8. must not OR couldn't OR can't have been
9. may OR might OR could have been
10. must have been

Quiz 10, p. 106

1. Mona may OR might OR could have forgotten her cell phone at home.
2. Mona can't OR couldn't have forgotten our meeting.
3. Mona must have left her office late.
4. Jim may OR might OR could have parked on a different street.
5. The police must have towed the car away.
6. Jim may OR might not have parked the car legally.
7. Jim may OR might OR could have had many unpaid parking tickets before this.

Quiz 11, p. 107

1. a. Jane
   b. Martha
   c. Mark
2. a. Alice's
   b. Jack's
   c. Kay's
3. a. Ms. Callahan
   b. Mr. Anton
   c. Mrs. Chu

Quiz 12, p. 108

1. may / might / could be talking
2. should have been listening
3. may / might / could have been taking
4. must be eating
5. should be cleaning
6. could / may / must have been driving
7. should have been sleeping
8. may / might / could be washing
9. must have been crying
10. should be paying

Quiz 13, p. 109

1. would rather take
2. would rather have
3. would rather not watch
4. would rather be sleeping
5. would rather have gone
6. would rather visit
7. would rather plant OR would rather have planted
8. would rather have gotten
9. would rather not be taking, would rather be playing
10. would rather have seen

Quiz 14, p. 110

1. must have forgotten
2. have got to
3. should
4. had better not
5. met
6. shouldn't have spent
7. will
8. borrow
9. may leave
10. couldn't be
11. has
12. be able to
13. drink
14. might
15. would

Test 1, p. 111

A.
1. could OR may OR might be
2. must be OR must have been
3. can OR could change, could OR may OR might be
4. may OR might need
5. should finish

B.
1. a. Linda
   b. Liz
   c. Sam
2. a. Mr. French
   b. Mrs. White
   c. Ms. Adams

C.
1. should be leaving
2. may / might / could be raining
3. must OR could / may / might be leaking
4. should be cleaning
5. may / might / could be meeting

D.
1. couldn't
2. can
3. can
4. can't
5. could, can

E.
1. would call
2. would rather be eating
3. would give
4. would play
5. would rather live

Test 2, p. 114

A.
1. may OR might OR could OR would rather go, should do
2. may OR might OR could change
3. must be OR must have been
4. can OR could leave, may OR might be able to
5. can OR may OR might not get

B.
1. a. Eva
   b. Ken
   c. Jeff
2. a. Kevin
   b. Julie
   c. Mr. Chang
   d. Tom

C.
1. must be looking
2. may OR might OR could be playing, may OR might OR could be reading
3. may OR might OR could OR must be studying
4. should OR must be going, should OR must be getting

D.
1. Can
2. could
3. can't
4. couldn't
5. can

E.
1. would take
2. would rather take
3. would rather have seen
4. would rather pass
5. would study

CHAPTER 11

Quiz 1, p. 116

1. P
2. P
3. A
4. P
5. A
6. P
7. A
8. P
9. A
10. P
11. A
12. P
13. P
14. A
15. P

Quiz 2, p. 117

1. a
2. b
3. a
4. a
5. b
6. b

Quiz 3, p. 118

2. is being answered
3. has been answered
4. was answered
5. was being answered
6. had been answered
7. will be answered
8. is going to be answered
9. Was ... answered
10. Has been answered
11. Will ... be answered

Quiz 4, p. 118

1. is enjoyed
2. are being studied
3. were stolen
4. is going to be discussed
9. Was ... explained
6. Are ... going to be given

Quiz 5, p. 119

1. are eaten
2. was invented
3. will be finished / is going to be finished
4. hasn't been elected
5. is being shown / will be shown / is going to be shown
6. were given
7. was featured
8. was written
9. were hit, were caught
10. is taught, are introduced

Quiz 6, p. 120

2. are read
3. (are) studied
4. were written
5. were performed
6. had not been published
7. have been translated
8. have been printed
9. are seen

Quiz 7, p. 120

1. The east coast of Florida was hit by Hurricane Betty two days ago.
2. Many houses were damaged in the storm.
3. Injured people were taken care of by aid workers.
4. The damage was evaluated the morning after the storm.
5. Some people were not allowed to go back to their homes.

Quiz 8, p. 121

1. a. may have been injured
   b. should have been driven
2. a. should not send / shouldn't send
   b. must be checked
3. a. has to be finished
   b. will be collected
4. a. should be divided / should have been divided
   b. could be chosen / could have been chosen
5. a. might have been started
   b. must have thrown

Quiz 9, p. 122

Sample answers:
1. All food must be rinsed from plastics, glass, and cans. OR
   Plastics, glass, and cans should be rinsed clean.
2. Clean boxes and paper items can / should be pressed flat.
3. Paper with food on it must not be recycled. It should be put in the trash. OR
   Paper with food on it should not be put in the recycle bin. It must be put in the trash.
4. All clean recyclable items can / should be put into your recycling bin.
5. Recycling bins should / must be put out for pick up by 7:00 A.M. on collection day.

Quiz 10, p. 123

1. with / in	6. to
2. about	7. of
3. to	8. to
4. with	
5. for	

Quiz 11, p. 123

1. am worried about
2. is located in
3. am finished with
4. is scared of / by
5. are excited about
6. is satisfied with
7. is exhausted from
8. am annoyed by / with

Quiz 12, p. 124

1. b, c	6. a
2. a, d	7. a, c, d
3. b, d	8. a, c, d
4. b, d	9. d
5. a, b	10. b, c

Quiz 13, p. 125

2. got arrested
3. didn't get killed
4. got done / has gotten done
5. am getting worried
6. got damaged
7. get (it) fixed
8. got finished
9. gets taken / will get taken
10. am getting accustomed / have gotten accustomed
11. get arrested

Quiz 14, p. 126

1. disappointing	5. embarrassing
2. surprised	6. annoyed
3. thrilling	7. shocked
4. excited	8. injured

Quiz 15, p. 126

1. entertaining	5. frustrated
2. satisfying	6. bored
3. surprised	7. fascinating
4. confusing	

Quiz 16, p. 127

1. a	7. b
2. c	8. a
3. c	9. c
4. d	10. b
5. c	11. d
6. a	12. d

Test 1, p. 128

A.

1. d	6. a
2. a	7. c
3. c	8. c
4. a	
5. c	

B.
1. was taken, was arrested
2. was made / will be made
3. are encouraged / have been encouraged / are being encouraged / were encouraged
4. has been given / was given / is going to be given / will be given
5. is being played

C.
1. Cell phones are used by nearly everyone these days.
2. The old book was lent to the university (by the museum). OR
   The university was lent the old book (by the museum).
3. The company president will be invited (by David) to speak at the meeting.
4. A visa is required (by the government) for tourists to visit the country.
5. Our car is being fixed (by the mechanic) at Maher's Auto Repair.

D.

1. should be obeyed	4. must be finished
2. could have been given	5. can be seen
3. should arrive	

E.
1. of
2. in
3. for
4. in / with
5. about
6. with / by
7. by / with / in

F.
1. interesting
2. exciting
3. fascinated, amazing
4. frightening
5. embarrassed

Test 2, p. 131

A.
1. c
2. b
3. a
4. b
5. b
6. a
7. b
8. a

B.
1. has been asked / was asked / is being asked / will be asked
2. will be given
3. is scheduled
4. were agreed / have been agreed
5. is being loaded, will be finished

C.
1. Scholarships are being given to many students from low-income families. OR
   Many students from low-income families are being given scholarships.
2. Michael was hit on the head by a falling pine cone.
3. Each computer is checked five times (by workers) before they pack it for shipping. OR
   Each computer is checked five times (by workers) before it is packed for shipping.
4. The weeds on the hill are going to be cut down.
5. The Cancer Foundation was given two million dollars (by an anonymous donor). OR
   Two million dollars was given to the Cancer Foundation (by an anonymous donor).

D.
1. should have been eaten
2. must have left
3. can always be counted
4. should be baked / should have been baked
5. may be invited / may have been invited

E.
1. about
2. with
3. for
4. for
5. from / by
6. with / by
7. in / with

F.
1. embarrassing
2. expected, surprising
3. balanced
4. Experienced
5. thrilling

CHAPTER 12

Quiz 1, p. 134
1. Mr. Murphy doesn't know how much the tickets are.
2. The students will ask their teacher when the final exam is.
3. Patricia wanted to know when her dad would give her a ride to school.
4. The police are trying to find out what happened.

5. We wondered why the woman had come to the meeting.
6. Can you tell me what time it is?

Quiz 2, p. 134
1. ALICE: did your tablet computer cost
   FATIMA: I paid
2. JEREMY: did Bill park / has Bill parked
   WILL: the car is
3. ARTURO: did you sell / have you sold
   PETER: Ted sold / Ted has sold
4. SIMON: does it say
5. OLIVER: the key is
   MIKE: is it
   OLIVER: it is

Quiz 3, p. 135
1. where the nearest post office is
2. who Pierre visited in Paris last year
3. how much Sue's car cost
4. which pages we are supposed to study
5. who left the door unlocked
6. how much time we have left
7. why they are going to the police station
8. why there is so much traffic today
9. how they will solve their financial problems
10. whose cell phone that is

Quiz 4, p. 136
2. d
3. a, c
4. a, b
5. a, d
6. a, b, d

Quiz 5, p. 137
1. if / whether / whether or not Alice is going to pass her math class
2. if / whether / whether or not an express mail package arrived today
3. if / whether / whether or not Andy likes the new basketball coach
4. if / whether / whether or not anyone has seen the new show at the Paramount Theater
5. if / whether / whether or not Jim and Marcia were at the party last night
6. if / whether you prefer coffee or tea for breakfast
7. if / whether / whether or not Ken had ever been to an opera before last night
8. if / whether / whether or not Max usually rides his bicycle to school
9. if / whether / whether or not the Smiths are coming over for dinner on Saturday
10. if / whether / whether or not she will go to Orlando with us

Quiz 6, p. 138
1. Mick showed me how to solve a Sudoku puzzle.
2. I can't decide whether or not to travel over the holidays.
3. Julie wanted to know when to start the barbecue.
4. I wondered what to do with my old clothes.
5. Sandy and Jack discussed where to go on vacation.

Quiz 7, p. 138
Possible answers:
1. how to do / how to solve / how to figure out
2. how to get / how to go / how to drive

3. where to find / where to get
4. what to do
5. whether to watch

Quiz 8, p. 139

1. Are you sure that you didn't leave your cell phone in the car?
2. It's a fact that there have been several robberies in our neighborhood recently.
3. That Steve failed his driving test is unfortunate.
4. Did I remind you that we are going shopping after work?
5. Ginger is excited that she will go to Costa Rica in March.

Quiz 9, p. 139

1. That Sarah won't be able to attend the celebration is too bad.
2. It is unlikely that the doctor gave you the wrong prescription.
3. It's a miracle that the little boy survived the plane crash.
4. That Rosa didn't finish the project on time surprises me.
5. That no one will pass this class without additional help from the teacher is clear.

Quiz 10, p. 140

Sample answers:

2. That Karen and Joe will arrive tomorrow is wonderful.
3. It's wonderful that Mary got an award for Teacher of the Year.
4. I'm lucky that I have a very loving and supportive family.
5. Martin is confident that our soccer team is going to do well this season.
6. Scientists believe (that) a meteorite hit the earth 65 million years ago.
7. It is unfortunate that a number of the tests were graded incorrectly.
8. That my daughter got a job as a flight attendant with Amazon Airlines is wonderful.
9. I promise that I will pay back the money I borrowed by the end of the month.

Quiz 11, p. 141

1. "Where are you going on your vacation?" Ruth asked.
2. "We are going on a road trip to Alaska," replied Anne.
3. "That sounds like fun," said Ruth. "How long will you be gone?"
4. "Around three weeks," answered Anne. "We are going to tour the southeast coast and visit a glacier. We also hope to go to one of the national parks."
5. "I hear Alaska is beautiful," said Ruth, "so you're sure to have a wonderful vacation."
6. "Yes," added Anne, "and we're sure to put lots of miles on our car."

Quiz 12, p. 141

1. (that) she doesn't want to eat her vegetables
2. (that) the earth has seven continents and five oceans
3. (that) she had a lot of work to do today / that day

4. if there were any new magazines available
5. (that) he thought that was an excellent book
6. what time the meeting started

Quiz 13, p. 142

1. (that) they might have pizza for dinner
2. how she could help me
3. (that) he had to be at work by 9:00 A.M.
4. (that) children ought to listen when adults are / were talking
5. when the movie would begin
6. (that) he was going to be here / there in fifteen minutes
7. (that) the local radio station would have a singing contest next month, (that) I should enter it
8. if he had to finish that project today / that day, (that) he might not have enough time

Quiz 14, p. 143

Sample answers:

1. David's mom asked him how his English test had been, and he replied that it hadn't been too hard.
2. When Harry said that he was so tired, Max told him that he should get more sleep.
3. Doug asked a clerk where the shoe department was, and she / he told him it was on the second floor. Doug thanked the clerk for his / her help.
4. Susan said that she had her first accounting class, and Carol asked her who her instructor was. Susan told her that her instructor was Professor Nelson. Carol replied that she had been in her class last year and thought she was great.

Quiz 15, p. 144

1. call
2. stay
3. go
4. talk
5. report
6. take
7. decide
8. get
9. pay
10. call

Quiz 16, p. 144

1. I don't know if we will buy a new car this year or not.
2. Can you tell me what time the concert starts?
3. Delia knows that I'm going to ride to Vancouver with her.
4. The student asked her counselor which class she should take.
5. After the flood, the president requested that everyone be helpful.
6. That Jordan was angry was obvious.
7. Marcy wants to know how much the bag costs.
8. I wonder if it is supposed to rain tomorrow.

Test 1, p. 145

A.

1. when Flight 2803 arrives
2. if / whether the mail has already been picked up
3. how the fire started
4. what grade I got on the last quiz
5. if / whether Jim would prefer a sweater or a shirt

B.

1. don't know what else to say
2. didn't know which way to go

3. wasn't sure what to do or how to begin
4. can't decide whether to go on a trip or visit his family during the holidays

C.
1. That James is lying is a shame. OR
   It is a shame that James is lying.
2. I am amazed that Sophie got 100% on the vocabulary quiz.
3. It is a fact that women live longer than men. OR
   That women live longer than men is a fact.
4. I agree that the coffee at the Campus Café is terrible.
5. That Max's father has six names is unusual. OR
   It is unusual that Max's father has six names.

D.
1. "I don't want to waste time," said Mary, "so let's hurry."
2. "Why did the mother bird fly away from the nest?" asked Jimmy.
3. Valerie told the tour group, "Please stay close together so no one gets lost."
4. "Mr. Donovan is our attorney," Margaret said. "He is very good."
5. When he saw the car coming towards them, James shouted, "Look out!"

E.
Sample answer:
When Anita asked the clerk if they sold computer accessories, he asked what she was looking for. Anita said she needed a wireless mouse for her laptop. The clerk asked Anita what kind of computer she had. When she said she had a MacBook Air, he showed her those that should work with her computer. Anita thanked him.

F.
1. go
2. choose
3. dress
4. buy
5. take

Test 2, p. 148

A.
1. how often you go to the gym
2. if / whether Teresa stayed after school to play table tennis
3. what time the movie starts
4. where Ana went after the lecture
5. if / whether Paul's meetings usually end on time

B.
1. can't decide which one to invite to the school dance
2. asked the doctor how often to take the medicine
3. told us how many paragraphs to write and when to turn it in
4. told the actors to rehearse their lines more before the performance

C.
1. That Mischa needs to study harder is the truth. OR
   It is the truth that Mischa needs to study harder.
2. It is too bad that Emma had to take her driving test three times before she passed. OR
   That Emma had to take her driving test three times before she passed is too bad.
3. Many Chinese are proud that the Chinese have used traditional medicines for thousands of years.
4. That too much sun can cause skin cancer is a well-known fact. OR
   It is a well-known fact that too much sun can cause skin cancer.
5. Jason is glad that the library is a quiet place to study.

D.
1. "Are you ready to order?" asked the waiter.
2. "Please help me," Doug begged. "This box is too heavy for me to carry."
3. "I don't want to go home!" cried the angry child.
4. "It is an unusual problem," said the scientist, "but I think we can find a solution."
5. Ms. Bell said to the students, "Please talk quietly in the library."

E.
Sample answer:
Mr. Thomas told Mary that she hadn't done well on the quiz, and he asked her what had happened. She said that she really hadn't had enough time to study, so Mr. Thomas asked her why. She told him that her mother had been sick and she had been taking care of her. Mr. Thomas said that Mary should have told him because she could have taken the quiz on a different day.

F.
1. have
2. wear
3. arrive
4. greet
5. do

CHAPTER 13

Quiz 1, p. 151
1. a, b, c
2. c, d, e
3. a, c
4. c, d
5. b
6. d
7. a, b, c, d
8. a, c, d
9. a, b, c
10. c, d

Quiz 2, p. 152
1. Robin told the children a story that / which made them laugh.
2. Jason applied for a job at the new café that / which / Ø I told you about.
3. The pianist played a Mozart concerto that / which was one of Mark's favorite pieces of music.
4. My roommate invited her brother who(m) / that / I had never met before to our party.
5. The new computer that / which / Ø I just bought last week makes my work easier.
6. Angela, who has three younger sisters and a younger brother, is the oldest child in her family.
7. The elderly woman who(m) / that / Ø Anne helped with yard work was grateful.
8. Julia's husband gave her some beautiful roses that / which / Ø he bought at the flower market.

Quiz 3, p. 153
1. who
2. whose
3. who
4. whose
5. whose
6. who
7. who
8. whose
9. whose
10. whose
11. who
12. whose
13. who
14. who
15. whose

Quiz 4, p. 154

1. The boy whose father is a dentist has beautiful teeth.
2. We want to do business with that company whose products are top quality.
3. Sarah feels sorry for her neighbors whose car was stolen last night.
4. The student whose homework was never done came to class late every day.
5. I have never met Meg's brother whose wife is the conductor of the symphony orchestra.
6. The dog whose back leg is injured always begs for food.
7. Ellen met a kind man whose parents died when he was very young.
8. The Johnsons, whose son goes to Stanford University, live in the apartment upstairs.
9. Claire, whose son goes to school in California, lives in New York.
10. Robert, whose favorite team made the finals, went to the big game.

Quiz 5, p. 155

1. which
2. where / in which
3. where / in which
4. which
5. where / in which

Quiz 6, p. 155

1. I have a job in the public relations department where / in which 14 people work.
2. Our department is in the east wing where / in which the advertising department is also located.
3. I share an office, where / in which we have our desks and computers, with another worker.
4. My boss has a large office where / in which she meets important clients.
5. This company is a good place where / in which employees are treated fairly.

Quiz 7, p. 156

1. where
2. when
3. where
4. where
5. when
6. when
7. where
8. when
9. where
10. when

Quiz 8, p. 157

1. My favorite season is spring when the colorful spring flowers bloom.
2. That is the furniture store where we bought our couch and coffee table.
3. I last saw David on that day when he got his new car.
4. Jim remembers a time when gasoline cost $1.25 per gallon.
5. The Chinese restaurant where we ate dinner served delicious seafood.
6. Do you know the name of the city where the Olympic games will be held?
7. Every student looks forward to the day when summer vacation begins.
8. A market where they sell many international products is near our house.
9. My favorite time of the year is fall when I play soccer.
10. That is the house where my best friend lives.

Quiz 9, p. 158

2. f
3. h
4. a
5. c
6. d
7. k
8. e
9. j
10. g
11. b

Quiz 10, p. 159

1. b
2. a
3. b
4. a
5. a
6. b

Quiz 11, p. 160

1. The city of Dubrovnik, which is on the Adriatic coast, is surrounded by an ancient stone wall.
2. no change
3. On our last family vacation we went to Disneyland, where we shook hands with Mickey Mouse.
4. I saw Alex and Alice, who are twins, at the shopping center.
5. The Mississippi River, which is one of the most important rivers in the United States, has an interesting history.
6. Mr. Mitchell, whom we saw at the flower show, is a fantastic gardener.
7. no change
8. *The Marriage of Figaro*, which is one of Mozart's comedic operas, is performed regularly on stages around the world.
9. no change
10. The book that I'm reading is from the Everett Public Library, where you can borrow books for up to three weeks.

Quiz 12, p. 161

1. Many people, most of whom bought their tickets online, were waiting to go inside.
2. Some moviegoers, several of whom looked sleepy, went to the midnight show.
3. The movie has three main characters, all of whom are interesting and funny.
4. The stars in the movie, most of whom studied acting, are very talented.
5. My sister saw the movies, both of which she liked, last week.
6. Most people, some of whom had tears in their eyes, laughed a lot during the movie.
7. There are many snacks, most of which are sweets, to choose from.
8. Theater employees, more than half of whom are college students, sell a lot of popcorn.
9. My friends, two of whom go to the movies every weekend, went to the theater with me.
10. After the movie, the building caretaker found two jackets, neither of which was mine.

Quiz 13, p. 162

1. a. the sentence
   b. a noun
2. a. the sentence
   b. a noun
3. a. a noun
   b. the sentence

Quiz 14, p. 162

1. Harold bought a newspaper, which he read on the train on the way to work.
2. On the way to work, Max stopped to get coffee, which was part of his morning routine.
3. After she got off the phone, Margaret typed an email, which was a message for her boss.
4. The receptionist answered the phone, which was a big part of her job.

Quiz 15, p. 163

1. The police officer responsible for directing traffic is very helpful.
2. Anyone passing the national exam will get a diploma.
3. Montana, the fourth largest state in the U.S., is on the border with Canada.
4. The boys playing soccer are preparing for a big tournament.
5. Instructors attending the workshop will learn about using cell phone apps in teaching.
6. How much are the tickets for the flight leaving at 11:30 P.M.?
7. The archeologists digging in an area in eastern China made an important discovery.
8. The Olympic official presenting the medals shook hands with the athletes.
9. There are more and more Americans driving cars that run on electricity.
10. Heather is the manager overseeing the accounting department.

Quiz 16, p. 164

1. b
2. a
3. a
4. b
5. a
6. b
7. a
8. b

Test 1, p. 165

A.
1. b
2. c, d
3. a, c
4. b
5. c, d

B.
1. a. whom
   b. who
2. a. whom
   b. who
3. a. whose
   b. who

C.
1. Connie finally finished preparing the documents that / which the department supervisor needs to sign.
2. My grandmother bought a lot of clothes that / which were on sale.
3. The red truck which / that caused the accident was driven by a drunk driver.
4. The young woman who / whom Sam just met seemed intelligent and pleasant.
5. Mrs. Tanaka is looking for the person whose car is blocking the driveway.

D.
1. *Little Women,* published in 1868, is my sister's favorite novel.
2. The science program showing on TV every night this week is a series about the brain.
3. People visiting the Taj Mahal are impressed that a man built it to honor his wife.
4. The director's new movie, opening in theaters this weekend, is sure to be entertaining.
5. People interested in French cooking often go to Paris to experience the food.

E.
1. Tom, who lives in Port Hadlock, is graduating from high school in June.
2. no change
3. Paul will call you at 5:30 P.M., when he will be home from work.
4. I have looked everywhere for my grammar book, which I thought I had left on the table. I can't find it anywhere.
5. no change

Test 2, p. 167

A.
1. c, d
2. a, d
3. b
4. c, d
5. a, c, d

B.
1. who
2. whose
3. whom
4. who
5. who
6. whom

C.
1. Joe's parents don't like the music that / which Joe / he listens to.
2. The printer that / which Matthew bought last week is fast and dependable.
3. The police talked to the woman whose car had been broken into.
4. The issue that / which many people are talking about is not important to our company.
5. People who have advanced technology skills are in great demand in today's job market.

D.
1. Students having high grades can apply for the scholarship.
2. The storms occurring in the eastern U.S. are the result of climate change.
3. Anyone having information about the robbery should call the police.
4. The lecture will most likely be attended by people interested in the Middle East.
5. The people not able / unable to see the lunar eclipse could look at photos of it online.

E.
1. We need to replace our roof, which is 20 years old and is leaking badly.
2. no change
3. no change
4. Jennifer's birthday cake, which had strawberries and cream on top, was enjoyed by everyone at the party.
5. The Red Cross, which provides humanitarian aid around the world, is Michele's favorite charity.

CHAPTER 14

Quiz 1, p. 169
Check numbers 1, 2 and 4.

Quiz 2, p. 169
Check numbers 2, 3 and 5.

Quiz 3, p. 170
1. shopping
2. playing
3. to celebrate
4. to go, barking
5. to call
6. to be
7. driving
8. calling
9. to have
10. planting
11. keeping
12. to grow
13. giving
14. to go
15. stopping
16. to study, to visit
17. going, to eat

Quiz 4, p. 171
1. us to come
2. to announce
3. them to play
4. to retire, him to stop
5. people to stay
6. students to try
7. to take
8. to pass
9. him to buy
10. to attend
11. her son to audition
12. to arrive, me to be

Quiz 5, p. 172
1. b
2. b
3. a
4. a
5. b
6. a, b
7. b
8. a, b
9. a
10. a

Quiz 6, p. 173
1. to
2. for
3. of
4. from
5. to
6. of
7. to
8. on

Quiz 7, p. 173
1. in coming
2. to helping
3. about / of taking
4. for coming
5. to wearing
6. for cleaning
7. about going
8. of standing

Quiz 8, p. 174
1. went dancing
2. will go sightseeing, go hiking
3. goes biking, goes jogging
4. go sailing
5. went fishing
6. gone snorkeling
7. go shopping
8. went sledding

Quiz 9, p. 174
1. Ms. Spring sat at her desk paying bills yesterday.
2. Every night Greg wastes a lot of time surfing the Internet.
3. We spent too much money eating in restaurants last month.
4. Stewart always has a hard time solving physics problems.
5. Carol had a good time traveling with her sisters last summer.

Quiz 10, p. 175
1. It's interesting to read about scientific discoveries.
2. It isn't easy to find a parking place downtown.
3. It takes a long time to learn a foreign language well.
4. It is impolite to talk when someone else is talking.
5. It costs a lot to fly first class.

Quiz 11, p. 175
1. Reading about scientific discoveries is interesting.
2. Finding a parking place downtown isn't easy.
3. Learning a foreign language well takes a long time.
4. Talking when someone else is talking is impolite.
5. Flying first class costs a lot.

Quiz 12, p. 176
1. a
2. a
3. a
4. b
5. a
6. a
7. b
8. a
9. b
10. b

Test 1, p. 177
A.
1. a
2. b
3. a
4. a
5. b

B.
1. about
2. on
3. for
4. about / of
5. to

C.
1. for borrowing
2. studying, to get
3. bringing
4. Listening
5. waiting, to go
6. sneezing
7. in learning
8. skiing
9. to buy, doing
10. to take / taking
11. Taking
12. relaxing

D.
1. to send
2. snowboarding
3. to lock, putting, hearing
4. telling
5. to buy

E.
1. My dad always takes his time choosing a new car.
2. It is uncomfortable to live in a hot climate without air-conditioning.
3. My sisters and I go swimming at the neighborhood pool twice a month.
4. Dennis sometimes has difficulty expressing his opinion.
5. Having a visa is necessary for traveling overseas.

Test 2, p. 180

A.
1. b
2. a
3. b
4. b
5. a

B.
1. to
2. in
3. of
4. about
5. from

C.
1. visiting
2. buying
3. to see
4. of telling, breaking
5. to be
6. eating
7. having
8. bothering, to take
9. for taking
10. to wear / wearing
11. to go
12. needing, to come

D.
1. smoking
2. to tell
3. seeing
4. to learn
5. doing
6. to sign

E.
1. It is terrible to wake up with a headache.
2. Living on their own is a good experience for young adults.
3. Jenny sometimes catches her children watching videos in the middle of the night.
4. It is dangerous for children to use fireworks without adult supervision.
5. The tourists are standing on the corner trying to figure out where to go.

CHAPTER 15

Quiz 1, p. 183
1. to
2. for
3. to
4. to
5. for
6. to
7. for

Quiz 2, p. 183
1. in order
2. Ø
3. Ø
4. in order
5. in order
6. Ø, in order
7. Ø, Ø

Quiz 3, p. 184
2. delighted to
3. surprised to
4. disappointed to
5. embarrassed to
6. proud to
7. unlikely to OR hesitant to
8. determined to
9. fortunate to
10. hesitant to or unlikely to
11. relieved to

Quiz 4, p. 185
1. b
2. a
3. a
4. b
5. a
6. b
7. a
8. a

Quiz 5, p. 186
1. painful enough
2. ripe enough
3. too bright
4. spicy enough
5. big enough
6. strong enough
7. too sweet
8. warm enough

Quiz 6, p. 186
1. to be married
2. being interviewed
3. being asked
4. to be invited
5. to be prepared
6. being driven
7. to be treated
8. being taken
9. to be remembered
10. being recognized

Quiz 7, p. 187
1. a
2. b
3. a
4. b
5. a

Quiz 8, p. 187
1. having lent
2. to have been asked
3. to have caused
4. having been told
5. to have been notified

Quiz 9, p. 188
1. washing OR to be washed
2. to buy
3. correcting OR to be corrected
4. to get
5. to find
6. repairing OR to be repaired
7. to fix
8. painting OR to be painted

Quiz 10, p. 188
2. ring or ringing
3. flashing
4. discuss / discussing
5. get, give
6. burning
7. tell

Quiz 11, p. 189
1. a, b
2. c
3. b
4. a
5. c
6. a
7. a
8. a
9. a, b
10. c

Quiz 12, p. 190
1. a
2. c
3. b
4. c
5. b
6. a

Quiz 13, p. 191

1. a. our
   b. us
2. a. my
   b. me
3. a. his
   b. him
4. a. their
   b. them
5. a. her
   b. her

Quiz 14, p. 192

1. ring
2. tall enough
3. too
4. borrow
5. to hear
6. to have been told
7. to be dusted
8. to introduce
9. waving
10. to pick
11. to being sent
12. to work
13. have
14. my
15. stop

Test 1, p. 193

A.
1. Ø
2. in order
3. in order
4. Ø
5. in order

B.
1. a
2. b
3. a
4. b
5. b

C.
1. to be washed
2. being seen
3. to be asked
4. to be introduced
5. being laughed

D.
1. hiding
2. burning
3. flying
4. brushing / brush
5. crying / cry

E.
1. stay
2. move
3. figure
4. to dance
5. return

F.
1. b
2. a
3. b
4. b
5. a

Test 2, p. 196

A.
1. in order
2. Ø
3. Ø
4. in order
5. Ø

B.
1. b
2. a
3. a
4. b
5. b

C.
1. being worried
2. to be invited
3. being allowed
4. to be thrown
5. to be treated

D.
1. standing
2. take / taking
3. report / reporting
4. blowing
5. beep / beeping

E.
1. find
2. use
3. to open
4. stretch
5. postpone

F.
1. b
2. a
3. a
4. b
5. a

CHAPTER 16

Quiz 1, p. 199

1. began
2. fit
3. trying
4. forgiveness
5. spoken
6. catch
7. sending
8. disappointed

Quiz 2, p. 199

1. High school graduation is an exciting, fun, and rewarding time for most students and their families.
2. Students are tired of high school, are ready for something new, and are looking forward to college or work.
3. Parents feel proud, satisfied, and relieved that their children have reached this milestone in their lives.
4. There are many events leading up to graduation day. For example, most graduates get their picture taken, send out graduation announcements, and invite friends and family to celebrate with them.
5. On graduation day there is a ceremony that includes speeches, awards, and music.
6. Parents, siblings, and friends look on as students receive their diplomas.
7. High school graduation is a sort of "coming of age" into the adult world of opportunity, independence, and responsibility.

Quiz 3, p. 200

1. Vienna, Austria, is famous for classical music, opera, and the waltz.
2. The new magazine was colorful and glossy and had lots of photographs and advertising.
3. The fireman put out a fire, rescued a cat stuck in a tree, and helped a man who had had a heart attack.
4. In Brazil, I saw white sand beaches, beautiful young women and men, and crystal clear blue water.
5. When Jane got home from work, she took off her suit and her high-heeled shoes and put on an old pair of jeans, an old pair of slippers, and a warm wool sweater.

Quiz 4, p. 201

1. My brother is an accountant. He can help us with our income taxes.
2. An Australian swimmer was attacked by a shark, but he scared the animal away by poking it in the eye.
3. Denny's computer stopped working while he was working on his college application. Fortunately, he had saved his documents, so he didn't lose any data.
4. A woman in Michigan got a $1 parking ticket in 1976. She finally paid it in 2008 by sending a twenty-dollar bill to the local police station. She also sent a note explaining the money, but she told the police not to try to find her.

5. People have been playing soccer since ancient times. The first soccer clubs were formed in England in the 1850s, but official soccer rules were not written until 1863. Many of those same rules still govern soccer today.

Quiz 5, p. 201
1. are
2. is
3. is
4. are
5. is
6. are
7. is
8. are

Quiz 6, p. 202
1. Neither Janice nor Erica has any brothers or sisters.
2. Both Greg and his twin brother are interested in studying medicine.
3. We can have either broccoli or cauliflower for dinner.
4. I have neither a passport nor money for travel.
5. Both the New York Yankees and the Tokyo Giants are great baseball teams.
6. Either my husband or my daughter and I will go to a movie tonight. OR
   Either my husband and I or my daughter and I will go to a movie tonight.
7. My English teacher had neither graded our essays nor returned our vocabulary quizzes.
8. During her speech, Lina spoke both loudly and clearly.

Quiz 7, p. 203
1. intelligent
2. either John or Linda
3. plane
4. slowly
5. likes
6. paid
7. work
8. facts
9. eat
10. is

Test 1, p. 204
A.
1. love, likes
2. were
3. is
4. appreciates

B.
1. Polly was looking for a new tablet computer for her brother's birthday. She wanted a large selection and good prices, so she used the Internet to do her shopping.
2. Both Silvia and her husband love the rock band Wind Tunnel, but they refuse to pay $125 a ticket to attend a concert.
3. Myron has written short stories and poems for the school literary magazine, and sports and feature articles for the school newspaper.
4. Acme Toy Company continues to produce dolls, metal cars, construction sets, and action figures, but it no longer makes bicycles or board games.
5. Flights 2058 and 2065 to Los Angeles have been delayed, but Flight 2061 is departing on time. I can get you a seat on Flight 2061.

C.
1. Linda has traveled by car, bus, and train, but she has not traveled by ship, plane, or balloon.
2. Thomas has read about computers and the Internet, and he has taken classes in computer programming and applications.

3. Next weekend, Shirley wants to visit her grandmother and spend time with friends, but she has to do her laundry and clean the bathroom, too.
4. Last year, I traveled to Germany and France on business, but this year I hope to find a new job and stop traveling so much.
5. At her surprise birthday party, Gloria was surprised to see her high school friends, her aunt and uncle from New York City, and her old college roommate, but she was disappointed not to see her sister or / and her niece.

D.
1. The terrible rainstorm both flooded basements and sewers and caused mudslides.
2. Either Cindy or Mrs. Smith will babysit the kids this evening.
3. Neither Arthur nor his cousins have ever been to Disneyland.
4. During the holiday weekend, the parking lots at both San Francisco International Airport and San Jose Airport were full.
5. Both bread and flour should be stored in the freezer instead of the refrigerator.
2061.

Test 2, p. 207
A.
1. save
2. live
3. have
4. is
5. wants

B.
1. I have tried the low fat diet, the low sugar diet, and the protein diet too, but none of them worked.
2. The weather forecaster predicts heavy fog and light drizzle for the morning, but clear skies and sunshine for the late afternoon.
3. Mary doesn't like to drink tea or decaffeinated coffee, so we need to pick up some regular coffee for her.
4. Bicycles, motorcycles, and handicapped drivers' cars can be parked in Lot A, but everyone else needs to park in Lots B or C.
5. Barbara has had many different jobs. She has been a flight attendant, a salesclerk, a waitress, and a receptionist, but now she has her MBA and is the regional manager for a large multinational corporation.

C.
1. Last night, Larry watched some TV, surfed the Internet, listened to some music, and read the newspaper, but today he has to do some serious work.
2. Mr. Kincaid owns real estate, stocks, and bonds, but he has to sell some stocks and bonds to pay his taxes.
3. Both Craig and Jean have good computer skills and can type 70 words a minute, and they both got jobs as executive assistants.
4. Both French and German are Indo-European languages, but Chinese and Korean are not.
5. Because it was an extremely cold day, Mark put on a heavy sweater and a warm jacket, but he didn't wear a hat or a scarf.

D.
1. The earthquake both knocked down several freeways and broke gas and water lines.
2. Philip wants neither to go to college nor find a job.

3. Both oranges and cabbage are good sources of vitamin C.
4. The contractor will either try to repair the broken fence or tear it down and replace it.
5. Neither mayoral candidate Jim Brown nor mayoral candidate Alicia Taylor talked about the homeless problem.

CHAPTER 17

Quiz 1, p. 210

1. As soon as I finish my report, I will email you.
2. Since it was hot today, Claire went swimming.
3. By the time I graduate, I will be 18 years old.
4. When Robert went to the game, he saw Marie.
5. As soon as I get home, I'm going to make dinner.
6. Just as I was about to leave, my sister called me.

Quiz 2, p. 210

1. Bryan and Cathy went to Rome after they visited Florence.
2. As soon as my plane arrives in Jakarta, I will call you.
3. Just as Ciela finished loading the game on her phone, the phone battery died.
4. Max was watching a video on his computer while he was folding his laundry.
5. By the time we see you next summer, you will have graduated from high school.
6. The police won't leave until the accident is cleared from the highway.
7. The first time Kevin tried to ride a motorcycle, he crashed into a fence.
8. I have been a *Star Wars* fan ever since I was a child.
9. Carol will return to her office once the meeting ends.
10. Since the 3M Company first made Post-It Notes, they have been sold in many sizes, shapes, and colors.

Quiz 3, p. 211

1. d	6. c
2. c	7. a
3. b	8. b
4. a	9. c
5. b	10. b

Quiz 4, p. 212

1. Whenever Sue comes home late, her parents are upset. OR
   Sue's parents are upset whenever she comes home late.
2. The chef heated up the barbecue before he grilled the steaks. OR
   Before the chef grilled the steaks, he heated up the barbecue.
3. After I showed my passport, the customs officer let me pass into the terminal. OR
   The customs officer let me pass into the terminal after I showed my passport.
4. Every time Shelley works out at the gym, she needs to drink a lot of water. OR
   Shelley needs to drink a lot of water every time she works out at the gym.
5. As soon as Mr. Arnold turns off the lights, we will be able to see the screen better. OR
   We will be able to see the screen better as soon as Mr. Arnold turns off the lights.

6. The crowd cheered when they saw the baseball fly over the stadium wall. OR
   When the crowd saw the baseball fly over the stadium wall, they cheered.
7. By the time I finish my homework, it will be midnight. OR
   It'll be midnight by the time I finish my homework.
8. The pilot got a message from the control tower just before the plane landed. OR
   Just before the plane landed, the pilot got a message from the control tower.
9. While Karen was shutting down her computer, the computer made a strange noise. OR
   Karen's computer made a strange noise while she was shutting it down.
10. Since Brad and Martha got married in 2012, they have played Scrabble once a week. OR
    Brad and Martha have played Scrabble once a week since they got married in 2012.

Quiz 5, p. 213

1. Because John arrived at the airport just ten minutes before his flight's departure time, he nearly missed his plane. OR
   John nearly missed his plane because he arrived at the airport just ten minutes before his flight's departure time.
2. Because we had never been to Scotland, we did a lot of research about it before our trip. OR
   We did a lot of research about Scotland before our trip because we had never been there.
3. Now that the rain has stopped, we can open the windows and get some fresh air. OR
   We can open the windows and get some fresh air now that the rain has stopped.
4. We will have to call or email Mr. Adams since he doesn't like to text. OR
   Since Mr. Adams doesn't like to text, we will have to call or email him.
5. Sue did not enjoy going to the movies because she had left her eyeglasses at home. OR
   Because Sue had left her eyeglasses at home, she did not enjoy going to the movies.
6. Larry has to do a lot of traveling now that he is the senior manager for his company. OR
   Now that Larry is the senior manager for his company, he has to do a lot of traveling.
7. We can stay up late and talk since we don't have to go to work tomorrow. OR
   Since we don't have to go to work tomorrow, we can stay up late and talk.
8. I need to find a new place to get my hair cut now that my barber has retired after 25 years. OR
   Now that my barber has retired after 25 years, I need to find a new place to get my hair cut.
9. Because I didn't pay my phone bill last week, the phone company sent me a notice today. OR
   The phone company sent me a notice today because I didn't pay my phone bill last week.
10. Since Rosa didn't have any cash, she paid for her groceries with a credit card. OR
    Rosa paid for her groceries with a credit card since she didn't have any cash.

Quiz 6, p. 214

1. even though
2. because
3. Even though
4. because
5. Because
6. even though
7. because, Even though
8. even though, because
9. Because, even though
10. Even though, because

Quiz 7, p. 215

1. b
2. c
3. d
4. a
5. b
6. d

Quiz 8, p. 216

2. c
3. a
4. h
5. k
6. d
7. f
8. i
9. g
10. j
11. l
12. b

Quiz 9, p. 217

1. a. so
   b. does
2. a. so
   b. are
3. a. not
   b. didn't
4. a. so
   b. is
5. a. so
   b. do
6. a. not
   b. wasn't

Quiz 10, p. 218

1. a. she cries a lot.
2. a. there is a traffic jam on the freeway
3. a. they have a game three times a week
4. a. I don't see you tomorrow
5. a. Steve gets nine hours of sleep a night
6. a. they lower the price
7. a. you support me
   b. you don't support me

Quiz 11, p. 219

1. unless
2. Only if
3. only if
4. unless
5. unless
6. only if
7. Unless
8. only if
9. only if
10. unless
11. Only if
12. only if
13. unless
14. only if
15. only if

Quiz 12, p. 220

1. b
2. c
3. d
4. b
5. a
6. c
7. d
8. a
9. c
10. d

Test 1, p. 221

A.
1. b
2. a
3. b
4. b
5. a

B.
1. c
2. a
3. e
4. b
5. d

C.
1. in case
2. Even if
3. in case / whether or not
4. even if / whether or not
5. even if

D.
1. Unless
2. unless
3. Only if
4. only if
5. Unless

E.
1. Now that the term is almost over, students can look forward to vacation. OR
   Students can look forward to vacation now that the term is almost over.
2. Because Shelley forgot her sister's birthday, she felt terrible. OR
   Shelley felt terrible because she forgot her sister's birthday.
3. Unless we repair our tent, we can't go camping. OR
   We can't go camping unless we repair our tent.
4. Even if I win the lottery, I won't quit my job. OR
   I won't quit my job even if I win the lottery.
5. The workers refused to work on New Year's Eve even though the company promised to pay them double their usual wage. OR
   Even though the company promised to pay them double their usual wage, the workers refused to work on New Year's Eve.

F.
1. After Teresa looked at a lot of college Web sites, she chose the college that she wants to attend. OR
   Teresa chose the college that she wants to attend after she looked at a lot of college web sites.
2. We were working on the new project when our boss returned from his vacation on Monday. OR
   When our boss returned from his vacation on Monday, we were working on the new project.
3. As soon as Joe gets up tomorrow at 6:00 A.M., he will do his exercises. OR
   Joe will do his exercises as soon as he gets up tomorrow at 6 A.M.
4. For her birthday, Martina is going to go out to dinner with her friends before they go dancing at a nightclub. OR
   Before Martina and her friends go dancing at a nightclub, they are going to go out to dinner for her birthday.
5. Kathy will have moved to Texas by the time her husband returns from his job in South America next month. OR
   By the time Kathy's husband returns from his job in South America next month, Kathy will have moved to Texas.

Test 2, p. 224

A.
1. a
2. b
3. b
4. b
5. a

B.
1. c
2. e
3. d
4. a
5. b

C.
1. Even if
2. In case / Whether or not
3. even if
4. whether or not / even if
5. Whether or not / Even if

D.
1. only if
2. Unless
3. unless
4. Only if
5. unless

E.
1. The accountant will re-calculate the taxes since he / she found an error in the calculations. OR
Since the accountant found an error in the calculations, he / she will re-calculate the taxes.
2. Even though the cake recipe was very easy, Patricia read it over three times to make sure that she didn't make any mistakes. OR
Patricia read the cake recipe over three times to make sure that she didn't make any mistakes even though the recipe / it was very easy.
3. Maria is going to marry Harry even if she doesn't really love him. OR
Even if Maria doesn't really love Harry, she is going to marry him.
4. Unless Sam improves his grades in math and chemistry, he won't get accepted to medical school. OR
Sam won't get accepted to medical school unless he improves his grades in math and chemistry.
5. While some people enjoy cycling for exercise, other people enjoy walking briskly. OR
While some people enjoy walking briskly for exercise, other people enjoy cycling.

F.
1. After I pick up my cousin at the airport, I am going to show him the Golden Gate Bridge. OR
I am going to show my cousin the Golden Gate Bridge after I pick him up at the airport.
2. Maurice was eating lunch in a restaurant when he dropped his napkin on the floor. OR
When Maurice dropped his napkin on the floor, he was eating lunch in a restaurant.
3. As soon as Ann gets over her bad cold, she will return to work. OR
Ann will return to work as soon as she gets over her bad cold.
4. Mary rinses the food off the dishes before she puts them in the dishwasher. OR
Before Mary puts the dishes in the dishwasher, she rinses the food off them.
5. Ali will have graduated from high school by the time his brother gets married in July. OR
By the time Ali's brother gets married in July, Ali will have graduated from high school.

CHAPTER 18

Quiz 1, p. 228
1. ✓
2. incorrect
3. ✓
4. incorrect
5. incorrect
6. ✓
7. ✓
8. incorrect
9. ✓
10. incorrect
11. incorrect
12. ✓
13. ✓
14. ✓
15. incorrect

Quiz 2, p. 229
1. Since moving to California a year ago, Harry has been to Disneyland five times.
2. Before leaving Milwaukee for Toronto, Calum filled up the gas tank.
3. no change
4. Usually after working an eight-hour shift at the busy department store, Katherine is exhausted.
5. While living in Los Angeles, Mary often ran into famous people.
6. George has quit his job and started traveling around the world since winning $1,000,000 on a TV game show.
7. no change
8. Mark used to watch videos on his phone while waiting for the bus.
9. Jason will do his laundry after finishing his accounting homework.
10. Before going to a new restaurant, Julie and Jay always read reviews and look at a sample menu online.

Quiz 3, p. 230
1. because
2. while
3. while
4. because
5. because

Quiz 4, p. 230
1. Being a talented singer, Phoebe often sings in local coffee houses on weekends.
2. While ice-skating with her son, Christine fell and broke her ankle.
3. Unable to finish writing his report at the office, Andy took it home with him.
4. Because fighting fires is a very demanding job, firefighters have to be in excellent physical condition.
5. While attending a seminar on Friday, the college administrators discussed goals for the coming year.

Quiz 5, p. 231
1. Upon hearing that the meeting was canceled, the teachers were very happy.
2. Upon passing her driving test, Maya breathed a sigh of relief.
3. Upon receiving an award for her performance, the actor gave a brief acceptance speech.
4. Upon finding a gold coin in the sand at the beach, Tom couldn't believe his good luck.
5. Upon being elected mayor of the city, Margaret Peters set up a committee to study the traffic problems.
6. Upon having her sixth baby, Tina said, "I think this will be my last one."
7. Upon being fired from his job, the plumber filed a complaint with his workers' union.
8. Upon returning from a trip to Ecuador, Mrs. Alexander started a small business that sold Ecuadorean handicrafts.

Quiz 6, p. 232
1. While lying in bed feeling depressed, Joe wondered what he should do about his problems.
2. Upon arriving in London, Jane will have afternoon tea at the Ritz Hotel.
3. Having no money to buy a present for his mother, Billy made her a birthday card.
4. After testing the drug on mice, the research scientists will test the drug on monkeys.

5. Since taking a course in public speaking, Alex has developed more self-confidence.
6. While working in her garden, Susan disturbed a wasp's nest and was stung several times.
7. (Being) confused about the directions to the party, Carol had to stop at a gas station to ask for help.
8. Before leaving for India, Brian had to get several shots to protect him from tropical diseases.
9. While talking with his accountant, Omar realized that starting his own business would be quite complicated.
10. Upon tasting Mrs. Wilson's blueberry pie, Louis said that it was the most delicious pie he had ever eaten.

Test 1, p. 233

A.
1. While cleaning out his garage, John found some old photos.
2. no change
3. Before throwing anything away, Mary consulted with John to make sure it was OK.
4. Since moving into their house in 2010, Mary and John have gotten a lot of furniture.
5. After finishing / Having finished their work in the garage, John and Mary drank some cold sodas.

B.
1. ✓
2. ✓
3. incorrect
4. ✓
5. incorrect
6. ✓

C.
1. Not wanting to interrupt your meeting, I left a message with your secretary.
2. After / Upon becoming a citizen, Mr. Santos registered to vote.
3. While George was standing on a ladder changing a light bulb, his dog ran by and knocked the ladder over.
4. After explaining the medical procedure, the doctor asked if the patient had any questions.
5. Being a single mom with three children, Mrs. Nguyen had to work at two jobs to support her family.

Test 2, p. 235

A.
1. Having had a car accident last summer, Joe had to ride his bike to work.
2. Riding to work every day, Joe was dreaming about buying a new car.
3. no change
4. While searching for information, Joe's sister found two cars that she thought would interest him.
5. After reading / Having read all the articles that his sister had found for him, Joe chose which car he wanted.

B.
1. incorrect
2. ✓
3. ✓
4. incorrect
5. ✓
6. incorrect

C.
1. While playing basketball with his friends, my brother fell and sprained his ankle.
2. Since reading a book about sharks, Sam has been afraid to swim in the ocean.

3. After / Upon finishing his homework assignment, Paul was free to watch TV for the rest of the evening.
4. Not having received a package that her brother sent, Luisa contacted the post office about tracking it.
5. Since graduating from the university with a degree in French history, George has been looking for a job in education.

CHAPTER 19

Quiz 1, p. 237
1. so, c
2. Therefore, b
3. Due to, d
4. so, c
5. Even though, a
6. but, c
7. Since, a
8. Because of, d
9. Consequently, b
10. Because, a

Quiz 2, p. 238
1. Because of
2. because
3. because of
4. Because
5. because of
6. because of
7. because
8. Because of
9. because
10. because
11. because of
12. because
13. Because
14. because of
15. Because

Quiz 3, p. 239
Sample answers:
1. the bad weather
2. her fever
3. (her) car problems
4. my mother's illness
5. the snow was deep
6. an 8:00 A.M. appointment tomorrow
7. a toothache
8. the caffeine
9. he is lazy
10. advances in medicine

Quiz 4, p. 240
1. My coffee got cold, so I reheated it in the microwave.
2. Fish was on sale at the market. Therefore, Pat bought three fillets to have for dinner. OR
   Fish was on sale at the market; therefore, Pat bought three fillets to have for dinner.
3. Andrea was upset that her favorite team was losing the match, so she turned off the TV.
4. The regular radio announcer had a sore throat. Consequently, another announcer was on the program. OR
   The regular radio announcer had a sore throat; consequently, another announcer was on the program.
5. Electricity, water, and gas are getting more expensive. People, therefore, are trying to conserve energy.
6. My little sister dropped my glasses and cracked a lens, so I had to replace it.

7. Jason really enjoyed reading stories by Tom Miller. Consequently, he was excited when one of them was made into a movie. OR
Jason really enjoyed reading stories by Tom Miller; consequently, he was excited when one of them was made into a movie.
8. Khanh speaks English every day. His pronunciation is improving, therefore.
9. The supervisor gave her employees a lot of freedom in doing their work. Consequently, they liked working for her. OR
The supervisor gave her employees a lot of freedom in doing their work; consequently, they liked working for her.
10. My doctor didn't have the right equipment for the medical test I needed. He, therefore, sent me to a specialist.

Quiz 5, p. 241

1. The chicken was left in the oven too long, so the meat was dry and chewy.
2. Because my husband doesn't like lima beans, we never eat them. OR
We never eat lima beans because my husband doesn't like them.
3. Due to the weak economy, many citizens are unhappy with the government. OR
Many citizens are unhappy with the government due to the weak economy.
4. A new book by Maggie's favorite author was just published. Consequently, Maggie bought it immediately. OR
A new book by Maggie's favorite author was just published; consequently, Maggie bought it immediately.
5. The manager has a cold. Therefore, the meeting is canceled. OR
The manager has a cold; therefore, the meeting is canceled.
6. Because of damage from the windstorm, many people have joined in the cleanup. OR
Many people have joined in the cleanup because of damage from the windstorm.
7. Hannah loves sweets. Consequently, she has gained back all the weight she lost. OR
Hannah loves sweets; consequently, she has gained back all the weight she lost.
8. Jason dropped his cell phone in the swimming pool. Therefore, his cell phone stopped working. OR
Jason dropped his cell phone in the swimming pool; therefore, his cell phone stopped working.
9. Due to the fact that it was very late, we decided not to go out for coffee after the play. OR
Due to the late hour, we decided not to go out for coffee after the play.
10. Because we didn't have any milk, we used ice cream in our coffee instead. OR
We used ice cream in our coffee because we didn't have any milk.

Quiz 6, p. 242

1. such
2. so
3. so
4. such
5. so
6. so
7. such
8. such

Quiz 7, p. 242

1. Mike's motorcycle is so loud that the neighbors have complained about the noise.
2. It was such a heavy desk that we needed three people to move it.
3. The weather in June was so cold that we had to wear our winter sweaters.
4. The store has such dirty windows that we can hardly see inside.
5. The Sunday paper has such great comics that Nick reads them every week.
6. Patrick ate so much chocolate ice cream that he got a stomachache.

Quiz 8, p. 243

1. I have a part-time job so that I can afford to go to college.
2. Jim will take the bus to the airport so that he doesn't have to pay for parking.
3. The mechanics at Sam's Garage do careful work so that their customers will come again.
4. Frank and Joan took a parenting class so that they would / could learn more about children.
5. The music director stood on a podium so that he could see all of the musicians.

Quiz 9, p. 243

1. Fahad doesn't enjoy video games, so he rarely plays them.
2. Rob practices kung fu three times a week so that he can stay in shape.
3. I need to use the spelling checker so that I don't have spelling mistakes in my emails.
4. Meg is going to be gone on vacation for three months, so a temporary worker will replace her.
5. Miki texts her parents in Japan almost every day so that they won't worry about her while she's in the U.S.

Quiz 10, p. 244

1. but
2. Nevertheless
3. even though
4. even though
5. Despite
6. Nevertheless
7. Even though
8. but
9. Despite
10. Nevertheless

Quiz 11, p. 245

1. I wasn't really hungry, but I ate lunch anyway.
2. Even though Emily skipped breakfast, she still has a lot of energy.
3. Mr. Kwan is a rich man. Nevertheless, he refuses to buy his daughter a new car. OR
Mr. Kwan is a rich man; nevertheless, he refuses to buy his daughter a new car.
4. In spite of the high cost of postage, Omar sends a package overseas every week.
5. Rosanne really wanted to learn to drive, yet she was too young to get a driver's license.
6. Helen always talks about losing weight. She constantly snacks, however.
7. Although Jamaal grew up in San Francisco, he prefers living in Oakland.
8. Despite the fact that Anthony had already lost two cell phones, his parents gave him another one.
9. Edward doesn't like to smoke. Nonetheless, he sometimes smokes a cigar with his business partners.

10. Pat was the most qualified person for the job. However, the company hired someone else.
11. Despite the fact that she studied for hours, Monica failed the exam.
12. Sean has a fear of heights. Nevertheless, he enjoys skydiving. OR
Sean has a fear of heights; nevertheless, he enjoys skydiving.
13. Although it's the middle of December, it's very warm today.
14. In spite of the storm that was approaching, we still started our morning jog.
15. Even though I don't like to swim, I love going to the beach in the summer.

Quiz 12, p. 246
Sample answers:
1. People who car camp pack everything into their cars, but backpackers carry everything on their backs.
2. People who backpack hike into their camp. On the other hand, people who car camp usually camp in a campground they can drive to.
3. People who prefer car camping often like meeting other campers, while backpackers often enjoy getting away from crowds.
4. Car campers can enjoy fresh food prepared in camp. However, backpackers eat mostly dried and canned foods in camp.
5. People who car camp often take their pets along. On the other hand, people who backpack rarely take their pets with them.

Quiz 13, p. 247
Sample answers:
1. Maria had better study for her quiz. Otherwise, she won't get a good grade.
2. I have to find my passport. Otherwise, I won't be able to cross the border.
3. You must have a reservation. Otherwise, you can't get a table for dinner.
4. Kathleen's flight from the Philippines had better arrive on time. Otherwise, she will miss her connecting flight to Boston.

Quiz 14, p. 247
1. Our teacher has to remember students' names, or (else) the whole class laughs.
2. Dan should work hard, or (else) the repairs on the house won't get finished by winter.
3. Mark must save money every month, or (else) he won't be able to afford a car.
4. Beth has to get a new car license, or (else) she'll get a ticket.

Test 1, p. 248
A.
1. The sweater Jane bought has a hole in it, so she needs to return it to the store.
2. The traffic on Highway 101 was jammed. Therefore, we took Highway 280 instead. OR
The traffic on Highway 101 was jammed; therefore, we took Highway 280 instead.

3. Because Ron was late for work for the third time, he was fired from his job. OR
Ron was fired from his job because he was late for work for the third time.
4. Due to injuring his lower back, Bill can't lift heavy objects. OR
Due to a lower back injury, Bill can't lift heavy objects.
5. The Mars *Rover* has many cameras. Consequently, scientists on Earth can see photos of Mars. OR
The Mars *Rover* has many cameras; consequently, scientists on Earth can see photos of Mars.

B.
1. but
2. In spite of the fact that / Even though
3. even though / in spite of the fact that
4. Nevertheless
5. Despite

C.
1. so
2. such
3. so
4. so
5. such

D.
1. such
2. Even though / Although
3. despite the fact
4. because of
5. While
6. although / even though
7. so
8. Because
9. Nevertheless
10. Otherwise

E.
1. Mary speaks Chinese and Japanese, while her sister Linda speaks Spanish and French.
2. Botanists study plants and plant life. On the other hand, zoologists study the animal kingdom.
3. I really wanted to go to New York, but I decided that the trip would be too expensive.
4. My wife is always telling me we need to save money. However, she spends as much money as she wants.

Test 2, p. 251
A.
1. Because Sally doesn't like the crowds at the shopping center, she usually shops online. OR
Sally usually shops online because she doesn't like the crowds at the shopping center.
2. I am an optimist, and my husband is a pessimist. Therefore, we sometimes disagree. OR
I am an optimist, and my husband is a pessimist; therefore, we sometimes disagree.
3. The previous owners of the house never took care of it. Consequently, it is now in bad condition. OR
The previous owners of the house never took care of it; consequently, it is now in bad condition.
4. Because of many construction delays, the subway line will not open on time. OR
The subway line will not open on time because of many construction delays.
5. Isaac majored in engineering due to pressure from his father. OR
Due to pressure from his father, Isaac majored in engineering.

B.
1. Although / Despite the fact that
2. yet
3. However
4. in spite of
5. Despite the fact that / Although

C.
1. so
2. so
3. such
4. so
5. such

D.
1. Nonetheless / However
2. due to
3. so
4. Because
5. in spite of
6. however / nonetheless
7. such
8. Otherwise
9. Even though
10. On the other hand

E.
1. Terry is very shy and quiet in class. On the other hand, Hannah is outgoing and very talkative with classmates.
2. Jan is interested in current events and listens to the news every day. However, Art never listens to the news and doesn't care much about what's happening in the world.
3. Mount McKinley, in Alaska, is the highest peak in North America, while Aconcagua, in Argentina, is the highest peak in South America and the Western Hemisphere.
4. Coffee is made from roasted and ground beans that grow on bushes, but tea is made from the leaves and flowers of a variety of plants.

CHAPTER 20

Quiz 1, p. 254
1. a
2. b
3. c
4. a
5. b
6. b
7. c
8. a
9. c
10. a

Quiz 2, p. 255
1. eats
2. don't gain, won't gain
3. will borrow
4. pay
5. will feel

Quiz 3, p. 255
1. wear
2. will pay
3. stays
4. calls
5. will wash

Quiz 4, p. 256
1. were
2. would enjoy
3. didn't have
4. wouldn't be
5. understood
6. would be
7. weren't / were not, would eat
8. lived, wouldn't see

Quiz 5, p. 256
1. will call
2. needed
3. doesn't come
4. would feel
5. receives
6. were, would be

Quiz 6, p. 257
3. R, If children are scared present / future
4. U, if we had called past
5. R, If Rebecca is tired present / future
6. U, If the dogs had stopped barking past

Quiz 7, p. 257
1. a. no
   b. no
   c. no
2. a. yes
   b. yes
3. a. no
   b. yes
4. a. yes
   b. no
5. a. yes
   b. no

Quiz 8, p. 258
1. had found
2. would have been
3. would have won
4. hadn't brought
5. would have trusted
6. wouldn't have died
7. had wanted, would have given
8. wouldn't have driven, hadn't been
9. had been, would have done
10. had had, would have bought

Quiz 9, p. 259
1. stays, will work
2. were, would enjoy
3. hadn't stayed, wouldn't have been
4. would quit, hated
5. wouldn't have gotten, had put
6. didn't have, wouldn't be
7. needs, will call
8. rains, don't get
9. had sent, would have known
10. weren't, would watch

Quiz 10, p. 260
1. did
2. hadn't
3. didn't
4. did
5. weren't
6. had
7. had
8. were
9. weren't
10. did

Quiz 11, p. 261
1. weren't sleeping
2. were using
3. hadn't been talking
4. were looking
5. had been enjoying
6. hadn't been sleeping
7. weren't blowing
8. hadn't been studying

Quiz 12, p. 262

1. If I had fed the cats, they wouldn't be hungry.
2. If the children hadn't practiced a lot, they couldn't sing the song by heart.
3. John would have paid his bills if he had enough money.
4. The house wouldn't be too hot inside if the heat hadn't been left on.
5. If I had bought stamps yesterday, I could mail these letters today.
6. If Paulo had contacted his parents, they wouldn't be worried about him.
7. Martha could check her online account if she hadn't forgotten her password.
8. Mark wouldn't be tired if he hadn't flown in from Hong Kong late last night.

Quiz 13, p. 263

1. Were Pat lazy, he wouldn't be so successful.
2. Should the phone ring, please answer it.
3. I would have come sooner had someone told me about the accident.
4. Were I you, I would look for a new hair stylist.
5. Had Abdul wanted to join us for dinner, he would have been welcome.

Quiz 14, p. 263

1. If I hadn't been so tired, I would have done the dishes last night.
2. Bob would have bought concert tickets if the show hadn't been sold out.
3. If Julio hadn't lent me $500, I wouldn't have been able to buy a plane ticket home.
4. It wouldn't have been as much fun if Talia hadn't been there.
5. Kate would have played the piano for us if she didn't have a broken finger.

Quiz 15, p. 264

1. could go
2. were going
3. weren't
4. could
5. would
6. had studied
7. had won
8. were
9. hadn't
10. did, turned

Quiz 16, p. 265

1. had
2. weren't
3. could speak
4. had been
5. could have (come)
6. hadn't forgotten / had remembered
7. had been listening
8. would call
9. were going / could go
10. could find

Quiz 17, p. 266

Sample answers:
1. If I could live anywhere in the world, I would live in Seattle.
2. If I hadn't learned English, I would have studied Italian.

3. If I don't understand my next English assignment, I will ask my teacher for help.
4. I wish all wars would end.
5. I wish I had known my grandparents better before they died.
6. If I were not taking this quiz, I would be drinking coffee with my friends.
7. If I were ten years older, I would be working at an interesting job.
8. If I could change anything about my past life, I would change the way I treated my little brother. I would have been nicer and more helpful.

Test 1, p. 267

A.
1. would be
2. pick
3. weren't studying
4. wouldn't have caught, had worn
5. paid
6. goes
7. would have visited, hadn't visited
8. will buy

B.
1. If Madeleine hadn't missed her flight, she wouldn't be feeling angry and frustrated.
2. If she had practiced, Saya could play the music for her piano lesson.
3. If Michael hadn't gotten three traffic tickets last year, his auto insurance rates wouldn't cost more.
4. If Tomás wanted to move to a different city, he would have accepted the job offer.
5. If Stacy Smith hadn't won the election, she wouldn't be the new mayor.

C.
1. If I weren't in a hurry, I would stop to chat with you.
2. If Fred hadn't had to work late, he would have met us for dinner.
3. If you hadn't helped me, I would never have completed this project on time.

D.
1. had gone
2. weren't
3. spoke
4. were
5. could
6. would
7. weren't
8. hadn't gone

Test 2, p. 269

A.
1. loses
2. would have gone, hadn't been
3. would visit
4. will see
5. got
6. wouldn't have pulled, had been
7. feel
8. were not cooking

B.
1. If Wendy had worked hard in high school, she would be going to college.
2. If Paula hadn't damaged the front wheel on her bike, she would / could ride it to work.

3. If the children weren't running and yelling, they would / could hear their teacher calling them.
4. If my computer were working, I would have finished the report.
5. If Roberta liked cheese, she would have eaten some pizza last night.

C.
1. If I hadn't been in the shower, I would have answered the door.
2. If Lisa didn't have a doctor's appointment, she wouldn't have left work early.
3. If the coach hadn't led the team, they couldn't have won the championship.

D.
1. could
2. lived
3. didn't
4. were
5. had
6. had
7. were
8. hadn't

MIDTERM EXAM 1
Chapters 1–10

M I D T E R M   E X A M   1 ,   p .   2 7 0

1. d	11. b	21. a	31. b	41. c
2. b	12. a	22. b	32. c	42. c
3. c	13. b	23. d	33. d	43. a
4. a	14. a	24. b	34. a	44. d
5. c	15. c	25. c	35. a	45. c
6. a	16. a	26. a	36. d	46. b
7. b	17. c	27. d	37. d	47. b
8. d	18. a	28. b	38. c	48. b
9. c	19. d	29. d	39. d	49. d
10. a	20. a	30. d	40. b	50. c

MIDTERM EXAM 2
Chapters 1–10

M I D T E R M   E X A M   2 ,   p .   2 7 5

A.
1. are
2. will make / is going to make
3. was working
4. will help
5. haven't had
6. bought
7. will speak / will be speaking
8. rained
9. am going to be attending
10. is studying
11. will have finished
12. has been surfing
13. has
14. hadn't talked
15. will celebrate

B.
1. b	6. a	11. a
2. b	7. b	12. b
3. a	8. a	13. b
4. b	9. a	14. a
5. b	10. b	15. b

C.
1. a. shouldn't have stayed
   b. may / might / could / must have been
   c. should / must / has to be
2. a. Can / Could / May, leave
   b. Would / Could / Will, ask

D.
1. a. Will	2. a. Max
b. Hannah	b. David
c. James	c. Ken

E.
1. must not
2. have to / must
3. could
4. don't have to
5. couldn't, must

FINAL EXAM 1
Chapters 1–20

F I N A L   E X A M   1 ,   p .   2 7 9

1. b	11. b	21. a	31. d	41. d
2. c	12. c	22. c	32. b	42. c
3. a	13. b	23. b	33. b	43. b
4. d	14. d	24. b	34. c	44. a
5. b	15. a	25. a	35. d	45. d
6. d	16. d	26. b	36. c	46. b
7. d	17. c	27. b	37. d	47. c
8. c	18. d	28. d	38. a	48. a
9. a	19. b	29. c	39. c	49. d
10. c	20. a	30. a	40. a	50. b

FINAL EXAM 2
Chapters 1–20

F I N A L   E X A M   2 ,   p .   2 8 5

A.
1. is going to go / will go / is going
2. didn't study
3. was waiting
4. had already started
5. will be given / is going to be given
6. hasn't arrived
7. will stay / are going to stay
8. is / will be
9. don't plan / aren't planning
10. is

B.
1. b	6. a
2. a	7. b
3. a	8. a
4. a	9. b
5. b	10. a

C.
1. Both Mary and John got 100% on their last grammar test.
2. Neither Barbara nor Steven can attend the meeting on Monday.
3. Stewart's team won not only the city championship but also the regional championship.
4. We can watch either a comedy film or a drama.

D.

1. what time the train for Edinburgh leaves
2. if / whether Kevin had gotten his driver's license
3. whose car that was
4. How that machine works

E.

1. Barbara wants to go to an island that has warm sandy beaches and lots of sunshine for her vacation.
2. Anne and Emily like to go shopping at the mall where their mom also shops.
3. The police are trying to find the man whose car was found near the scene of the crime.

F.

1. e
2. g
3. j
4. f
5. h
6. d
7. c
8. i
9. a
10. b

G.

1. studying
2. playing
3. to meet
4. to get
5. swimming
6. to admit
7. to go
8. traveling
9. to drive
10. getting / to get